Laboratory experimentation in economics

Laboratory experimentation in economics

Six points of view

Edited by
ALVIN E. ROTH
University of Pittsburgh

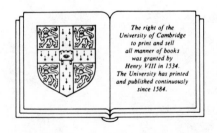

The right of the
University of Cambridge
to print and sell
all manner of books
was granted by
Henry VIII in 1534.
The University has printed
and published continuously
since 1584.

CAMBRIDGE UNIVERSITY PRESS

Cambridge
New York   New Rochelle   Melbourne   Sydney

Published by the Press Syndicate of the University of Cambridge
The Pitt Building, Trumpington Street, Cambridge CB2 1RP
32 East 57th Street, New York, NY 10022, USA
10 Stamford Road, Oakleigh, Melbourne 3166, Australia

First published 1987

Printed in the United States of America

Library of Congress Cataloging-in-Publication Data
Laboratory experimentation in economics.
1. Economics – Experiments. I. Roth, Alvin E.,
1951–
HB131.L32   1987   330'.0724   87–10343

British Library Cataloguing in Publication Data
Laboratory experimentation in economics:
six points of view.
1. Economics, Mathematical   2. Game theory
I. Roth, Alvin E.
330'.01'5193   HB144

ISBN 0 521 33392 X

Contents

Acknowledgments   *page* vii
List of contributors   viii

1 Introduction and overview   1
  Alvin E. Roth

2 Bargaining phenomena and bargaining theory   14
  Alvin E. Roth

3 Equity and coalition bargaining in experimental
  three-person games   42
  Reinhard Selten

4 The psychology of choice and the assumptions of
  economics   99
  Richard Thaler

5 Hypothetical valuations and preference reversals in the
  context of asset trading   131
  Marc Knez and Vernon L. Smith

6 Economics according to the rats (and pigeons too): what
  have we learned and what can we hope to learn?   155
  John H. Kagel

7 Dimensions of parallelism: some policy applications of
  experimental methods   193
  Charles R. Plott

Acknowledgments

The chapters in this volume were commissioned following a conference entitled "Laboratory Experimentation in Economics" at the University of Pittsburgh on May 16–18, 1985. I particularly want to thank President Wesley Posvar, Dean Jerome Rosenberg, and my colleague Professor Jack Ochs, all of the University of Pittsburgh, whose support was invaluable.

Contributors

JOHN H. KAGEL is Professor of Economics and Director of the Center for Experimental Economics at the University of Houston. He received his Ph.D. from Purdue University in 1970. He has been a National Fellow at the Hoover Institution and an Earhart Foundation Fellow.

MARC KNEZ is a graduate student at the University of Pennsylvania. He began his collaboration with Vernon Smith when he was at the University of Arizona.

CHARLES R. PLOTT is Professor of Economics and Director of the Program for the Study of Enterprise at the California Institute of Technology. He received his Ph.D. from the University of Virginia in 1965. He has been a Guggenheim Fellow and a Fellow at the Center for Advanced Study in the Behavioral Sciences and is a Fellow of the AAAS and the Econometric Society.

ALVIN E. ROTH is A. W. Mellon Professor of Economics at the University of Pittsburgh. He received his Ph.D. from Stanford University in 1974. He received the 1980 Founders' Prize of the Texas Instruments Foundation, has been a Guggenheim Fellow and an Alfred P. Sloan Research Fellow, and is a Fellow of the Econometric Society.

REINHARD SELTEN is Professor of Economics at the University of Bonn in the Federal Republic of Germany. He received his Ph.D. in mathematics from the University of Frankfurt in 1961 and his habilitation in economics, also from the University of Frankfurt, in 1968. He is a member of the Northrhine-Westfalian Academy of Sciences and a Fellow of the Econometric Society.

VERNON L. SMITH is Professor of Economics and Research Director, Economic Science Laboratory at the University of Arizona. He received his B.S.E.E. from the California Institute of Technology in 1949 and his Ph.D. in economics from Harvard University in 1955. He has been a Ford Foundation Fellow, Fellow at the Center for Ad-

vanced Studies in the Behavioral Sciences, and Sherman Fairchild
Distinguished Fellow (California Institute of Technology).

RICHARD THALER is Professor of Economics at Cornell University's
Johnson Graduate School of Management. He received his Ph.D. from
the University of Rochester in 1974. He has been a visiting scholar at
the National Bureau of Economic Research in Stanford, California,
and a visiting professor at the University of British Columbia.

CHAPTER 1

Introduction and overview

ALVIN E. ROTH

Each of the chapters in this volume concerns some aspect of economists' use of controlled experiments. Since the mid-1970s this kind of work has been transformed from a seldom encountered curiosity to a small but well-established and growing part of the economic literature. This transformation has been rapid. For example, when I began my own experimental work about a dozen years ago, it was most convenient to publish the results in journals of psychology and business. Today it is no longer unusual for controlled experiments to be reported in any of the major American economics journals. Experimental work has become well enough represented in the literature so that, in 1985, the *Journal of Economic Literature* established a separate bibliographic category, "Experimental Economic Methods."

However, as might be expected of any newly developing field of scientific endeavor, there are at least as many points of view about the role of experiments in economics as there are economists who conduct them. One of the reasons for this is that "economics" encompasses quite a diversity of activities and methodologies, and controlled experimentation appears to have the potential to play at least a supporting role, and in some cases a far larger part, in many of these.

At the time that I was organizing the conference that led to the publication of this volume, I was preparing a paper on experimental economics to present at one of the symposia of the Fifth World Congress of the Econometric Society, which was held in the summer of 1985. (World congresses are held every five years and are organized around a group of symposia on significant recent advances. A sign of the times, and of the distance experimental economics has come in so short a time, is the fact that this was the first such symposium to be devoted to experimentation.) In that paper (Roth, 1985) I tried to organize some of the experiments that have been conducted by classifying them according to the kinds of dialogues they were a part of, that is, according to how they were motivated and who they were

1

trying to persuade. Although it became increasingly evident that no classification scheme would be adequate to the task of demonstrating the relationships as well as the differences between different bodies of work, I organized the paper around three principal kinds of dialogues, which I referred to as "Speaking to Theorists," "Searching for Facts," and "Whispering in the Ears of Princes."

The category "Speaking to Theorists" was meant to include experiments motivated by well-articulated formal theories. These experiments are designed to test the predictions of those theories, as well as to reveal unpredicted regularities, in a controlled environment where observations can be unambiguously interpreted in relation to theory and incorporated if necessary into the construction of new theory. The requirement that the observations be interpretable in relation to a particular theory or group of theories imposes constraints on the experimental designs that are perhaps the chief characteristic of these experiments. Such experiments are typically motivated by the theoretical literature and are intended to feed back into that literature; that is, they are part of a dialogue between experimenters and theorists.

The category "Searching for Facts" includes experiments on the effects of variables about which existing theory may have little to say. These experiments are consequently often designed without reference to a specific body of theory, but might be motivated instead by some interesting unexplained phenomenon. They tend to be part of the dialogue that experimenters carry on with one another, and indeed many experiments of this sort are designed to help us understand earlier experimental observations.

The category "Whispering in the Ears of Princes" deals with the dialogue between experimenters and policymakers. These experiments might be motivated, for example, by questions raised by government regulatory agencies about the effect of changes in the organization of some market. Their characteristic feature is that the experimental environment is designed to resemble closely the natural environment that is the focus of the policy question at hand. In my symposium paper, I wrote, "These investigations offer the possibility of bringing scientific methods to bear on one of the traditional nonscientific vocations of economists, which is whispering in the ears of princes who require advice about pressing practical questions whose answers lie beyond the reliable scientific knowledge of the profession."

Although these categories seem useful for distinguishing different kinds of work, most extended experimental studies cannot be confined to a single category. Experiments that test formal theories may identify unanticipated phenomena for which existing theory offers no explanation and suggest other experiments designed to reveal more about those phenomena. Experiments that are not motivated primarily by theoretical considerations may eventually lead to the construction of new theories and to further experiments that test them. And experiments that are motivated by questions of policy may nevertheless have some (perhaps informal) theoretical motivation and may uncover empirical regularities that require further experimentation.

In general, no simple classification scheme can do full justice to the variety of uses to which experimentation is presently being put in economics. This is at least in part because economics does not have a long-established tradition of experimental work, and experimenters are forced to develop their methodology and philosophy at the same time they investigate particular phenomena. So all these matters are in flux: Not only may different experimenters have different points of view, but any given experimental economist may approach experimentation differently over time or in different situations.

My purpose in organizing this volume and the conference that preceded it was to provide an opportunity for a number of "veteran" experimental economists to discuss and compare their views. In my initial letter to one of the participants, I wrote, "I'm hoping to get papers that exemplify the different points of view from which the six of us have conducted experiments." Although a number of these investigators have engaged in a wide variety of experimental work, I solicited papers from each one on an aspect of his work that would otherwise not have been adequately represented. Regarding this book, I wrote, "My hope is that the volume will be useful to two quite different audiences. For economists already involved in experimentation, I hope that this project will make it easier to discern the essential differences and similarities among the several approaches to experimentation now becoming well represented in the literature. And for economists and others who are not involved in this kind of investigation, such a volume should provide an otherwise unavailable kind of window on this literature."

Thus the hope for this book is that the whole will be more than the sum of the parts. Though each speaks about a particular group of experiments, together these contributions convey a preliminary picture – a snapshot in time – of the shape of experimental economics. That is not to say that the work here covers all, or even a large part, of the experimental work to date. On the contrary, no broad surveys have been included; each chapter is concerned with a specific study or series of related studies. But the *kinds* of work discussed go a long way toward exhibiting the different types of experimental work that economists are doing. Also, the contributors were encouraged to express their opinions – something that is sometimes difficult to do in journals – and they have availed themselves of this opportunity. So a reader of this book should come away with a good idea of the variety of reasons that lead economists to the laboratory.

With this in mind, readers might find the following questions useful in their reading of each of the chapters. What was it about the phenomena being studied that called for an experimental approach? What were the chief problems of design and implementation? What was the character of the data, and what difficulties were encountered in analyzing and interpreting them? How do the results change and inform our understanding of the problem that motivated the experiment and give rise to new problems?

Chapter 2 describes a series of experiments that my colleagues and I have conducted, experiments directly motivated by a body of formal theory about bargaining. These are by no means the first bargaining experiments to have been published in the economics literature, nor the first experiments concerned at least in part with the same body of theory (see, e.g., Stone, 1958; Siegel and Fouraker, 1960; Rapoport and Perner, 1974). But they do appear to be the first experiments designed so that the results can be interpreted unambiguously in terms of the parameters in which the theory is expressed, namely the preferences and risk postures of the bargainers. The fact that these data are virtually impossible to observe in natural bargaining situations makes experimental methods particularly appropriate for testing such theories, and obtaining the necessary control even in a laboratory environment presented the chief problem in experimental design. Unpredicted effects, due to variables that the theory predicts should have had no influence, were observed early in the experiments and further explored in later experiments. However, experiments designed to test predictions about those variables that the theory predicts *are* important yielded positive conclusions. So the experimental results lend support to some of the predictions of existing theory and tend to disconfirm others, while yielding a body of empirical evidence about systematic bargaining phenomena that seems likely to lead to new theory.

A point about how experimental evidence accumulates struck me as I was preparing this chapter. One of the clearest bargaining phenomena to emerge from these experiments (the "deadline effect"), which can be observed in the data of virtually all these experiments, escaped serious examination until a great deal of evidence had accumulated. Although my colleagues and I had informally observed this phenomenon, we had not formally analyzed it and had consequently failed to realize how pronounced it is in the data. For example, I did not refer to this aspect of the data at all in my discussion (Roth, 1983) of the initial experiments in this series. Yet it now seems possible that this will prove to be a very significant bargaining phenomenon, for two reasons. The first is simply the fact that it appears so plainly and robustly in the data. The second reason (which is both more subtle and more speculative) is that this phenomenon, although unpredicted by existing theory, may lend itself to modeling with familiar theoretical tools. Thus it may help to provide a bridge between existing theoretical models and the body of empirical regularities (both predicted and unpredicted) that are emerging from this work.

Chapter 3, by Reinhard Selten, starts from a different point in the dialogue between theorists and experimenters. Selten's concern is with coalition formation in three-person games of the sort that game theorists call "characteristic function games." These are games in which, loosely speaking, the actions available to each group of players are independent of what other players may do and in which the available gains can be "monetized" and freely divided among the members of the coalition, so that the options available to a coalition can be summarized by a single number equal to the maximum amount of money available to it. These games have attracted considerable theoretical interest, because they are in some sense the simplest environments in which coalition formation can be studied. By the same token, natural economic environments can, at best, be modeled only very approximately as characteristic function games, so that artificial laboratory environments provide an otherwise unavailable opportunity to test theories of coalition formation in their simplest form. Selten considers a body of data from a number of experiments involving such games conducted under various experimental conditions by different experimenters. He identifies some empirical regularities in this diverse set of experimental data and proposes a formal theory to describe and explain them. He also proposes novel statistical tests with which to compare the descriptive accuracy of the new theory with that of existing theories applicable to the same data. (The problem of developing appropriate statistical tests for comparing the descriptive accuracy of alternative hypotheses arises in many economic experiments.) These comparisons seem promising for the new theory, which therefore seems likely to suggest further experiments. (For some related work, see Rapoport et al., 1979, and the papers referenced there.)

Two remarks about the background of this chapter seem in order. First, experimental economics in Europe seems to have developed for a time separately from similar work in the United States. Some of Selten's early work on this topic was published in a continuing series of volumes, *Contributions to Experimental Economics*, the first of which, edited by Heinz Sauermann, appeared in 1967. (Selten earlier collaborated with Sauermann on an experimental study of oligopolistic market behavior; see Sauermann and Selten, 1959.) Second, Selten is perhaps best known among economic theorists for his theoretical work on perfect equilibria, which forms the basis for much of the current theoretical work on rational and "hyperrational" behavior. It is therefore noteworthy that the theory of coalition formation that he proposes here is a theory of *limited* rationality. His chapter emphasizes his conclusion that limitations of human rationality must be taken seriously in descriptive theories of behavior. In my 1985 symposium paper I wrote in this regard that "it is the mark of a committed scientist to be able to adjust his theoretical ideas in the face of compelling evidence, and I think that a characteristic of experimental evidence is that it will often have the power to compel such adjustments in economic theories."

The next chapter, by Richard Thaler, deals with the assumptions about individual choice behavior that implicitly or explicitly underlie most of contemporary economic theory. Specifically, Thaler is concerned with systematic deviations of individual choice behavior from the predictions of subjective expected utility theory and from predictions derived from utility theory in conjunction with various auxiliary assumptions that are often used in applying it to economic models. The study of systematic departures of observed individual choice behavior from predicted behavior began not long after the introduction of formal theories of individual behavior – see, for example, the famous papers of Maurice Allais (1953) and Daniel Ellsberg (1961). Some attempts to observe and explain certain of these departures were made in a systematic way, and theoretical explanations were offered for at least some of the observed phenomena (see, e.g., the work of Kenneth May, 1954, and Amos Tversky, 1969, on intransitive preferences). Tversky and Daniel Kahneman, among others, subsequently turned to the investigation of a wider range of individual choice phenomena that are anomalous from the point of view of existing theory, some of which they attempted to codify into a descriptive theory (Kahneman and Tversky, 1979). (An alternative approach being pursued by other investigators attempts to deal with observed empirical anomalies by extending and "reconstructing" utility theory so as to preserve many of the appealing properties of the original versions of the theory; see, e.g., Machina, 1982.)

Thaler is interested in exploring some of the implications for economic theory that would follow if we adopted the position that, because of the weight of the empirical evidence, utility theory will have to be abandoned as a useful model of individual choice behavior. He begins with a description of what he believes are the most telling phenomena that cannot be accommodated by traditional economic theory and goes on to discuss the experimental methodology that has given rise to these conclusions.

The discussion of methodology is particularly interesting, because many of the data come from subjects' responses to hypothetical questions. This contrasts with the methodology adopted by most experimental economists, who typically take pains to control for subjects' economic incentives when making choices in the laboratory, in order to guard against the possibility that subjects' verbal responses to hypothetical questions about their choice behavior might differ systematically from the choices they would make if actually faced with the indicated situation. (In this regard it seems to me that the kinds of hypothetical questions put to experimental subjects in these studies place different demands on their imaginations. Some of the questions are relatively straightforward – for example, "Which of the following options do you prefer?" Some require a little more imagination – "Imagine that you are about to purchase a jacket . . ." and some call for considerable insight – "Assume yourself richer by $500 than you are today.") However, a number of the phenomena initially identified via hypothetical questions have also been observed in experiments in which incentives were controlled. Thaler's remarks on this subject are thought provoking (as are his reflections on the trade-off between gathering data from experienced vs. inexperienced subjects). It seems likely that more experimental work will be needed to clarify the potential strengths and weaknesses of these methods for different categories of choice phenomena. In the meantime, the survey methods Thaler discusses seem to offer the possibility of obtaining at least certain kinds of data inexpensively and quickly.

The chapter by Marc Knez and Vernon Smith arose out of the discussion that followed Thaler's presentation at the conference. Smith, who had earlier spoken about another experimental study, remarked that he had some data that might be related to the evaluation of the significance, for general economic theory, of the kind of individual choice phenomena Thaler had discussed. The data Smith was referring to had to do with the way subjects responded when they were asked how much they would be willing to pay to acquire a certain object that they did not have or how much they would be willing to accept in exchange for a certain object that they did have. One of the observed phenomena was that the price individuals said they would be willing to accept (WTA) for some object was often much higher than the price they said they would be willing to pay (WTP) for the same object. Another observed phenomenon, called preference reversal, is that subjects sometimes report a higher WTP (or WTA) for one object than for another but nevertheless say that they prefer the second object to the first.

The question that motivated the Knez and Smith chapter was, How would these phenomena be reflected in transactions occurring in a market environment? To examine this question, they allowed buyers and sellers to trade with one another in a double-auction market, after soliciting WTP information from the buyers and WTA information from the sellers. This process was carried out several times, allowing the same buyers and sellers to interact with one another repeatedly in the same market environment. Knez and Smith observed that, although anomalous WTPs and WTAs were often reported and although the associated preference reversal phenomenon persisted, these reported prices did not seem to be a reliable indicator of subjects' market trading behavior, in that traders were often observed to sell below their reported WTA and buy above their reported WTP. Although numerous WTPs violated the predictions of expected utility theory, all but a few market transactions were at prices consistent with the theory. Knez and Smith conclude that these results "call into question the interpretation, reliability, and robustness of preference reversal phenomena in the joint context of repetitive responses and market trading."

There is now a considerable body of experimental evidence about various aspects of market behavior. (An early market experiment was reported in Chamberlin, 1948.) Smith has been a prolific experimenter, and this study is representative of much of his work, with its emphasis on the function of markets as economic institutions and its close attention to the "texture" of the complex observations that result from a repeated market interaction by a group of subjects. (An account of much of Smith's work can be found in Smith, 1982, and a discussion of some of the dialogue among experimenters of which it is a part can be found in Roth, in press.)

Chapter 6, by John Kagel, is different from the others in this volume in that the experimental subjects are rats and pigeons rather than people. Kagel and his colleagues have conducted many experiments on individual choice behavior of laboratory animals in which animals make choices (pigeons by pecking keys, rats by pressing levers) that influence how much food and water is delivered to them. The "price" of goods is controlled by varying the amount of effort needed (e.g., the number of times a lever must be pressed) to obtain a given amount of a given commodity. (Thus Kagel observes that "rats clearly prefer root beer to water at equal effort price.") Experiments of this kind have long been conducted by psychologists, and Kagel and his colleagues have found that the predictive power of economic theories of consumer demand compare favorably with those of theories found in the behavioral psychology literature. Also, economic theories have been a fruitful source of conjectures about animal behavior, which then motivate novel kinds of animal experiments. So one role of animal experiments motivated by economic theory that should be relatively uncontroversial (at least among economists) is that of establishing the extent to which the predictions of economic theory apply to, and further the study of, animal behavior.

It is another use, however, that Kagel primarily addresses in his chapter, in which he discusses the implications of animal experiments for economic theory as it applies to people. The underlying view is that many aspects of human choice behavior have a biological component that might be shared with other species of animals. Kagel reports that animals can be experimentally observed to exhibit transitive and risk-averse preferences and to share with people the kind of anomalous choice behavior observed in the Allais paradox.

He further notes that animal experiments can be designed to avoid one of the criticisms frequently leveled at economic experiments conducted with humans – that the incentives offered to subjects may not be sufficient to command their utmost attention. (Kagel cites a number of studies suggesting that experiments based on hypothetical questions may be unreliable.) However, in the experiments he discusses, the animals are maintained at approximately 80% of their natural body weight to ensure that the edible commodities involved in the experiment will be highly desirable. Thus phenomena in which strong incentives might play a critical role may sometimes be easier to study in animals than in humans. Kagel reports the results of two experiments motivated by hypotheses about the effects of poverty. The "welfare trap hypothesis" is that agents who have unearned income will get "hooked on leisure" and subsequently reduce their labor supply. Kagel reports observing a small effect in this direction among pigeons who had earlier been given "unearned income" in the form of free access to food and water. The "cycle of poverty hypothesis" is that low-income agents tend to discount the future more heavily than high-income agents, and Kagel reports the opposite effect among liquid-deprived rats.

Kagel notes that many economists question whether direct implications about human behavior can be drawn from observations of animal behavior. (Cognitive psychologists may also find this controversial for some kinds of behavior.) But he argues that this question is not logically different from the question of whether an experiment with people will generalize from one subject population (e.g., college students) to another (e.g., business executives) and that both questions lend themselves to further empirical investigation.

The last chapter, by Charles Plott, deals with experiments designed to help make and evaluate policy decisions, mainly involving economic activity subject to government regulation. Some of these laboratory experiments are thus related in spirit to the kinds of field experiments that have occasionally been conducted to evaluate policy questions. (Field experiments, which are often viewed as demonstration projects, have concerned peak-load pricing of electricity and the operation of various forms of public assistance. See Ferber and Hirsch, 1982, for a review of such experiments, the most famous of which is the New Jersey Income-Maintenance Experiment.) Plott discusses a number of experiments that he and his colleagues have conducted. His discussion is organized around the different experimental "strategies" that were adopted in response to the different ways these experiments were intended to influence the process of making and evaluating policy.

For example, Plott discusses experiments that were designed to demonstrate to policymakers, who would normally find the academic literature inaccessible or unpersuasive, some point that economists already regarded as relatively well established. Other experiments were meant to "shift the burden of proof" in an adversarial debate (e.g., court testimony), and still others were meant to guide the design of policies for new situations (such as those arising after deregulation of the airlines).

These experiments differ from the others discussed in this volume in that each was interpreted with respect to some "target" market. Consequently, Plott considers very carefully the kinds of conclusions that can be drawn about the target market from the laboratory market, which is necessarily different in many respects and inevitably much simpler than the natural target market. Such questions of interpretation are of more than academic concern, since the experiments that were meant to be introduced into adversarial debates were conducted with the anticipation that their interpretation might be actively disputed. These concerns are reflected in the design of the experiments. Since it might not be clear which features of the economic environment would be germane to the question at hand, the experimental markets were often constructed to resemble scale models of the target market. In this way, the results of the experiment could not be attributed to some obvious structural difference between the laboratory and target markets. In some experiments, the experimental subjects were individuals employed in the industry in question, so that the results could not be attributed to some difference between a subject pool of, say, college students and one consisting of individuals with relevant experience. Consequently, many of these experiments have the look and feel of the scale models and simulations found in many branches of engineering. Plott remarks that this kind of experimentation "is a source of experience similar to the experience one acquires as one practices the piano before a concert or that a team acquires as it practices before a game."

Of course, although there are some differences between these policy-oriented experiments and the others discussed in this volume, there are at least equally clear similarities. After all, it is not just in adversarial circumstances that one wants to be able to distinguish among plausible alternative explanations of the data, and the purpose of good experimental design is to make this possible. Plott has been an active contributor to many aspects of experimental economics, and the policy-oriented work he discusses here is related to his other work (some of which he discusses in Plott, 1982).

There is a certain family resemblance among all the experiments discussed in this volume that, despite the differences among them, distinguishes them from the variety of experiments found in other sciences. So although it is still too early to know what roles experimentation will come to play in economics, it is safe to speculate that the distinctive character of economics as a science will be reflected in the development of economic experimentation. There are nevertheless instructive parallels with other sciences. For example, the connection between experimental economics and the rest of economics has some things in common with the connection between experimental biology and the rest of biology. Like economics, some parts of biology, such as evolutionary biology, deal primarily with historical data about very large and complex systems that cannot be brought into the laboratory. Like economics, biology is called on to answer policy-related questions, such as those in medicine and public health, which go beyond what is reliably understood. But experimental methods and results have had an impact even on problems of this kind and of course a profound impact on biology generally. I think the same may one day be said of experimentation in economics.

This is not to say that developments in experimental economics will ever proceed in lock step with developments in other kinds of economic research. One does not have to be a philosopher of science to recognize, for example, that well-established theoretical edifices do not fall merely because some evidence begins to accumulate showing that they are not completely true, or even that they are largely false on some part of the domain to which they were supposed to apply. There are at least several reasons for this. First, science and scientists abhor a vacuum, and so an existing theory is most easily replaced by an alternative theory or group of theories, not by a collection of anomalous observations, however reliable. Second, established theories typically have become established because they explain some phenomena well, and if these phenomena are important, then any proposed replacement theory suffers a serious handicap if it cannot also address them. Finally, theories in economics frequently serve as building blocks from which to construct theories of larger scope, and any proposed replacement for an existing theory also suffers a handicap if it does not mesh well with the body of theory of which the existing theory is a part.

Conversely, neither the most pressing empirical phenomena in the economy at large nor the most powerful constructs in contemporary theory will necessarily be closely connected at any time with the most productive lines of experimental research (any more than they need to be closely connected to one another). Different kinds of research seem to set their own agendas, just as they establish different standards by which competing claims can be evaluated. One of the disciplines that experimentation imposes is that, in order even to begin an experiment, it is necessary to specify many details of the environment that are not addressed by most economic theories. Much of the work of experimental economics therefore concerns aspects of economic phenomena that are not addressed by other kinds of economic research.

Among the pleasures of the academic life must be counted the opportunity not only to pursue one's own work, but also to have a good vantage point from which to appreciate the work of one's colleagues and the evolution of one's field. I hope that this volume will make clear why the past few years, which I think have been formative for experimental economics, have been particularly exciting. I think that each of the directions explored in this volume has the potential to lead to significant changes in the way we understand economic phenomena.

References

Allais, Maurice (1953). "Le comportement de l'homme rationnel devant le risque: Critique des postulats et axiomes de l'école americaine." *Econometrica, 21*, 503–46.
Chamberlin, Edward H. (1948). "An Experimental Imperfect Market." *Journal of Political Economy, 56* (2), 95–108.

Ellsberg, Daniel (1961). "Risk, Ambiguity and the Savage Axioms." *Quarterly Journal of Economics*, 75, 643–69.

Ferber, Robert, and Werner Z. Hirsch (1982). *Social Experimentation and Economic Policy*, Cambridge Surveys of Economic Literature. Cambridge University Press.

Kahneman, Daniel, and Amos Tversky (1979). "Prospect Theory: An Analysis of Decision Under Risk." *Econometrica*, 47, 263–91.

Machina, Mark J. (1982). " 'Expected Utility' Analysis Without the Independence Axiom." *Econometrica*, 50, 277–323.

May, Kenneth O. (1954). "Intransitivity, Utility, and the Aggregation of Preference Patterns." *Econometrica*, 22, 1–13.

Plott, Charles R. (1982). "Industrial Organization Theory and Experimental Economics." *Journal of Economic Literature*, 20, 1485–1527.

Rapoport, Amnon, J. P. Kahan, S. G. Funk, and A. D. Horowitz (1979). *Coalition Formation by Sophisticated Players*, Lecture Notes in Economics and Mathematical Systems, No. 169. Berlin: Springer-Verlag

Rapoport, Anatol, and J. Perner (1974). "Testing Nash's Solution of the Cooperative Game," in *Game Theory as a Theory of Conflict Resolution*, A. Rapoport (ed.). Dordrecht: Reidel, pp. 103–115.

Roth, Alvin E. (1983). "Toward a Theory of Bargaining: An Experimental Study in Economics." *Science*, 220, 687–91.

 (in press). "Laboratory Experimentation in Economics," in *Advances in Economic Theory 1985 (Symposia of the 5th World Congress of the Econometric Society)*, T. Bewley (ed.). Cambridge University Press. Preprinted in *Economics and Philosophy*, 2, 245–73 (1986).

Sauermann, Heinz, ed. (1967). *Contributions to Experimental Economics* (Beitrage zur Experimentellen Wirtschaftsforschung), Vol. 1. Tübingen: Mohr.

Sauermann, Heinz, and Reinhard Selten (1959). "Ein Oligopolexperiment." *Zeitschrift für die Gesamte Staatswissenschaft*, 115, 427–71.

Siegel, Sidney, and Lawrence E. Fouraker (1960). *Bargaining and Group Decision Making: Experiments in Bilateral Monopoly*, New York: McGraw-Hill.

Smith, Vernon L. (1982). "Microeconomic Systems as an Experimental Science." *American Economic Review*, 72, 923–55.

Stone, Jeremy J. (1958). "An Experiment in Bargaining Games." *Econometrica*, 26, 286–97.

Tversky, Amos (1969). "Intransitivity of Preferences." *Psychological Review*, 76, 31–48.

CHAPTER 2

Bargaining phenomena and bargaining theory

ALVIN E. ROTH

2.1 Introduction

I first began to plan an experimental study of bargaining while I was preparing a monograph (Roth, 1979) concerned with what was then (and is probably still) the most comprehensively articulated body of formal theory about bargaining in the economics literature. I am referring to the game-theoretic work that followed in the tradition begun by John Nash (1950).[1]

A number of experiments had already investigated bargaining situations of the kind addressed by this set of theories, and some were even explicitly concerned with testing the predictions of the theory that Nash had proposed.[2] However, none of these experiments corresponded closely to the conditions assumed by Nash's theory or measured those attributes of the bargainers that the theory predicted would influence the outcome of bargaining. This was largely because, taken literally, Nash's theory applies to bargaining under conditions unlikely to obtain in natural bargaining situations and depends on attributes of the bargainers that are difficult to measure. Specifically, Nash's theory assumes that bargainers have available to them the

Almost all of the work described in this chapter has been done in collaboration with various colleagues: the theoretical work with Richard Kihlstrom, Uriel Rothblum, and David Schmeidler and the experimental work with Michael Malouf, J. Keith Murnighan, and Francoise Schoumaker. I owe them all a great debt, particularly Keith Murnighan. This work has also been supported by grants from the National Science Foundation and the Office of Naval Research and by a Fellowship from the Alfred P. Sloan Foundation.

[1] But see Roth (1985b) for a collection of papers concerned with new directions in the theory of bargaining.

[2] These were reviewed in Roth and Malouf (1979). Some connections between the results of those experiments and the ones presented in this chapter are discussed in Roth and Malouf (1982).

information contained in one another's expected utility functions (i.e., each bargainer's preferences and risk posture), and it depends on this information to generate a prediction about the outcome of bargaining. Some of the earlier experimenters had elected to examine bargaining under conditions they believed more closely approximated natural situations, and all had assumed, for the purpose of obtaining predictions from Nash's theory, that the preferences of all bargainers were identical and risk neutral.

Important aspects of the predictions of the theory obtained in this way were disconfirmed by the experimental evidence.[3] This evidence, however, was almost uniformly discounted by game theorists, who felt that the results simply reflected a failure to measure the relevant parameters. Nash's theory, after all, is a theory that predicts that the preferences and risk aversion of the bargainers exercise a decisive influence on the outcome of bargaining (and, furthermore, that these are the *only* personal attributes that can influence the outcome when bargainers are adequately informed). If the predictions made by Nash's theory *under the assumption* that bargainers had identical and risk-neutral preferences were disconfirmed, this merely disconfirmed the assumption. The theory itself had yet to be tested.

It was therefore clear that, in order to provide a test of the theory that would withstand the scrutiny of theorists,[4] an experiment would have to either measure or control for the differences among individuals in their willingness to bear risks. Such experiments would make it possible to test for the first time whether these differences influenced the outcome of bargaining in the manner predicted and whether they were the attributes of the bargainers that were the most important explanatory variables.

In the intervening years, my colleagues and I have conducted a series of experiments concerned with these issues. The first of these (Roth and Malouf, 1979) employed a design in which individual differences in risk aversion were controlled for, and the most recently completed (Murnighan, Roth, and Schoumaker, 1986) employed a design in which these differences were measured. It would not have been possible to plan from the outset or even to anticipate the need for each experiment in this series. But the results of each raised questions and suggested new hypotheses that guided the design of subsequent experiments. It was sometimes necessary to develop the implications

---

[3] Although the qualitative predictions about which bargainer would do better were sometimes supported.

[4] Among whom I am happily prepared to be counted, at least part time.

of the theory further before a particular experiment could be designed and to reassess, in the light of subsequent experiments, what had been learned from earlier ones. Sometimes unanticipated regularities were serendipitously observed. One purpose of this chapter is to shed some light on this process.

Only in the most recently completed experiment have we finally been able to test directly whether differences in individuals' risk aversion influence the outcome of bargaining in the manner predicted by Nash's theory. It turns out that these predictions are quite robust, in the sense that virtually all of the standard economic theories of bargaining make the same qualitative predictions about differences in risk aversion. The experimental results support these predictions.

However, the overwhelming evidence of all the experiments taken together points to the conclusion that some of the most important bargaining phenomena are neither predicted nor easily accommodated by such theories. As a theorist, I am inclined to believe that entirely new classes of theories will have to be explored. A second purpose of this chapter is to try to present in a coherent fashion the phenomena that have led me to this conclusion.

The remainder of this chapter is organized as follows. Section 2.2 briefly reviews the principal elements of theory that are necessary to understand the experiments and discusses some elements of procedure and experimental design shared by a number of our experiments. Section 2.3 reviews the results of some of these experiments, namely Roth and Malouf (1979), Roth, Malouf, and Murnighan (1981), Roth and Murnighan (1982, 1983), Roth and Schoumaker (1983), and Murnighan et al. (1986). Section 2.4 briefly discusses the serendipitous observation of what appears to be a very robust bargaining phenomenon, which I call the "deadline effect," and Section 2.5 concludes with a brief discussion of directions in which further experimentation may prove fruitful.

2.2   Theory and experimental design

2.2.1   Game-theoretic models of bargaining

John von Neumann and Oskar Morgenstern introduced, in their seminal 1944 book, not only the outlines of a theory of interactive behavior, but also a model of goal-oriented, "rational" behavior that has become the dominant model of individual choice behavior in economics.[5] They modeled individual choice by means of a binary

[5] But see Chapter 4 by Thaler and my comments in Chapter 1.

preference relation defined on the set of alternatives and established conditions on preferences that, if satisfied, implied that the corresponding choice behavior could be viewed as the result of maximizing an *expected utility* function. That is, a utility function represents the preferences by assigning every alternative α a number $u(\alpha)$, with $u(\alpha)$ being greater than $u(\beta)$ if and only if alternative α is preferred to alternative β. Lotteries between alternatives – that is, probability distributions over alternatives – are themselves alternatives over which preferences are defined, and von Neumann and Morgenstern showed how utility representations could be constructed so that the utility of a lottery was equal to the expected value of the utility of the outcome of the lottery. That is, if p is a probability and $L = [p\alpha; (1 - p)\beta]$ is the lottery that yields the alternative α with probability p and the alternative β with probability $(1 - p)$, then $u(L) = pu(\alpha) + (1 - p)u(\beta)$ is the utility of participating in the lottery L.

For preferences that obey the regularity conditions they proposed, their method of construction involves scaling the utility of any alternative in terms of an arbitrarily chosen origin and unit. Consider any two alternatives α and β such that α is preferred to β, and set the utilities $u(\alpha) = 1$ and $u(\beta) = 0$. Now consider an alternative γ such that α is preferred to γ, which is in turn preferred to β. Then finding the utility $u(\gamma)$ consists of finding the probability p such that the preferences are indifferent between γ and the lottery $L(\gamma) = [p\alpha; (1 - p)\beta]$, so that $u(\gamma) = u(L(\gamma)) = p$. A utility function constructed in this way conveys not only an individual's preferences among nonrisky alternatives, but also the individual's willingness to undertake risky ventures. The latter property has come to be called the individual's "risk posture."

For various reasons, it was convenient to represent the feasible outcomes of multiperson decision problems – "games"– as numerical outcomes representing the utilities of the players. Nash (1950) followed this tradition when he considered what is sometimes called the "pure bargaining problem," in which two bargainers must agree on one alternative from a set A of feasible alternatives over which they have different preferences. If they fail to reach agreement, some fixed disagreement alternative δ results. Nash modeled such a problem by a pair (S, d), where S is a subset of the plane and d a point in S. The set S represents the feasible utility payoffs to the bargainers – that is, each point $x = (x_1, x_2)$ in S corresponds to the utility payoffs to players 1 and 2 from some alternative α in A, and $d = (d_1, d_2)$ corresponds to the utility payoffs to the players from the disagreement alternative δ.

Nash proposed to model the bargaining process by a function f that would associate with each pair (S, d) a point in S. That is, for each

18   Alvin E. Roth

bargaining problem represented in terms of the utilities of the bargainers, such a function f would predict what agreement would be reached, also in terms of the utilities of the bargainers. In fact, Nash characterized a particular function f as the unique such function possessing certain properties (axioms) that he proposed. However, for our purposes here, it will be sufficient to note that any of this class of functions constitutes a theory of bargaining that takes as its data the set (S, d). That is, such a function f embodies a theory of bargaining that predicts that the outcome of bargaining will be determined by the preferences of the bargainers over the set of feasible alternatives, together with their willingness to tolerate risk.[6]

2.2.2   Binary lottery games

To test theories that depend on the von Neumann–Morgenstern utilities of the bargainers, an experiment must be designed so that these utilities can be determined. An experimental design of this kind was discussed in Roth (1979) and first implemented in Roth and Malouf (1979). In these *binary lottery games*, each agent i can eventually win only one of two monetary prizes: a large prize λ_i or a small prize σ_i (with $\lambda_i > \sigma_i$). The players bargain over the distribution of "lottery tickets" that determine the probability of receiving the large prize; for example, an agent i who receives 40% of the lottery tickets has a 40% chance of receiving the amount λ_i and a 60% chance of receiving the amount σ_i. Players who do not reach agreement in the allotted time each receive σ_i. Since the information about preferences conveyed by an expected utility function is meaningfully represented only up to the arbitrary choice of origin and scale, there is no loss of generality in normalizing each agent's utility so that $u_i(\lambda_i) = 1$ and $u_i(\sigma_i) = 0$. The utility of agent i for any agreement is then precisely equal to his probability of receiving the amount λ_i, that is equal to the percentage of lottery tickets he has received.

Of course, so far we have not addressed the (empirical) question of whether a given individual's choice behavior can indeed be summarized by a preference relation exhibiting the regularity conditions needed for it to be accurately represented by an expected utility

[6] This was the traditional assumption in cooperative game theory. Indeed, games in which the players know both the rules of the game and one another's preferences and risk posture are referred to as games of "complete information" (the assumption being that there is nothing else that is important to know). The tacit assumption underlying Nash's work (although it plays no part in the mathematics) is that the games he considers are played under conditions of complete information.

function. In fact, a substantial body of empirical work has recorded a number of systematic ways in which individual preferences often fail to exhibit these regularities. However, the most serious of these departures from expected utility maximization involve the way trade-offs are made among three or more riskless alternatives (see Machina, 1983). Since only two such alternatives are feasible in a binary lottery game, these departures at least do not arise.

2.2.3   Procedures

The following procedures, taken from Roth and Murnighan (1982), are fairly typical of those used in each of our experiments:

Each participant was seated at a visually isolated terminal of a computer system, called PLATO. . . . Participants were seated at scattered terminals . . . and received all of their instructions and conducted all communication via the terminal. . . . Pretests were run with the same subject pool to make sure that the instructions were clear.

Background information including a brief review of probability theory was presented first. The procedures for sending messages and proposals were then introduced. A proposal was a pair of numbers, the first being the sender's probability of receiving his prize and the second the receiver's probability. . . . The proposal was displayed on a graph of the feasible region, along with the expected monetary value of each proposal. [In each information condition, PLATO displayed the expected monetary value which the player would receive from any proposal he made or received. The opponent's expected value was only displayed in those conditions in which the player knew his opponent's prize.] Bargainers could cancel a proposal before its transmittal. . . . An agreement was reached whenever one of the bargainers returned a proposal identical to the one he had just received.

Messages were not binding. Bargainers could send any message they wished, with one exception. To insure anonymity, the monitor intercepted any messages that revealed the identity of the players. Intercepted messages were returned to the sender's terminal with a note that participants were not permitted to identify themselves.

Not all of the experiments discussed in the next section used precisely the same procedures, and significant variations are noted where they occurred. Except as noted, the allotted time for each bargaining game was from 9 to 12 minutes. A clock came on the screen to mark the last 3 minutes.

With any set of procedures, there must be some concern as to which of the experimental results might be artifacts of the procedures. Of particular concern to us was the fact that the automatic computation of the expected monetary values made those values extremely salient. Pilot studies showed that the results obtained without providing this computation went in the same direction as those reported below, but with more variance. We decided to make the computation of the expected values automatically available because we did not want arithmetic ability to be a determinant of the relative success of the bargainers. However, the experiment reported in Section 2.3.2 was designed in part to verify that the results reported in Section 2.3.1 did not depend critically on the availability of this computation.

2.3   A series of experiments

2.3.1   Is "complete information" complete?

Note that the set of feasible utility payoffs to the players of a binary lottery game is insensitive to the magnitudes of λ_i and σ_i for each agent i. Furthermore, the bargainers have "complete" information whether or not they know the value of one another's prizes, since knowing a bargainer's probability of winning λ_i is equivalent to knowing his utility. Thus a theory of bargaining under conditions of complete information that depends only on the utility payoffs to the bargainers predicts that the outcome of the game will depend neither on the size of the prizes nor on whether the bargainers know the monetary value of one another's prizes. The experiment of Roth and Malouf (1979) was designed in part to test this prediction and determine whether changes in the size of the prizes, and whether the bargainers knew one another's prizes, influenced the outcome.

Each bargainer played games with different prizes[7] against different opponents in one of two information conditions. In the "full-information" condition, each bargainer knew both his own prize and his counterpart's; bargainers who were assigned to the "partial-information" condition knew only their own prize value. In the partial-information condition, messages concerning the value of the prizes were not allowed.[8] Tables 2.1 and 2.2 describe the games and give the mean and standard deviations of the observed outcomes.[9]

[7] In all the games of this experiment the small prize was equal to zero for both bargainers. The experiment also included some games in which the maximum percentage of lottery tickets obtainable by one of the bargainers was restricted in order to test a property of Nash's model – "independence of irrelevant alternatives" – which is not discussed here.

[8] Thus in addition to the anonymity restriction discussed in Section 2.2.3, this experiment imposed a further restriction on messages.

[9] The statistics are presented in terms of the quantity $D = p_2 - p_1$, where p_i is the percentage of lottery tickets obtained by player i. Thus if the bargainers split the lottery tickets 50–50 (as predicted by Nash's solution), D will equal 0.

Table 2.1. *Prizes and feasible distributions for games 1 to 4*

Game	Prize for player 1 ($)	Prize for player 2 ($)	Maximum % allowed player 1	Maximum % allowed player 2
1	1	1	100	100
2	1	1	100	60
3	1.25	3.75	100	100
4	1.25	3.75	100	60

Source: Roth and Malouf (1979).

Table 2.2. *Means and standard deviations for* $D = p_2 - p_1$

Statistic	Game			
	1	2	3	4
	Full information (11 pairs)			
Mean	0.0	−1.9	−34.6	−21.6
SD	0.0	12.2	19.3	22.5
	Partial information (8 pairs)			
Mean	0.0	1.3	2.5	−2.5
SD	0.0	8.3	4.6	4.1

Note: The mean and standard deviation are reported after the removal of an outlier [$D = +98$ resulting from a (1, 99) agreement] that is 6.8 standard deviations from the mean.
Source: Roth and Malouf (1979).

In the partial-information condition, in which the bargainers did not know one another's prizes, and also in those games of the full-information condition in which the two bargainers had equal prizes, agreements were observed to cluster around the "equal probability" agreement that gives each bargainer 50% of the lottery tickets, often with extremely low variance. In the full-information condition, in those games in which the bargainers' prizes were not equal, agreements tended to cluster around two "focal points": the equal probability agreement and the "equal expected value" agreement that gives each bargainer the same expected value. That is, in these games the bargainer with the lower prize tended to receive a higher share of the lottery tickets. The mean agreement in these games tended to fall approximately halfway between the (50%, 50%) agreement (with

$D = 0$) and the (75%, 25%) agreement ($D = -50$) that yields equal expected monetary payoffs (since player 2's prize was three times the size of player 1's). These means were significantly different from those of other games.

Contrary to the prediction of the theory, the monetary value of the bargainer's prizes, and whether the bargainers knew the value of each other's prizes, were thus clearly observed to influence the agreements reached in the full-information condition. The next experiment was designed in part to determine whether this effect was an artifact of the experimental design.

2.3.2   Focal points: strategic or sociological?

One difference between the two information conditions of the previous experiment that might account for the different outcomes observed has to do with the kinds of messages the players can formulate. The transcripts of the messages exchanged show that the value of the prizes, and the disparity between them, played a considerable part in the negotiations in the full-information condition. The equal probability (50, 50) proposal and the equal expected value (75, 25) proposal occupied prominent places in these negotiations. Although both parties mentioned notions of "fairness," the way they employed these notions clearly had a strategic aspect since the player advancing the (50, 50) outcome as fair could be reliably counted on to be the player with the larger prize. One natural question is whether the different agreements reached in the two conditions might be *entirely* due to the different strategies available to the bargainers or whether some sociological factors related to notions of equity recognized by both bargainers might be an essential ingredient in the effectiveness of the strategic appeals to "fairness."

The experiment of Roth et al. (1981) was designed to reveal whether arbitrary focal points could be created. It employed binary lottery games with prizes stated in terms of an intermediate commodity, "chips," having monetary value. Each player always knew the number and value of chips in his own prize, but a player's information about his opponent's prize was an experimental variable. The conditions of the previous experiment were essentially replicated, there being "low-information" and "high-information" conditions, and in addition there was an "intermediate-information" condition, in which each player knew the number of chips in his opponent's prize, but not their value. As in the previous experiment, messages that revealed information

Table 2.3. *Prizes in chips and dollars*

	Player 1			Player 2		
	Number of chips	Value per chip ($)	Value of prize ($)	Number of chips	Value per chip ($)	Value of prize ($)
Game 1	60	0.05	3.00	20	0.45	9.00
Game 2	80	0.03	2.40	240	0.04	9.60
Game 3	100	0.09	9.00	300	0.01	3.00
Game 4	150	0.08	12.00	50	0.06	3.00

Source: Roth, Malouf, and Murnighan (1981).

about the prize values not contained in the instructions were not allowed. The experiment was conducted so that the intermediate-information condition was strategically equivalent to the full-information condition of Roth and Malouf (1979), "equal expected number of chips" in this experiment being strategically equivalent to "equal expected value" in that experiment. In particular, in the intermediate-information condition, the expected value of each proposal *in chips* was automatically computed in precisely the same way that the expected monetary value was handled in the full-information condition of the previous experiment.

If the results of the previous experiment were an artifact of the procedures or if they could be explained entirely in terms of the strategies available to the players in formulating messages, the results of bargaining in the intermediate-information condition should resemble the results of bargaining in the full-information condition of the previous experiment. In that case, the player with the smaller prize *in chips* should receive a significantly higher share of the lottery tickets in the intermediate-information condition than the player whose prize contains more chips. However, if the results of the previous experiment depended on the players sharing some social conventions of what might constitute "fair" (or credible) bargaining positions, proposals for "equal expected value in chips" should not meet with the same success as did proposals for "equal expected value in money" in the previous experiment, even though the expected values were displayed in the same way and equivalent messages could be transmitted about the two commodities in the corresponding information conditions.

The games are described in Table 2.3, and the results are graphed in Figure 2.1.

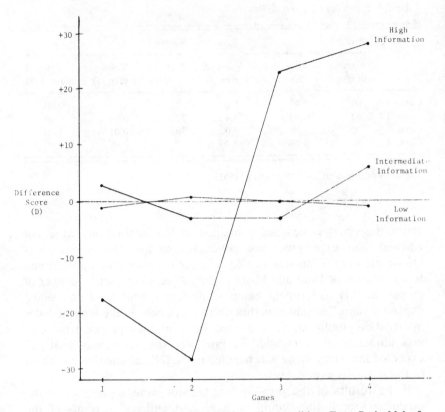

Figure 2.1. Means for games by information condition. From Roth, Malouf, and Murnighan (1981).

The observed results were that the low- and high-information conditions replicated the partial- and full-information conditions of the previous experiment, but the outcomes observed in the intermediate-information conditions did *not* differ significantly from those in the low-information condition: The observed agreements tended to give both players equal probabilities, regardless of the size of their prize in chips. The means in each game do reflect a small tendency for the player with the smaller number of chips in his prize to receive a higher percentage of the lottery tickets; however, this effect is approximately an order of magnitude smaller than the difference between the prizes of the players with low and high *monetary* values in either the full-information condition of the previous experiment or the high-information condition of this one (see Figure 2.1).[10] Thus information about the artificial commodity, chips, did not affect the outcomes in the same way as did strategically equivalent information about money.

This supports the hypothesis that there is a "social" aspect to the focal point phenomenon that depends on the players' shared perceptions of the credibility of any bargaining position.

2.3.3   Common knowledge and the fine structure of shared information

The experiments described above revealed an effect of information that cannot be explained as an artifact of the experimental procedures and demonstrated that information about an artificial commodity does not play the same role as information about money. To the extent that this effect depends on the players' *shared* perceptions, it is likely to depend on the detailed nature of their information and the extent to which it is "common knowledge."[11]

In the earlier experiments, either each bargainer knew his opponents' prize or neither bargainer knew his opponent's prize, and each player always knew what information his counterpart possessed in this regard. The next experiment was conducted to separate the observed effect of information into components that could be attributed to the possession of specific information by specific individuals.

Each game of the experiment of Roth and Murnighan (1982) was a binary lottery game in which one player had a $20 prize and the other

[10] Note that the experiment is designed so that in two of the four games the player with the higher number of chips has the smaller monetary prize, and in the other two games the player with the higher number of chips has the larger monetary prize (see Table 2.3). The results from the intermediate-information condition can thus be unambiguously interpreted as giving the players with the smaller number of chips a slightly higher mean percentage of lottery tickets. If the difference in the bargainers' success in this condition had somehow been due to their monetary payoffs, the intermediate-information curve in Figure 2.1 would have had the same shape as the high-information curve.

[11] A piece of information is common knowledge between us if not only do we both know it, but I know you know it and you know I know it, and I know you know I know it, etc. Knowledge of an event can be thought of as becoming common knowledge when the event occurs in public, so not only do we see it, but we see each other seeing it, etc. The notion of common knowledge, which has become familiar in economic theory, seems to have been first formally considered by the philosopher David Lewis (1969) in his treatment of social conventions.

a $5 prize. In all eight conditions of the experiment, each player knew at least his own prize. The experiment employed a 4 (information) × 2 (common knowledge) factorial design. The information conditions were (1) neither knows his opponent's prize; (2) the $20 player knows both prizes, but the $5 player knows only his own prize; (3) the $5 player knows both prizes, but the $20 player knows only his own prize; and (4) both players know both prizes. The second factor made this information common knowledge for half the bargaining pairs but not common knowledge for the other half. For example, when the $20 player is the only one who knows both prizes, the (common) instructions to both players in the common-knowledge condition reveal that both players are reading the same instructions and that, after the instructions are presented, one player will be informed of only his own prize, and the other will be informed of both prizes. In the non-common-knowledge condition, the instructions simply state that each player will be informed of his own prize and may or may not be informed of the other prize. Note that the two conditions that made it common knowledge that neither player knew both prizes or that both players knew both prizes provide a replication of the experiment of Roth and Malouf (1979).[12]

We drew three principal conclusions from the results of this experiment: First, the equal expected value agreement becomes a focal point if and only if the player with the smaller prize knows both prizes. When the $5 player knew that the other player's prize was $20, this was reflected not only in his messages and proposals, but also in the mean agreements (i.e., mean percentage of lottery tickets obtained by each player) when agreement was reached (see Table 2.4), and in the shape of the distribution of agreements (see Figure 2.2). Note that, in the four conditions in which the $5 player does *not* know his opponent's prize, the distribution of agreements has a single mode, corresponding to the (50, 50) equal probability agreement. However, in the four conditions in which the $5 player *does* know that the other player has a $20 prize, the distribution of agreements is *bi*modal, with a second mode corresponding to the (20, 80) equal expected value agreement. Note also that the mean agreements reached when neither player knows both prizes and when both players know both prizes replicate the results of Roth and Malouf (1979), in both direction and magnitude.

[12] Except that, in all conditions of this experiment, bargainers were free to send any messages they wished about their prizes. The only messages that were illegal in any condition were those in which a bargainer sought to identify himself.

Table 2.4. *Mean percentage of lottery tickets to the $20 and $5 players in each information–common-knowledge condition when agreements were reached (disagreements excluded)*

Information	Common knowledge		Non-common knowledge	
	$20 player	$5 player	$20 player	$5 player
Neither player knows both prizes	48.8	51.2	47.5	52.5
Only the $20 player knows both prizes	43.6	56.4	49.1	50.9
Only the $5 player knows both prizes	33.6	66.4	37.2	62.8
Both players know both prizes	32.6	67.4	34.3	65.7

Note: Outcomes are the mean lottery percentages obtained by the $20 player (expressed first) and the $5 player when they reached agreement.
Source: Roth and Murnighan (1982).

Second, whether it is common knowledge what information the bargainers possess influences the frequency of disagreement (Table 2.5). The frequency of disagreement in the two non-common-knowledge conditions in which the $5 player knows both prizes is significantly higher than in the other conditions. The highest frequency of disagreement (33%) occurs when the $5 player knows both prizes, the $20 player does not, but the $5 player does not *know* that the $20 player does not know both prizes. (In this situation the $5 player cannot accurately assess whether the $20 player's honest skepticism about his opponent's prize being only $5 is just a bargaining ploy.)

Third, in the non-common-knowledge conditions, the relationship among the outcomes is consistent with the hypothesis that the bargainers are rational utility maximizers who correctly assess the trade-offs involved in the negotiations. That is, in the non-common-knowledge conditions there is a trade-off between the higher payoffs demanded by the $5 player when he knows both prizes (as reflected in the mean agreements in Table 2.4) and the number of agreements actually reached (as reflected in the frequency of disagreement). One could imagine that, when $5 players knew both prizes, they might have tended, as a group, to persist in unrealistic expectations about how high a percentage of lottery tickets they could obtain. The mean overall (utility) payoffs (i.e., percentage of lottery tickets) given in Table 2.6 (which include both agreements and disagreements) indicate that this is not the case. The increase in the number of disagreements just offsets

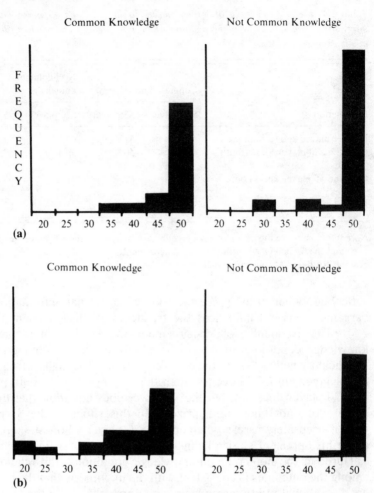

Figure 2.2. Frequency of agreements in terms of the percentage of lottery tickets obtained by the $20 player. (a) Neither player knows both prizes; (b) only the $20 player knows both prizes; (c) only the $5 player knows both prizes; (d) both players know both prizes. From Roth and Murnighan (1982).

the improvement in the terms of agreement when the $5 players know both prizes, so that the overall expected payoff to the $5 players does not change. This means that the behavior of $5 players observed in any one of these conditions could not profitably have been substituted for the behavior observed in any other condition.

Consider, for example, a $5 player who knows his opponent's prize is $20 but does not know if his opponent knows both prizes. (In

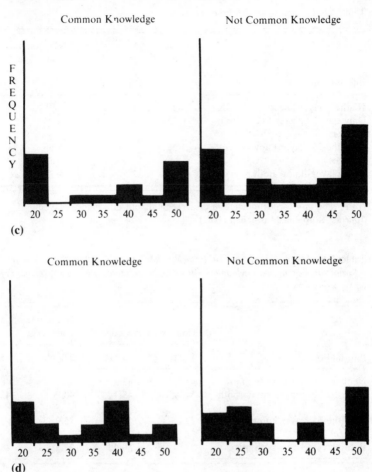

(c)

(d)

general, $20 players who did know their opponent's prize tried to conceal this knowledge.) Suppose the $5 player thinks it is equally likely that his opponent does or does not know his prize. Then, looking at Table 2.6 we see that he faces a 50–50 gamble between 48.8 or 42.0% if he acts as if he knows both prizes and a 50–50 gamble between 42.4 and 48.2% if he acts as if he does not. Since the expected values of these two gambles do not significantly differ, the $5 players who knew both prizes could not have profited if they had behaved as if they did not.

The same is true of the $20 player. In particular, the expected payoff of $20 players who knew both prizes does not differ from that of those who knew only their own prize (although it is significantly affected by what the $5 player knows), so that a $20 player who knew both prizes,

Table 2.5. *Frequency of disagreements*

	Common knowledge		Non-common knowledge	
Information	*m/n*	Percentage	*m/n*	Percentage
Neither player knows both prizes	4/27	14	3/36	8
Only the $20 player knows both prizes	6/30	20	4/24	17
Only the $5 player knows both prizes	5/26	19	18/55	33
Both players know both prizes	5/30	17	9/35	26

Note: The *m/n* values indicate *m* disagreements out of *n* games played.
Source: Roth and Murnighan (1982).

Table 2.6. *Mean percentage of lottery tickets to the $20 and $5 players in each information–common-knowledge condition over all interactions (disagreements included as zero outcomes)*

	Common knowledge		Non-common knowledge	
Information	$20 player	$5 player	$20 player	$5 player
Neither player knows both prizes	41.6_{ab}	43.3_c	43.5_a	48.2
Only the $20 player knows both prizes	34.9_{bc}	45.1_{bc}	40.9_a	42.4
Only the $5 player knows both prizes	27.2_c	53.6_{ab}	25.0_b	42.0
Both players know both prizes	27.2_c	56.4_a	25.5_b	48.8

Note: Within a column, means with common subscripts are not significantly different from one another using the Mann–Whitney U test ($a = .01$); none were significantly different in the non-common-knowledge conditions for the $5 player.
Source: Roth and Murnighan (1982).

for example, could not have profited from behaving as he would have if he knew only his own prize. The situation facing $20 players is slightly different from that facing $5 players, since $5 players who knew both prizes were virtually always quick to say so (often in their very first message). So a $20 player who knew both prizes should not have been in much doubt about whether his opponent knew both prizes also. Looking at Table 2.6 again we see that a $20 player whose opponent knew both prizes had an expected payoff of 25.5% if he knew his

Table 2.7. *Mean first demands of the players in the different information conditions when the players had common knowledge*

	Mean first demands (percentage of lottery tickets) by	
Information condition	$20 player	$5 player
Neither knows	67.4$_b$	69.4$_b$
$20 player knows	67.6$_b$	71.7$_b$
$5 player knows	62.9$_b$	80.8$_a$
Both know	61.6$_b$	83.8$_a$

Note: Cells with common subscripts are *not* significantly different from one another at the .05 level using the Newman–Keuls procedure.
Source: Roth and Murnighan (1983).

opponent's prize and 25.0% if he did not, the two payoffs not being significantly different. A $20 player whose opponent knew only his own prize had an expected payoff of 40.9% if he knew his opponent's prize and 43.5% if he did not, again the two payoffs not being significantly different. So, like a $5 player, a $20 player who knew both prizes could not profit by behaving as he would have if he had known only his own prize.

The situation is somewhat different in the common-knowledge conditions. The ability of players to misrepresent what they know is more limited in these conditions, but the strategies available to the $20 player when it is common knowledge that only he knows both prizes are the same as those available to the $5 player when it is common knowledge that he is the only one who knows both prizes. However, the expected overall payoff to the $20 player in this situation is only 34.9% of the lottery tickets (see Table 2.6) compared with an expected payoff of 53.6% for the $5 player in the corresponding situation.

In order to understand why this is the case, Roth and Murnighan (1983) undertook a more detailed analysis of the record of negotiations. Both the proposals and messages generated by the bargainers were analyzed. Table 2.7 gives the mean demand made by each player in his first proposal in these negotiations, which gives some idea of the bargainers' maximal objectives. These figures tell much of the story: $5 players who knew both prizes got a higher mean payoff than any other players in these conditions because they demanded more. No other players made demands of nearly 80%, as the informed $5 players did. This is not to say that other players did not demand more than their "fair share." Analysis of the messages and proposals shows that they did. But when informed $20 players who knew that the $5 player was uninformed chose to misrepresent their own prize, they did not claim that their own prize was only one-quarter of their opponent's, and they did not stick to their demands with the tenacity of the informed $5 players. In view of the success of the $5 players when it was common knowledge that only they were informed, it seems likely that the $20 players could have increased their expected payoff by being more demanding and more insistent.

2.3.4   Expectations and reputations

Together, these experiments demonstrate an effect that is consistent with rational (equilibrium) behavior but that cannot be accounted for simply in terms of players' preferences over consequences (lotteries) or by the set of available actions (strategies). Thus if we continue to hypothesize that the players are (approximately) Bayesian utility maximers, it must be that the effect of information about the value of the prizes on the observed outcome is due to a change in the players' subjective beliefs.

The experiment of Roth and Schoumaker (1983) was conducted to investigate this hypothesis; the point was to determine if either one of the two observed focal points could be obtained as a stable equilibrium by directly manipulating the bargainers' expectations about what agreements were most likely to be achieved. To this end, the bargainers were asked to play a sequence of 25 identical binary lottery games, nominally against a sequence of different opponents. In fact, in each of two experimental conditions, the subjects played the first 15 games against a programmed opponent designed to reinforce their expectations of either the equal probability agreement or the equal expected value agreement. A third group of subjects constituted the control group and played all 25 of their games against different opponents from the same subject pool.

In order to make it difficult to detect that a programmed opponent was involved in the first 15 trials while at the same time ensuring that the program behaved in a consistent manner, the games were simplified by the elimination of messages. Instead, only proposals were allowed to be transmitted, in two stages. In the first stage, each player made any proposal he wished. In the second stage, each player could choose only between repeating his first-stage proposal and agreeing to the proposal he had been offered in the first stage. Two minutes were allotted for the first stage, and one minute for the second. An

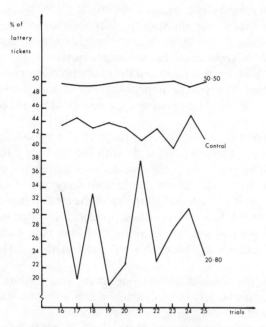

Figure 2.3. Average percentage of lottery tickets obtained by the $40 player when agreement was reached in trials 16 to 25. From Roth and Schoumaker (1983).

agreement was reached only when at least one of the bargainers accepted the proposal he had been offered.

The results (Figure 2.3) clearly supported the "expectations" hypothesis, since the observed agreements in the three conditions diverged as predicted: In the last 10 plays, the agreements in the control condition fell between those in the two experimental conditions, whose outcomes were concentrated on the focal point expected on the basis of experience of the first 15 games against the programmed opponent. This experiment shows that by manipulating the expectations of the players we can sort them between the two previously observed focal points. The results are consistent with (and provide some indirect support for) the hypothesis that the effect of players having information about one another's prizes observed in the previous experiments is due to the way in which this information affects each player's expectations about what agreements his opponent will accept.

2.3.5 Risk aversion and bargaining ability

Although the experiments described above reveal a number of ways in which the existing models of bargaining systematically fail to describe observed behavior, these experiments primarily involve the effects of variables that the theories in question predict will not influence the outcome of bargaining. As such, the experimental results demonstrate that these theories have serious shortcomings. However, in order to evaluate a theory fully, we must also test the predictions it makes about those variables that it says *are* important. For theories based on bargainers' von Neumann–Morgenstern expected utilities, risk posture is such a variable.

To put it another way, the success of these classical models in the theoretical economics literature has to do with the kinds of intuitively appealing *qualitative* predictions they make in a variety of circumstances. Some of these qualitative predictions may prove to have descriptive power even though many aspects of the overall model from which they are derived do not. Since these models are stated in terms of the von Neumann–Morgenstern utilities of the bargainers, the bargainers' risk postures are inevitably involved in their qualitative predictions.

The predictions of these models relating to the risk posture of the bargainers had not previously been developed in a way that lent itself to direct experimental testing. A systematic theoretical study of these issues was therefore carried out by Roth (1979, 1985a), Kihlstrom, Roth, and Schmeidler (1981), and Roth and Rothblum (1982). Rather surprisingly, a very broad class of apparently quite different models, including all the standard axiomatic models[13] and the strategic model of Rubinstein (1982)[14] yield a common prediction regarding risk aversion. Loosely speaking, these models predict that risk aversion is disadvantageous in bargaining, except when the bargaining concerns potential agreements that have a positive probability of yielding an outcome that is worse than disagreement. That is, these models predict that a personal attribute of the bargainers – their risk aversion – will have a decisive influence on the outcome of bargaining. This prediction concerning risk aversion is important to test not only because it is a central and robust prediction of existing bargaining theories, but also because it connects the theory of bargaining with what has proved to be one of the most powerful explanatory variables in a number of other areas of economics.

From the point of view of developing the experimental design, the

---

[13] Including those of Nash (1950), Kalai and Smorodinsky (1975), and Perles and Maschler (1981).

[14] See Binmore, Rubinstein, and Wolinsky (1986) for a somewhat different interpretation.

crucial theoretical development was the demonstration by Roth and Rothblum (1982) that there are situations in which theories of bargaining like Nash's predict that risk aversion will be advantageous to a bargainer. Before that theoretical demonstration, it had not been clear how to design an experiment that would separate the predicted (*dis*advantageous) effects of risk aversion from the possible effects of other personal attributes that might be correlated with risk aversion. For example, if risk aversion is predicted to be disadvantageous in all the bargaining situations under examination and if an experiment is conducted in which it is observed that more risk averse bargainers do worse than less risk averse bargainers in these situations, risk aversion might still be correlated with, say, a lack of aggressiveness, and aggressiveness might account for bargaining success.

Three closely related experimental studies exploring the predicted effects of risk aversion on the outcome of bargaining are reported in Murnighan et al. (1986). Whereas binary lottery games were employed in the earlier experiments precisely in order to control the individual variation due to differences in risk posture, these studies employed *ternary* lottery games having *three* possible payoffs for each bargainer i. These are large and small prizes λ_i and σ_i obtained by lottery when agreement is reached and a disagreement prize δ_i obtained when no agreement is reached in the allotted time. (In binary lottery games, $\sigma_i = \delta_i$.)

We measured the bargainers' risk postures by having them make a set of risky choices. Significant differences in risk aversion were found among the population of participants, even on the relatively modest range of prizes available in these studies (in which typical gambles involved choosing between receiving $5 for certain or participating in a lottery with prizes of $\lambda_i = \$16$ and $\sigma_i = \$4$).

Those bargainers with relatively high risk aversion bargained against those with relatively low risk aversion in pairs of games such that $\delta_i > \sigma_i$ in one game and $\delta_i < \sigma_i$ in the other. The prediction of game-theoretic models such as Nash's is that agreements reached in the first game should be more favorable to the more risk averse of the two bargainers than agreements reached in the second game.[15]

[15] In contrast, the hypothesis that bargaining ability is a personal attribute uncorrelated with risk aversion would lead to the prediction that whichever bargainer did better in one game would do better in the other, whereas the hypothesis that bargaining ability is related to a personal attribute correlated with but distinct from risk aversion might predict, e.g., that the less risk aversion bargainer would do better in both games. It was in order to design an experiment that would distinguish between such hypotheses that we

The results of these experiments support the predictions of the game-theoretic models that more risk averse bargainers do better when the disagreement prize is high than when it is low. But these results also suggest that, in the (relatively modest) range of payoffs studied here, the effects due to risk aversion may be much smaller than some of the "focal point" effects observed in previous experiments.

Because the effects of risk aversion were not large in this range of payoffs, the work reported in Murnighan et al. (1986) turned out to be both difficult and time-consuming to complete.[16] The reason we reported three studies in that paper is that we found it necessary to make small changes in the experimental design as we went along in order to better separate the effects of risk aversion from other influences on the outcome of bargaining. It would be worthwhile to conduct further experiments designed to improve our understanding of both the nature and magnitude of the influence of risk aversion on the outcome of bargaining.

2.4   The "deadline effect"

Although some of the experimental results reported in the preceding sections were unexpected, they were not entirely unanticipated, in the sense that they concern phenomena that the experiments were specifically designed to elicit. For example, it was not expected that information about the prizes would lead to a bimodal distribution of agreements, but the experiments that uncovered this phenomenon were designed to reveal the effects of such information. In this section we report a phenomenon that the experiments were not designed to investigate but that we noticed in passing in each of the experiments: Whatever the time limit on the bargaining, many agreements were reached very near the end, just before the deadline. When we (belatedly) made a formal examination of the distribution of agreements over time in each of our experiments (see Roth, Murnighan, and Schoumaker, 1987), the phenomenon that we now call the "deadline effect"

decided to measure subjects' risk aversion, rather than control it, since a design that induced arbitrary risk postures would mask any correlation between risk posture and some other personal attribute that was instead responsible for the outcome. One set of laboratory procedures that could be used to implement a binary lottery game design to control for various risk postures has been independently described by Berg et al. (1986).

[16] The experiments were begun very shortly after the theoretical work reported in Roth and Rothblum (1982) was completed.

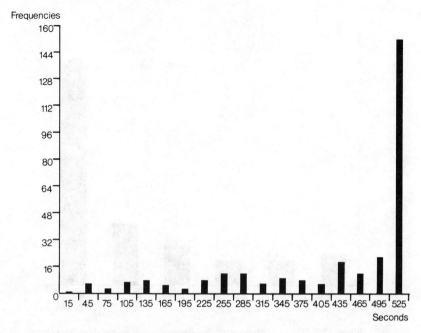

Figure 2.4. Distribution of agreement times. Numbers on the horizontal axis indicate the midpoint of 30-second intervals. Thus 525 indicates agreements in the last 30 seconds of bargaining, i.e., 511–540. From Murnighan, Roth, and Schoumaker (1986).

literally leaped out at us: There is a pronounced concentration of agreements in the last seconds before the deadline.[17]

Figures 2.4 and 2.5, which show the distribution over time of the agreements in the experiment of Murnighan et al. (1986), are fairly typical. Bargaining in that experiment had a time limit of 9 minutes (540 seconds), and Figure 2.4 shows clearly that agreements were overwhelmingly concentrated in the last 30 seconds. Figure 2.5 shows the distribution of agreements reached in the last 30 seconds and reveals that most of the action took place in the last 5 seconds.

The important thing to note here is that, although we were not looking for this deadline effect, it is clearly and consistently observed

[17] It is worth recalling in this connection that each bargainer could make proposals at any time during the bargaining period (regardless of what the other bargainer was doing) and that an agreement was reached whenever a bargainer made a proposal identical to one he had just received.

Frequencies

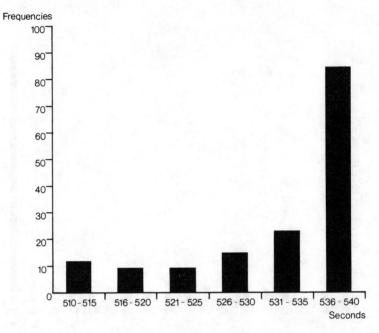

Figure 2.5. The distribution of agreement times in the last 30 seconds of negotiations. From Murnighan, Roth, and Schoumaker (1986).

in a range of experiments.[18] Although much more experimental and theoretical work must be done before we will understand what is involved, some sort of deadline effect will probably be an important and robust phenomenon whenever bargaining takes place with an approaching deadline and it is not too costly to the bargainers to continue bargaining up until the deadline.[19]

2.5   Where do we go from here?

The kinds of experiments described in this chapter, which are intimately connected with a body of theory, are by nature a part of a continuing

[18] Casual empiricism leads me to believe that a similar phenomenon is observed in many natural bargaining situations, when agreements are reached in the final days, hours, or even minutes before some deadline is reached.

[19] Of course, in waiting until the last moments before the deadline the bargainers incurred some costs, since sometimes a bargainer would try to make a concession or accept a proposal too late, and time would run out before he could transmit it.

dialogue. Directions in which to develop theory become clearer as experimental evidence builds up about systematic bargaining phenomena, and developments in theory suggest questions to investigate experimentally. No long-term experimental agenda (at least none that I can formulate) would be likely to survive intact the unanticipated developments that are characteristic of this kind of work. At the same time, new directions in the evolving theory of bargaining raise new questions and may cause us to interpret some of the empirical evidence in a new way.

Undoubtedly, new directions for experimental investigation will arise from the modern body of theory that has focused on the problem of bargaining when time is of the essence. This work, which traces its recent inspiration to the influential 1982 paper of Rubinstein, models bargaining in environments in which bargaining is costly in the sense that negotiation takes time (but may continue indefinitely), consumption does not occur until agreement takes place, and future payoffs are discounted relative to present payoffs. (For example, labor–management negotiations after a strike has begun might fall into this category.)[20] Some preliminary experimental work motivated by these models has already been conducted.[21] The bargaining environments of these models are different from those of the models discussed in this chapter, which are formulated without reference to costs of delay and are usually thought of as modeling negotiations that take place over a fixed period of time throughout which the gains to bargaining will remain available. (For example, labor–management negotiations taking place before the existing contract has expired might fall into this category.) Nevertheless, it seems likely that a better understanding of bargaining in either kind of environment will illuminate issues that arise in the other. For example, an understanding of the role of time when each second is costly but bargaining may continue indefinitely should shed light on the role of time when there is a deadline, as discussed in section 2.4.

It is also not hard to anticipate additional experiments designed to elucidate some of the experimental observations discussed in this chapter. For example, the bimodal distribution of agreements dis-

---

[20] Some earlier results for a related finite horizon model are those of Stahl (1972). For a collection of papers on modern directions in the theory of bargaining, see Roth (1985b).

[21] See Binmore, Shaked, and Sutton (1985) and Neelin, Sonnenschein, and Spiegel (1986), who offer contradictory conclusions based on preliminary evidence.

cussed in Section 2.3.3 and the fact that this seems related to players' expectations about what constitutes a credible agreement (recall Section 2.3.4) suggest that credible bargaining positions play a substantial role in the negotiations we have observed. However, little is known either about how credible positions are established or about how, once established, they influence the outcome of negotiations. Although these questions are obviously related, we can also attack them separately, by focusing on particular questions. (For example, does the distance between the two bargainers' negotiating positions influence the frequency of disagreement? Preliminary evidence indicates that it does; see Roth, 1985c.) Similarly, I have already commented on the need for more experiments concerned with the effects of risk aversion and with the deadline effect.

The most exciting source of new experiments may well arise from new theory that is able to explain how some of these experimentally observed phenomena are *related* to one another. We are not so far from having theoretical models that will display many of the phenomena discussed here. Such a model (or, better yet, several such models) would give us a source of testable hypotheses about how, say, the risk aversion of bargainers is related to the frequency with which they disagree or to the manner in which they react to an approaching deadline. The results of these experiments would in turn help us select among existing theories and suggest further observable regularities on which new theory might be built. This kind of interaction between theory and experimentation has the potential to change the way theory is developed in economics, and this largely untapped potential represents one of the most exciting prospects for the long-term role of laboratory experimentation in the discipline.

References

Berg, Joyce E., Lane A. Daley, John W. Dickhaut, and John R. O'Brien, "Controlling Preferences for Lotteries on Units of Experimental Exchange." *Quarterly Journal of Economics*, *101*, 1986, pp. 281–306.

Binmore, Ken, Ariel Rubinstein, and Asher Wollinsky, "The Nash Bargaining Solution in Economic Modelling." *Rand Journal of Economics*, *17*, 1986, pp. 176–188.

Binmore, Ken, Avner Shaked, and John Sutton, "Testing Noncooperative Bargaining Theory: A Preliminary Study." *American Economic Review*, *75*, 1985, pp. 1178–80.

Kalai, Ehud, and Meir Smorodinsky, "Other Solutions to Nash's Bargaining Problem." *Econometrica*, *43*, 1975, pp. 513–18.

Kihlstrom, R., A. E. Roth, and D. Schmeidler, "Risk Aversion and Solutions to Nash's Bargaining Problem," in *Game Theory and Mathematical Economics*, O. Moeschlin and D. Pallaschke, eds. Amsterdam: North Holland, 1981, pp. 65–71.

Lewis, D., *Convention: A Philosophical Study*, Cambridge, Mass.: Harvard University Press, 1969.

Machina, Mark J., "The economic Theory of Individual Behavior Toward Risk: Theory, Evidence, and New Directions," Technical Report No. 433. Stanford University, Institute for Mathematical Studies in the Social Sciences, 1983.

Murnighan, J. K., A. E. Roth and F. Schoumaker, "Risk Aversion in Bargaining: An Experimental Study," University of Montreal, mimeo (revised), 1986.

Nash, John, "The Bargaining Problem," *Econometrica, 28*, 1950, pp. 155–162.

Neelin, Janet, Hugo Sonnenschein, and Matthew Spiegel, "An Experiemental Test of Rubinstein's Theory of Bargaining," Princeton University, mimeo, 1986.

Perles, M. A., and M. Maschler, "The Super-Additive Solution for the Nash Bargaining Game." *International Journal of Game Theory, 10,* 1981, pp. 163–93.

Roth, A. E., *Axiomatic Models of Bargaining,* Lecture Notes in Economics and Mathematical Systems No. 170. Berlin: Springer-Verlag, 1979.

"A Note on Risk Aversion in a Perfect Equilibrium Model of Bargaining." *Econometrica, 53,* 1985a, pp. 207–11.

(ed.) *Game-Theoretic Models of Bargaining.* Cambridge University Press, 1985b.

"Toward a Focal-Point Theory of Bargaining." in *Game-Theoretic Models of Bargaining,* A. E. Roth, ed. Cambridge University Press, 1985c, pp. 259–68.

Roth, A. E., and M. K. Malouf, "Game-Theoretic Models and the Role of Information in Bargaining." *Psychological Review, 86,* 1979, pp. 574–94.

"Scale Changes and Shared Information in Bargaining: An Experimental Study." *Mathematical Social Sciences, 3,* 1982, pp. 157–77.

Roth, A. E., M. Malouf, and J. K. Murnighan, "Sociological Versus Strategic Factors in Bargaining." *Journal of Economic Behavior and Organization 2,* 1981, pp. 153–77.

Roth, A. E., and J. K. Murnighan, "The Role of Information in Bargaining: An Experimental Study," *Econometrica, 50,* 1982, pp. 1123–42.

"Information and Aspirations in Two Person Bargaining," in *Aspiration Levels in Bargaining and Economic Decision Making,* R. Tietz, ed. Berlin: Springer-Verlag, 1983.

Roth, A. E., J. K. Murnighan, and F. Schoumaker, "The 'Deadline Effect' in Bargaining: Some Experimental Evidence," University of Pittsburgh, mimeo, 1987.

Roth, A. E., and U. Rothblum, "Risk Aversion and Nash's Solution for Bargaining Games with Risky Outcomes." *Econometrica, 50,* 1982, pp. 639–47.

Roth, A. E., and F. Schoumaker, "Expectations and Reputations in Bargaining: An Experimental Study." *American Economic Review, 73,* 1983, pp. 362–72.

Rubinstein, Ariel, "Perfect Equilibrium in a Bargaining Model." *Econometrica, 50,* 1982, pp. 97–109.

Stahl, Ingolf, *Bargaining Theory,* Stockholm: Economic Research Institute, 1972.

von Neumann, J., and O. Morgenstern, *Theory of Games and Economic Behavior.* Princeton, N.J.: Princeton University Press, 1944.

CHAPTER 3

Equity and coalition bargaining in experimental three-person games

REINHARD SELTEN

3.1 Introduction

Games in characteristic function form were introduced by von Neumann and Morgenstern (1944). Laboratory experiments on such games have led to descriptive theories of coalition bargaining. No theory proposed up to now is completely satisfactory in light of the data. However, the evidence clearly suggests that equity considerations have a strong influence on observed payoff divisions. The purpose of this chapter is to elucidate this phenomenon.

The formal structure of equity considerations can be expressed by an "equity principle," which is explained in Section 3.2. This principle is well known in the social psychology literature (Homans, 1961; Adams, 1963; Leventhal and Michaels, 1969; Walster, Walster, and Berscheid, 1978; Harris, 1976; Mikula, 1980). The terminology used here is based on a paper published elsewhere (Selten, 1978).

To some extent the influence of equity considerations on the behavior of subjects in coalition experiments may be due to the subjects' desire to conform to social norms. However, a different explanation of the phenomenon seems to be more adequate for most of the experimental results.

In a unanimity game where the players can either all agree on the division of a fixed sum of money or else end up with zero payoffs for everyone, the inherent symmetry of the situation points to equal shares for all players. Clearly, in this case an equal payoff division does not in any way contradict the assumption that the players are exclusively motivated by their own payoffs.

In many experimental coalition games, obvious differences in the profitability of coalition opportunities immediately establish a ranking of the players with respect to their strength. Clearly, the strongest player can expect at least his equitable share. In this way equitable shares can serve as upper or lower bounds of payoff expectations.

It is unreasonable to suppose that experimental subjects perform complicated mathematical operations in an attempt to understand the strategic structure of the situation. It seems plausible to assume that they look for easily accessible cues, such as obvious ordinal power comparisons and equitable shares, in order to form aspiration levels for their payoffs. This is the basic idea of the theory of equal division payoff bounds (Selten, 1982). A revised version of the theory of equal division payoff bounds is presented in Section 3.9.

Even if the desire to conform to social norms is occasionally strong enough to lead to payoff sacrifices, the main importance of equity considerations seems to lie in their usefulness for establishing baselines in strategic reasoning. One looks at what could be obtained in the absence of power differences in order to obtain bounds on power-adequate payoff distributions.

The explanations favored in this chapter are based on the methodological point of view that the limited rationality of human decision behavior must be taken seriously. Experiments have shown again and again that the way in which human beings choose among alternatives is not adequately described by the theory of subjectively expected utility maximization. The reader is referred to a psychological investigation and the literature quoted there (Huber, 1982). In view of this literature, it has become clear that making cosmetic changes in the usual picture of Bayesian rationality is not a sufficient approach to the problem of limited rationality. It would be better to look for theories that do not even mention such constructs as subjective probabilities.

In this chapter attention is concentrated on zero-normalized three-person games in characteristic function form. Mainstream game theory has produced many solution concepts for such games that do not seem to have much descriptive relevance. In this respect Aumann–Maschler bargaining set theory is a notable exception (Aumann and Maschler, 1964). Since its beginnings, this theory has been linked to an attempt to explain experimental data, even if Maschler's experimental paper has been published only much later (Maschler, 1978).

Bargaining set theory in its original form does not make use of the equity principle. However, Maschler argues that, for the purpose of deriving behavioral predictions, this theory may have to be applied to a "power transformation" of the original game rather than directly to the unmodified characteristic function. Maschler's power transformations make explicit use of equity considerations (Maschler, 1963, 1978).

Different theories often aim at different types of predictions. An "area theory" is one that predicts a range of outcomes. Other kinds of theories predict only average outcomes or are even less specific. The advantage of area theories is that for every single play of the game one can check whether the prediction was correct or false. This is a great heuristic advantage if one wants to improve theories in the light of data. In every case in which a prediction fails one can ask oneself what went wrong. This is the reason for restricting attention in this chapter to area theories.

A method for comparing the predictive success of different theories has been proposed (Selten and Krischker, 1982). This method solves the problem of different area theories predicting regions of different size. A measure of predictive success is defined that is based on the relative frequency of correct predictions and a correction for the size of the predicted region. The measure is explained in Section 3.10.

This chapter focuses on two area theories: a version of the bargaining set that takes into account power transformation where this is possible and the theory of equal division payoff bounds in its revised form. Results obtained elsewhere (Selten and Krischker, 1982; Selten, 1982) will be complemented by evaluations of additional experimental data. A third area theory, equal share analysis (Selten, 1972), has proved to be quite successful. However, comparisons have shown that equal division payoff bounds yield better predictions for zero-normalized three-person games (Selten, 1982).

There are in the literature several other descriptive theories based on equity considerations, namely bargaining theory (Komorita and Cherkhoff, 1973), equal excess theory (Kormorita, 1979), and the equal division kernel (Crott and Albers, 1981). Even if these theories might permit a reinterpretation as area theories, they are not intended to serve this purpose. Komorita has compared several theories proposed in the social psychology literature, among others bargaining theory and equal excess theory (Komorita, 1984). He is interested mainly in the question of which coalition should be considered the most likely. Therefore, he does not look at area theories, which generally do not predict a most likely coalition.

The influence of prominence in the sense of Schelling results in a tendency to form agreements specifically "round" numbers as payoffs for some or all members of a coalition (Schelling, 1960). Descriptive theories of coalition formation should take this phenomenon into account. Therefore, the descriptive version of the bargaining set considered here explicitly permits small deviations caused by prominence effects. The theory of equal division payoff bounds also incorporates the influence of rounding. Both theories depend on a parameter, the prominence level, whose integer multiples are considered to be "round" numbers. Section 3.11 is devoted to the question of how the prominence level should be determined on the basis of the data.

It will be shown in this chapter that the predictive success of bargaining set theory is improved if power transformations are taken into account. The "united bargaining set" based on the union of three bargaining sets for the unmodified characteristic function and for two power transformations yields better predictions than the ordinary bargaining set alone. Moreover, it will be shown that the predictive success of the theory of equal division payoff bounds is clearly superior to that of the united bargaining set.

3.2   The equity principle

The equity principle applies to situations in which benefits or costs have to be distributed among the members of a group. Consider a group of n members $1, \ldots, n$ and an amount r of money or some other commodity that has to be distributed among the members $1, \ldots, n$. A *division* of r is a vector $(r_1, \ldots, r_n)$ with $r_i \geq 0$ for $i = 1, \ldots, n$ and with $r_1 + \cdots + r_n = r$. We call r_i the *share* of i. We speak of an *equal division* in the case of $r_i = r/n$ for $i = 1, \ldots, n$.

Only in special cases does the application of the equity principle give rise to an equal division. In many situations there are good reasons for an uneven split of r. As an example consider a quota cartel of n firms producing the same commodity. Here r is the total supply agreed upon and r_i is the supply quota of firm i. In practical cases quota bargaining is concerned mainly with proposals to divide r in proportion to some key numbers like the firm's capacity or its average sales in the past five years (Kastl, 1963). A specific selection of key numbers (e.g., the capacities) was called a *standard of comparison* in an earlier paper (Selten, 1978). A standard of comparison determines a system of nonnegative *weights* $w_1, \ldots, w_n$ for the group members such that $w_i > 0$ holds for at least one i. The *equity principle* requires

$$r_i = \mu w_i \qquad (3.1)$$

with

$$\mu = r \bigg/ \sum_{i=1}^{n} w_i \qquad (3.2)$$

A standard of comparison provides a ratio scale with a natural zero point. The same scale is applied to each group member. In some cases it is not clear from the outset how the shares r_i should be measured. In a quota cartel for coal it may be a point of dispute whether the quotas should include or exclude coal delivered to steel mills owned by the same company. We call a method of computing shares r_i a *standard of distribution*. Here, too, measurement is on the level of a ratio scale with a natural zero point.

A standard of distribution measures shares and a standard of comparison assigns weights. Both are needed for an application of the equity principle. A standard of distribution together with a standard of comparison is called an *equity standard*. Once the equity standard is known, the application of the equity principle is trivial. However, the equity principle does not tell us how the equity standard should be determined. Nevertheless, the principle is not without predictive power. In practical applications the number of reasonable equity standards is often quite small. Standards of distribution and comparison are not completely arbitrary. They cannot serve their purpose unless they are *relevant*, in the sense that they are substantially connected to the problem, and *accessible*, in the sense that the variables to be measured can be easily observed by all members of the group.

A relevant standard of distribution must be a meaningful measure of the rewards to be distributed (or the burdens to be shared in cost division problems). A standard of comparison that yields unequal weights must be based on good reasons for differences in shares. If there are no such reasons, only the *egalitarian* standard of comparison, which gives equal weights to all members, can be applied. The application of the equity principle with the egalitarian standard of comparison leads to an equal division.

The equity principle together with an equity standard can be looked upon as a social norm. Social norms must be controllable and consequently cannot be based on hidden variables like utilities. Therefore, accessibility is an important requirement for standards of distribution and comparison. The shares r_i and the weights w_i must be observable without any ambiguity by all members of the group.

In the literature the rule expressed by the equity principle is interpreted as a norm of distributive justice (Homans, 1961). However, it should be pointed out that this may be too narrow a view of the equity principle. It is possible that an equity standard is an assessment of the power situation rather than an expression of justice. In a bargaining situation it may be appropriate to give more to those who are more powerful, whether or not this is ethically justified. In such cases the "justice" achieved by the equity principle is at best relative.

Perhaps it would be better to call the equity principle a rule of distributive appropriateness rather than distributive justice.

In practice it is often difficult to tell whether the behavior of persons involved in a bargaining situation is motivated by ethical considerations. In an experiment performed by Nydegger and Owen (1974) two subjects had to agree on the division of one dollar. Invariably the subjects agreed to split evenly. Why did they apply the egalitarian standard of comparison? One may say that in this case the reason was the lack of any justification for an uneven split. Neither ethical nor power-related considerations give rise to another system of weights.

3.3   Characteristic function games, notations, and definitions

A *characteristic function* v assigns a real number $v(C)$ to every element C of a set P of nonempty subsets of a player set $N = \{1, \ldots, n\}$, where P contains at least all one-element subsets of N. The nonempty subsets of N are called *coalitions*, and those in P are *permissible coalitions*. The number of elements in a finite set S is denoted by $|S|$. Coalitions C with $|C| = 1$ are called *solo coalitions*, and those with $|C| \geq 2$ are referred to as *genuine coalitions*. The set of all permissible genuine coalitions is denoted by Q. A *characteristic function game* is described by a triple $G = (N, Q, v)$, where N is the player set, Q the set of permissible genuine coalitions, and v a characteristic function defined on the set P of permissible coalitions, which contains the elements of Q and all solo coalitions. Since no other games are considered here, a characteristic function game is often simply called a *game*. A game with n players is called an *n-person game*.

In a play of a characteristic function game, a genuine coalition C can be formed by an agreement of its members on the division of $v(C)$ among themselves; if several genuine coalitions $C_1, \ldots, C_m$ are formed, they must be pairwise nonintersecting.

A *coalition structure* for (N, Q, v) is a list $C_1, \ldots, C_m$ of pairwise nonintersecting permissible genuine coalitions $C_j \in Q$. The end result of a play is described by a *configuration*,

$$\alpha = (C_1, \ldots, C_m; x_1, \ldots, x_n) \tag{3.3}$$

which shows the coalition structure $C_1, \ldots, C_m$ and the payoffs $x_1, \ldots, x_n$ reached by the players. In a configuration the payoffs x_i are subject to the following restrictions:

$$x_i = v(i) \quad \text{if} \quad i \notin C_j \quad \text{for} \quad j = 1, \ldots, m \tag{3.4}$$

$$x_i \geq v(i) \quad \text{if} \quad i \in C_j \quad \text{for} \quad j = 1, \ldots, m \tag{3.5}$$

$$\sum_{i \in C_j} x_i = v(C_j) \quad \text{for} \quad j = 1, \ldots, m \tag{3.6}$$

Here $v(i)$ stands for $v(\{i\})$. A simplified notation will be used for coalitions in three-person games: i stands for $\{i\}$; ij for $\{i, j\}$; and 123 for $\{1, 2, 3\}$. The set of all configurations for $G = (N, Q, v)$ is denoted by K.

A characteristic function v is called *admissible* if we have

$$v(C) \geq \sum_{i \in C} v(i) \tag{3.7}$$

for every permissible genuine coalition $C \in Q$. A genuine coalition $C \in Q$ is called *profitable* if the following is true:

$$v(C) > \sum_{i \in C} v(i) \tag{3.8}$$

A game $G = (N, Q, v)$ is called *essential* if Q contains at least one profitable coalition. (Only essential games are of interest for experimentation.) A coalition structure $C_1, \ldots, C_m$ is called a *null structure* if none of the coalitions $C_1, \ldots, C_m$ is profitable. (Such coalition structures merit special attention, since they are rarely observed in experimental results.)

For every game $G = (N, Q, v)$ we define a *zero-normalized* game $G_0 = (N, Q, v_0)$ with

$$v_0(C) = v(C) - \sum_{i \in C} v(i) \tag{3.9}$$

for every permissible coalition C (including solo coalitions). A one-to-one mapping f from the configuration set K of G onto the configuration set K_0 of G_0 is defined as follows. A configuration in K,

$$\alpha = (C_1, \ldots, C_m; x_1, \ldots, x_n) \tag{3.10}$$

is mapped to the following configuration $\beta = f(\alpha)$ in K_0

$$\beta = f(\alpha) = (C_1, \ldots, C_m; y_1, \ldots, y_n) \tag{3.11}$$

with

$$y_i = x_i - v(i) \tag{3.12}$$

The mapping f is called the *zero-normalization mapping*.

Normative theories for characteristic function games are invariant with respect to the zero-normalization mapping. However, this is not a good property for descriptive theories. In the first experiments on characteristic function games it was observed that subjects pay special attention to equal shares $v(C)/|C|$ of coalition values and that this tendency destroys zero-normalization invariance (Kalish et al., 1954).

A game $G = (N, Q, v)$ is called *zero-normalized* if $v(i) = 0$ holds for $i = 1, \ldots, n$. This chapter concentrates on experiments performed with zero-normalized three-person games. However, in the theoretical treatment of such games we have to look at Maschler's power transformations, which do not preserve zero-normalization.

A player is called a *dummy* in $G = (N, Q, v)$ if the following is true for every $C \in Q$ with $i \in C$. We have $C \setminus i \in P$ and

$$v(C) = v(C \setminus i) + v(i) \tag{3.13}$$

As far as the author knows, no experimental games with dummies have been performed. However, it is reasonable to suppose that a dummy should not be able to obtain more than $v(i)$ if the game structure is sufficiently simple. In very complicated games this may be different.

A game $G = (N, Q, v)$ is called *superadditive* if all coalitions are permissible and if the following is true for every pair of nonintersecting coalitions C and D:

$$v(C \cup D) \geq v(C) + v(D) \quad \text{for} \quad C \cap D = \emptyset \tag{3.14}$$

In experimental games that fail to be superadditive the players sometimes develop ingenious schemes to circumvent the lack of superadditivity (Maschler, 1978). They may find a way to form a nonpermissible coalition, and they may also overcome limitations imposed by a violation of (3.14). In such cases it may be advantageous to base the theoretical analysis not on the experimental game $G = (N, Q, v)$, but on its *superadditive cover* $\overline{G} = (N, \overline{Q}, \overline{v})$, where $\overline{Q}$ is the set of all genuine coalitions and $\overline{v}$ is defined as follows. For every coalition C let $\phi(C)$ be the set of all partitions $(C_1, \ldots, C_m)$ of C into pairwise nonintersecting permissible coalitions; with this notation we have

$$\overline{v}(C) = \max_{(C_1, \ldots, C_m) \in \Phi(C)} \sum_{j=i}^{m} v(C_j) \tag{3.15}$$

If $G = (N, Q, v)$ is a superadditive game, there is no difference between G and its superadditive cover $\overline{G}$.

The core of a game $G = (N, Q, v)$ is the set of all configurations $\alpha = (C_1, \ldots, C_m; x_1, \ldots, x_n)$ such that for no permissible genuine coalition $C \in Q$ we have

$$v(C) > \sum_{i \in C} x_i \tag{3.16}$$

In view of (3.4) and (3.5) there cannot be any solo coalition C with (3.16). Therefore, it is sufficient to exclude (3.16) for $C \in Q$. Note that here the core is defined as a set of configurations rather than a set of payoff vectors.

In many games the core is empty. In such cases the core cannot serve as a reasonable predictive theory. The theoretical importance of the core lies in its relationship to other solution concepts.

3.4   The bargaining set for three-person games

The bargaining set (Aumann and Maschler, 1964) is one of the most important theories for characteristic function games, from both the normative and the descriptive points of view. The bargaining set in its original form has no connection to the equity principle. However, the way in which it is applied to experimental data involves Maschler's theory of the power of a coalition (Maschler, 1963, 1978), which is based on equity considerations. This is explained in Section 3.5.

The literature presents many versions of the bargaining set. However, in the special case of the three-person game, they coincide. Since we do not look at more general cases we can speak of "the bargaining set." The definition of the bargaining set is based on auxiliary concepts named "objections" and "counterobjections," and a configuration is considered stable in the sense of the bargaining set if for every objection there is a counterobjection. Definitions can be found in the original literature or in textbooks on game theory (e.g., Rosenmüller, 1981; Owen, 1982) and will not be repeated here. We shall restrict ourselves to the description of the bargaining set for three-person games, and even there we will not consider the most general case. At first we shall look at superadditive zero-normalized three-person games; later we shall see how the description can be generalized to other three-person games.

It is convenient to introduce special notational conventions for superadditive zero-normalized three-person games:

$$v(12) = a \tag{3.17}$$

$$v(13) = b \tag{3.18}$$

$$v(23) = c \tag{3.19}$$

$$v(123) = g \tag{3.20}$$

Let $G = (N, Q, v)$ be a superadditive zero-normalized three-person game with

$$g \geq a \geq b \geq c \geq 0 \tag{3.21}$$

Assumption (3.21) does not entail any loss of generality since $a \geq b \geq c$ can always be achieved by a suitable renumbering of the players.

Three numbers q_1, q_2, and q_3 called *quotas* can be attached to the players of a three-person game. (These numbers are important not only for the bargaining set but also for other normative theories.) Consider a general three-person game $G = (N, Q, v)$ and let $\overline{G} = (N, \overline{Q}, \overline{v})$ be the superadditive cover of G. For $i = 1, 2, 3$ player i's *quota* q_i is defined as

$$q_i = \frac{\overline{v}(ij) + \overline{v}(ik) - \overline{v}(jk)}{2} \tag{3.22}$$

where i, j, k is a permutation of 1, 2, 3. The quotas are characterized by the property

$$q_i + q_j = \overline{v}(ij) \tag{3.23}$$

for every permutation i, j, k of 1, 2, 3. In the special case of a superadditive zero-normalized three-person game we have

$$q_1 = (a + b - c)/2 \tag{3.24}$$

$$q_2 = (a - b + c)/2 \tag{3.25}$$

$$q_3 = (-a + b + c)/2 \tag{3.26}$$

If (3.21) holds, q_1 and q_2 are nonnegative. However, q_3 may be negative. The right side of (3.26) is nonnegative if and only if the following *triangular inequality* holds:

$$b + c \geq a \tag{3.27}$$

A *quota game* is a three-person game in which the quotas are all nonnegative.

Table 3.1 shows the bargaining set for superadditive zero-normalized three-person games with (3.21). The top two lines indicate the case distinctions that have to be made. The core is nonempty if and only if we have

$$2g \geq a + b + c \tag{3.28}$$

The second case distinction separates quota games from other games. The coalition structures are indicated on the left. The table can also be applied to zero-normalized three-person games in which not all coalitions are permissible. Of course, the players must be numbered in a way that is consistent with those inequalities implied by (3.21) that concern permissible coalitions. One simply has to ignore those configurations whose coalition structure contains nonpermissible coalitions.

Table 3.1. Bargaining set for superadditive zero-normalized three-person games with (3.21)

Coalition structure	Conditions		
	$b + c \geq a$		$b + c < a$
	$2g < a + b + c$ Quota games	$2g \geq a + b + c$	Nonempty core
—		$(-; 0, 0, 0)$	
12	$(12; q_1, q_2, 0)$		$(12; x_1, x_2, 0)$ with $x_1 \geq b$ and $x_2 \geq c$
13	$(13; q_1, 0, q_3)$		$(13; b, 0, 0)$
23	$(23; 0, q_2, q_3)$		$(23; 0, c, 0)$
123	$(123; x_1, x_2, x_3)$ with $x_i = q_i - \dfrac{q_1 + q_2 + q_3 - g}{3}$	$(123; x_1, x_2, x_3)$ with $x_1 + x_2 \geq a,\ x_1 + x_3 \geq b,\ x_2 + x_3 \geq c$	

In order to determine the bargaining set of a three-person game $G = (N, Q, v)$ that is not zero-normalized, one has to find the bargaining set of the zero-normalized game $G_0 = (N, Q, v_0)$ of G and to apply the inverse of the zero-normalization mapping.

3.5 Power transformations

In discussing the results of his experiments, Maschler observed that the application of bargaining set theory to experimental characteristic function games does not yield good predictions (Maschler, 1978). He argued that this does not necessarily mean that bargaining set theory must be rejected. The game representation rather than the theory may be wrong. A game that is given in the form of a characteristic function v may actually be described in a more appropriate way by a different characteristic function v', in the sense that $v'(C)$ rather than $v(C)$ is a reasonable expectation of the joint payoff obtainable by coordinated action.

Maschler (1963) proposed a theory of the "power of a coalition." This theory describes several ways to compute a transformed characteristic function v' for every given characteristic function v. These transformations will be called power transformations, since Maschler refers to $v'(C)$ as the "power" of C. Formally a power transformation is a function ψ that assigns a new characteristic function $v' = \psi(v)$ to every characteristic function v; the transformed function $v' = \psi(v)$ is defined on the same set P of permissible coalitions as v.

Let $G = (N, Q, v)$ be a superadditive n-person game. A *bargaining arrangement* $D_1, \ldots, D_m$ for G is a list of coalitions that form a partition of N. (Some of these coalitions may be solo coalitions.) The interpretation of a bargaining arrangement is as follows. The players want to bargain on the formation of the grand coalition N, and for this purpose they have organized themselves into m *bargaining groups* $D_1, \ldots, D_m$, each of which speaks with one voice.

The bargaining groups $D_1, \ldots, D_m$ bargain on the distribution of $v(N)$. They have to agree on joint payoffs $x(D_1), \ldots, x(D_m)$ for each of the bargaining groups. These payoffs must sum to $v(N)$. The distribution of $x(D_j)$ is an internal matter of D_j and does not concern the discussion among the bargaining groups.

Maschler defines several "standards of fairness," which can be thought of as different social norms for the solution of such bargaining problems. In the terminology used here a standard of fairness is an equity standard.

Two standards of distribution suggest themselves. They define the

Table 3.2. *Equitable shares for bargaining groups according to four equity standards*

	Equal	Size proportional
Gross payoff split	$\dfrac{1}{m} v(N)$	$\dfrac{|D_j|}{n} v(N)$
Surplus split	$\dfrac{1}{m}\left[v(N) - \displaystyle\sum_{j=1}^{m} v(D_j)\right]$	$\dfrac{|D_j|}{n}\left[v(N) - \displaystyle\sum_{j=1}^{m} v(D_j)\right]$

share $r(D_j)$ of bargaining group D_j in two different ways: as a *gross payoff* share,

$$r(D_j) = x(D_j) \tag{3.29}$$

and as a *surplus* share,

$$r(D_j) = x(D_j) - v(D_j) \tag{3.30}$$

These two standards of distribution can be combined with two standards of comparison, which also immediately suggest themselves. One definition of weights demands an *equal split:*

$$w_j = 1 \quad \text{for} \quad j = 1, \ldots, n \tag{3.31}$$

The other asks for a *size-proportional split:*

$$w_j = |D_j| \quad \text{for} \quad j = 1, \ldots, n \tag{3.32}$$

One obtains four equity standards: (1) equal gross payoff split, (2) size-proportional gross payoff split, (3) equal surplus split, (4) size-proportional surplus split.

Table 3.2 shows the equitable shares arising from these four equity standards. The two equity standards based on gross payoff shares do not necessarily guarantee at least $v(D_j)$. Therefore, they cannot serve as a general rule applicable to all games and all bargaining arrangements. Moreover, gross payoff shares are not invariant with respect to zero normalization. Therefore, Maschler considers only one standard of distribution, namely surplus shares.

In the interpretation of his experimental data, Maschler puts the most emphasis on his "cooperative standard of fairness," which is nothing other than our equal surplus split. He also considers size-proportional splits, but he does not find any evidence for this equity standard in the protocols written by his subjects (Maschler, 1978, p. 260n).

There are two ways in which these ideas can be used to generate power transformations. The simpler approach looks at bargaining arrangements with only two bargaining groups C and $N \backslash C$. Here one takes the point of view that players who want to coordinate their bargaining activities have to bargain as one group and the remaining players cannot avoid forming only one opposing group. We refer to this approach as the *polarization view*. The polarization view can be defended by the idea that a situation in which there are more than two bargaining groups creates insurmountable difficulties of multilateral fighting. Bargaining groups must unite to form larger bargaining groups until finally there are only two opposing ones left.

According to the polarization view the power transformation should express the joint payoff expectation of a coalition C for the case in which it is one of the two bargaining groups in the final stage of bargaining before agreement is reached. This together with the two equity standards based on surplus split leads to two power transformations ψ_1 and ψ_2, called *equal surplus split power transformation* and *size-proportional surplus split power transformation*. For superadditive games $G = (N, Q, v)$ the transformed characteristic function $v_1 = \psi_1(v)$ and $v_2 = \psi_2(v)$ are defined as follows:

$$v_1(C) = v(C) + \tfrac{1}{2}[v(N) - v(C) - v(N \backslash C)] \tag{3.33}$$

$$v_2(C) = v(C) + \frac{|C|}{n}[v(N) - v(C) - v(N \backslash C)] \tag{3.34}$$

Maschler takes a different point of view. He does not think that multilateral bargaining among more than two bargaining groups is too difficult. He maintains that a coalition C whose members want to bargain in a coordinated way should consider splitting into several bargaining groups in order to improve its joint payoff. We call Maschler's approach the *strategic view*.

In this chapter the implications of the strategic view are discussed only for the special case of zero-normalized three-person games. Let $G = (N, Q, v)$ be a superadditive game of this kind. Consider a two-person coalition ij. The players i and j can choose whether they want to form one bargaining group ij or two bargaining groups i and j. Suppose that in both cases bargaining results in an equal surplus split. Then in the first case, ij can expect $v_1(ij)$ and, in the second one, two-thirds of $v(123)$. Players i and j will choose the more advantageous possibility if both do not yield the same joint payoff. This leads to a power transformation ψ_3, which will be called *Maschler's power transformation*. We define $v_3 = \psi_3(v)$ as

$$v_3(ij) = \max[v_1(ij), \tfrac{2}{3}g] \qquad (3.35)$$

$$v_3(i) = g - v_3(jk) \qquad (3.36)$$

for every permutation i, j, k of 1, 2, 3 and for every zero-normalized three-person game $G = (N, Q, v)$.

The strategic view can also be combined with the equity standard of size-proportional surplus split. However, it can be seen immediately that no new power transformation results in this way. Size-proportional surplus split does not offer any incentive for a coalition to subdivide into several bargaining groups.

Up to now power transformations have been discussed for superadditive games only. A natural way to extend a power transformation ψ from superadditive games to more general games is based on the application of the power transformation to the superadditive cover $\bar{v}$ of the original characteristic function:

$$\psi(v) = \psi(\bar{v}) \qquad (3.37)$$

In this way ψ_1 and ψ_2 can be extended to all games and ψ_3 can be extended to all zero-normalized three-person games.

As long as N is a permissible coalition, it is not unreasonable to replace a game by its superadditive cover in order to compute the power transformation. The members of a nonpermissible coalition C may still be able to coordinate their bargaining activities. Bargaining groups are not necessarily permissible coalitions.

It is doubtful whether power transformations should be applied to games in which the grand coalition N is not permissible. After all, the interpretation of power transformations is based on the idea that a coalition may be able to get more than its value in an agreement on the formation of the grand coalition N. Nevertheless, in some cases power transformations may be relevant even if N is not permissible.

In experimental games with unrestricted face-to-face communication, subjects sometimes find ingenious ways to circumvent the prohibition of the grand coalition. An example is described by Maschler (1978). The example concerns a zero-normalized three-person game in which 12, 13, and 23 are permitted, but 123 is not. The two-person coalition values are $a = b = 50$ and $c = 10$. Sometimes players 2 and 3 threw a coin in order to allocate the right to form a two-person coalition with player 1. Thereby each of them would obtain half a chance to get 25. Obviously, it makes sense here to apply ψ_1 in order to compute the power of 23. One may say that the coin-throwing scheme is a way of forming the nonpermissible grand coalition with payoffs of 25, 12.5, and 12.5 for players 1, 2, and 3, respectively.

If one wants to take account of such possibilities, it becomes very difficult to say under what conditions a final outcome is correctly predicted by an area theory. Neither the final coalitions nor the final payoffs can be taken at face value. One would have to consider all possible ways of forming nonpermissible coalitions in order to explore the implications of theories on final outcomes. It is not clear how this could be done in a systematic way. Therefore, it seems to be advisable to avoid power transformations of games in which the grand coalition is not permissible. Experimental procedures with restricted formalized communication like those used by Kahan and Rapoport (1974) practically exclude the formation of nonpermissible coalitions. Under such conditions it makes no sense to apply power transformations to games without the grand coalition.

It should be pointed out that all three power transformations considered here are counterintuitive for some types of games. In superadditive three-person games with large cores, $v_1 = \psi_1(v)$ often fails to be admissible. Let $G = (N, Q, v)$ be a superadditive zero-normalized three-person game. In the special notation introduced in (3.17) to (3.20) we have

$$v_1(1) + v_1(2) + v_1(3) = (3g - a - b - c)/2 \tag{3.38}$$

As a consequence,

$$v_1(1) + v_1(2) + v_1(3) > v_1(123) \tag{3.39}$$

holds for

$$g > a + b + c \tag{3.40}$$

Clearly, it is doubtful whether in such cases ψ_1 is a reasonable power transformation. The other two power transformations avoid this difficulty in view of $v_2(i) \leq g/3$ and $v_3(i) \leq g/3$. However, neither ψ_2 nor ψ_3 preserves dummies in the sense that a dummy in v may fail to be a dummy in $\psi_2(v)$ and $\psi_3(v)$. Consider the following superadditive three-person game:

$$v(1) = v(2) = v(3) = v(13) = v(23) = 0 \tag{3.41}$$

$$v(12) = v(123) = 60 \tag{3.42}$$

In this game player 3 is a dummy. Both transformations ψ_2 and ψ_3 yield the same result, $v' = \psi_2(v) = \psi_3(v)$:

$$v'(1) = v'(2) = 20 \tag{3.43}$$

$$v'(3) = 0 \tag{3.44}$$

$$v'(12) = 60 \tag{3.45}$$

$$v'(13) = v'(23) = 40 \tag{3.46}$$

Obviously player 3 is a dummy in v but not in v'. It is difficult to understand why the addition of a dummy should increase the power of a coalition. Unlike ψ_2 and ψ_3 the power transformation ψ_1 preserves dummies.

The discussion of these difficulties seems to indicate that one should not look at a power transformation as a general rule to be applied to all possible cases. This does not necessarily mean that power transformations are irrelevant to the description of behavior in experimental games. Experimental subjects probably do not look for reasonable general rules but rather for ad hoc solutions to specific problems. If one equity standard does not work, they will look for another one. It is not unreasonable to suppose that in the bargaining process different players propose different equity standards. If finally one of these equity standards determines the agreement, this may be due to the fact that other equity standards do not reflect the power situation sufficiently well. One cannot exclude the possibility that sometimes an agreement is reached as a compromise between several equity standards.

Maschler's theory of power transformation is an ingenious attempt to capture the influence of equity considerations on strategic reasoning in characteristic function games. Undoubtedly this approach merits examination in the light of experimental data.

3.6   Power bargaining sets

Maschler proposed that bargaining set theory should not necessarily be applied to the original characteristic function; one should also consider applications to various power transformations. In order to do this we define "power bargaining sets" for zero-normalized three-person games in which the grand coalition is permissible. The symbol B is used for the ordinary bargaining set and B_1, B_2, and B_3 denote the power bargaining sets derived from the three power transformations ψ_1, ψ_2, and ψ_3, respectively, discussed in the preceding section.

Let $G = (N, Q, v)$ be a zero-normalized three-person game with $123 \in Q$. Consider the power transformation $v' = \psi_m(v)$ where m is 1, 2, or 3. Let $G' = (N, Q', v')$ be the transformed game and B' the bargaining set of G'. A configuration for G' may not be a configuration for G. First of all, Q' may contain more coalitions than Q, but even if G is superadditive, configurations for G' are not necessarily configurations for G. Whenever $v(ij)$ is smaller than $v(123)$, we have

$$v'(ij) > v(ij) \tag{3.47}$$

If (3.47) holds, a configuration of the form $(ij; x_1, x_2, x_3)$ for the transformed game G' cannot be a final result of a play of G. Clearly, only configurations for G can serve as predictions for G. Therefore, B_i is defined as follows. The *power bargaining set* B_m for G is the set of all configurations in B' that are configurations for G ($m = 1, 2, 3$). The power bargaining set B_m implies that in G no permissible two-person coalition ij can be formed unless we have $v(ij) = g$. For $g > a + b + c$, the consequence of inequality (3.39) is that the power bargaining set B_1 is empty. This difficulty does not arise with respect to B_2 and B_3.

The transformed characteristic function $v' = \psi_i(v)$ always has the *constant sum property*

$$v'(ij) + v'(k) = g \tag{3.48}$$

for every permutation i, j, k of 1, 2, 3. The transformed game is always a quota game with an empty core. Therefore, a power bargaining set B_m contains at most one configuration for every coalition structure.

3.7 Descriptive bargaining sets

In the discussion of his experimental data, Maschler suggests that one should neglect small deviations from theoretical predictions. He observed that his subjects did not seem to care much about payoff differences up to five points. This results in a tendency to agree on round payoffs, where "round" means divisibility by 5. He concludes that deviations of up to five points should not be considered violations of the theory.

Maschler's suggestion to neglect deviations up to 5 is probably appropriate for his data. For other experiments one may need another specification of permissible deviations. Section 3.11 is devoted to the question how one should approach this problem. For the time being we shall consider the maximal size of permissible deviations as a parameter Δ that has to be adjusted to the experiments under consideration.

Suppose that T is a set of configurations predicted by a theory. If one wants to say that deviations up to m do not matter, one really predicts a larger set $T[\Delta]$, which is called the Δ-neighborhood of T. Formally the Δ-neighborhood of T is defined as the set of all configurations

$$\alpha = (C_1, \ldots, C_m; x_1, \ldots, x_n) \tag{3.49}$$

for which in T a configuration

$$\beta = (C_1, \ldots, C_m; y_1, \ldots, y_n) \tag{3.50}$$

with the same coalition structure can be found, such that the inequalities

$$|x_i - y_i| \leq \Delta \tag{3.51}$$

hold for $i = 1, \ldots, m$. It is important that here β is required to have the same coalition structure as α. This means that T is enlarged for every coalition structure separately by taking a neighborhood with respect to the "city block distance." The *bargaining set with deviations up to* Δ, denoted by $B[\Delta]$, is the Δ-neighborhood of the bargaining set B. Analogously, $B_m[\Delta]$, called the *power bargaining set with respect to* ψ_m *with deviations up to* Δ, is the Δ-neighborhood of B_m. The bargaining set does not exclude any coalition structures, not even the null structure in which no genuine coalition is formed. The null structure is very rarely observed in experiments. In order to give bargaining set theory the best possible chance, a modified version of the bargaining set will be introduced that excludes the null structure.

Let K_0 be the set of all configurations with the null structure as coalition structure. We call $B \backslash K_0$ the *bargaining set without null structure*. The symbol B_0 is used for $B \backslash K_0$. The Δ-neighborhood of B_0, the *bargaining set without null structure and with deviations up to* Δ, is denoted by $B_0[\Delta]$. Analogously, B_{0m} denotes $B_m \backslash K_0$, the *power bargaining set with respect to* ψ_m *without null structure*, and $B_{0m}[\Delta]$ is the Δ-neighborhood of B_{0m}.

In the case of games where the grand coalition is permitted, one should also consider power transformations. This does not necessarily mean that predictions should be based on one of the power bargaining sets only. As we shall see, for the samples investigated here the best predictions are obtained by following set $U[\Delta]$:

$$U[\Delta] = B_0[\Delta] \cup B_{01}[\Delta] \cup B_{02}[\Delta] \tag{3.52}$$

We call $U[\Delta]$ the *united bargaining set with deviations up to* Δ. One may ask why $B_{03}[\Delta]$ is not included in $U[\Delta]$. We shall look at only one sample in which for some games B_3 is different from B_1, namely,

Maschler's 27 superadditive games (Maschler, 1978). There, no additional correct prediction is obtained by the inclusion of $B_{03}[\Delta]$. These data are discussed in Section 3.12.

3.8 A look at an experiment by Murnighan and Roth

Murnighan and Roth (1977) performed an experiment on a special zero-normalized three-person game. This game $G = (N, Q, v)$ with $N = \{1, 2, 3\}$ and $Q = \{12, 13, 123\}$ has the following characteristic function:

$$v(1) \; = v(2) = v(3) = 0 \tag{3.53}$$

$$v(12) = v(13) = v(123) = 100 \tag{3.54}$$

The procedure used by Murnighan and Roth excludes the coalition 23. However, the grand coalition is permitted.

Thirty-six triads of subjects played the game 12 times in the same roles. No money payoffs were offered. Repeated play might lead to cooperation beyond one play, and the lack of money payoffs might reduce competitiveness. In spite of these disadvantages it is interesting to look at the data of Murnighan and Roth. To a limited extent subjects can be relied on to aim for a large number of points if they are told to do so. Since full cooperation is possible within one play, it is not immediately clear why repetition should drastically change the strategic situation.

The games were played with formal anonymous communication. The procedure was not the same for all plays, and the variation of communication rules had some influence on the outcomes. For the purpose of testing cooperative theories that do not even mention details of communication rules, it is justifiable to ignore the procedural variations. Actually, formal bargaining procedures define extensive games that could be analyzed with the help of noncooperative game theory. Maybe this would be the right way to approach questions of procedural variation. Cooperative game theory tries to avoid the analysis of the extensive game and therefore must aim for rough predictions that are relatively robust with respect to procedural detail.

The unusually large number of 432 plays of the same game is a good reason for reevaluating the data gathered by Murnighan and Roth. Moreover, the game structure is of considerable theoretical interest.

The bargaining set coincides with the core and predicts a payoff of 100 for player 1 if a genuine coalition is formed. In view of the extreme character of this game, one should expect power transformations to be relevant.

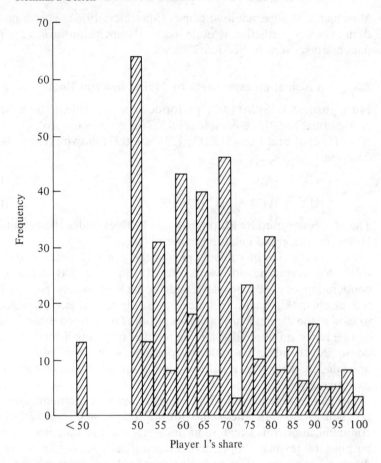

Figure 3.1. Frequency distribution of player 1's share in two-person coalitions. Frequencies are shown for shares divisible by 5 for open intervals bordered by such payoff values. From Murnighan and Roth (1977).

Of the 432 plays, 412 ended in two-person coalitions 12 or 13. Since 123 was formed in only 4.6% of all cases it is most interesting to look at the plays with two-person coalitions as outcomes. The game is symmetric with respect to players 2 and 3. As far as theoretical predictions are concerned it does not matter whether 12 or 13 has been formed. A two-person coalition outcome is sufficiently characterized by x_1, the share of player 1.

Figure 3.1 shows the distribution of x_1. Frequencies of values divisible by 5 are shown as separate columns alternating with columns for aggregate frequencies for groups of the form $5k < x_1 < 5k + 5$ with

Table 3.3. *Player 1's payoff in two-person coalitions*

Theory	Range for player 1's payoff in two-person coalitions	Number of observed cases
$B_0[5]$	$95 \leq x_1 \leq 100$	16
$B_1[5]$	$70 \leq x_1 \leq 80$	113
$B_2[5]$	$61.67 \leq x_1 \leq 71.66$	103
$B_3[5]$	$61.67 \leq x_1 \leq 71.66$	103
$U[5]$	$95 \leq x_1 \leq 100$ or $61.67 \leq x_1 \leq 80$	188
	$0 \leq x_1 \leq 100$	412
	$0 \leq x_1 \leq 50$	13
	$50 \leq x_1 \leq 100$	399

Source: Murnighan and Roth (1977).

$k = 10, \ldots, 19$. There are only 13 cases with $x_1 < 50$ shown separately as one column. Obviously, divisibility by 5 is a very frequent feature of agreed-upon payoffs. Therefore, Maschler's proposal to neglect payoff differences up to 5 seems to be appropriate here, too.

In the experiments by Roth and Murnighan it was possible to agree on broken payoffs up to 1/100 of one point. Sometimes the subjects made use of this possibility. This has to be taken into account in the determination of 5-neighborhoods.

Table 3.3 shows the ranges predicted by various bargaining sets with deviations up to 5 and the number of observed cases within these ranges. The ordinary bargaining set $B_0[5]$ contains only 3% of all 412 cases. The power bargaining set $B_1[5]$ contains 27% and $B_2[5]$ contains 25% of the 412 cases. In the game under consideration there is no difference between $B_2[5]$ and $B_3[5]$. The united bargaining set $U[5]$ contains 46% of all 412 cases.

At least at first glance the performance of bargaining set theory for the data gathered by Murnighan and Roth is not impressive. Figure 3.1 reveals that there is no extraordinary concentration of observations in the ranges predicted by the various bargaining sets with deviations up to 5. Apart from prominence effects connected to divisibility by 5 and 10, frequencies seem to have the tendency to decrease from left to right in the range from 50 to 100, even if 70 has a slightly higher frequency than 60.

In the face of Figure 3.1, one might ask oneself what payoff range one would like to predict for future experiments of the same kind. It seems to be best to avoid any attempt at exaggerated precision. It is quite safe to predict that player 1's share in a two-person coalition should be at least 50. About 97% of all 412 cases in Table 3.3 satisfy this condition. Any further restriction of player 1's share does not seem to make much sense in the light of the data. The discussion of the measure of predictive success proposed by Krischker and the author will confirm this impression.

Player 1 has more profitable coalition opportunities than either player 2 or player 3. In this sense he is stronger than the other two players. It is reasonable to expect that he, as the stronger partner, should get at least as much as the weaker one in a two-person coalition. This simple commonsense argument immediately yields the lower bound of 50 for player 1's share in a two-person coalition. The theory of equal division payoff bounds, which is explained in Section 3.9, is an attempt to exploit such arguments in order to derive predictions for all zero-normalized three-person games.

3.9   Equal division payoff bounds

The theory of equal division payoff bounds intends to reflect the limited rationality of human decision making. Players are portrayed as satisficing rather than maximizing. The behavior of a satisficer is guided by aspiration levels. In the tradition of limited rationality theory going back to H. A. Simon, aspiration levels are lower bounds on goal variables (Simon, 1957; Sauermann and Selten, 1962). A satisficer tries to obtain at least as much as his aspiration level.

In the context of an experimental characteristic function game an aspiration level can be thought of as the smallest payoff a player is willing to accept in a genuine coalition. A player who wants to make up his mind on the minimum payoff acceptable to him is involved in a decision problem that requires an analysis of the strategic structure of the game. Experimental subjects who do not perform complicated computations must base their strategic reasoning on simple commonsense arguments. The theory of equal division payoff bounds is an attempt to describe the commonsense reasons that influence the aspiration levels of the players.

In zero-normalized three-person games it is easy to make crude power comparisons among the players. Such power comparisons can be combined with equity considerations in order to arrive at lower bounds for acceptable payoffs. The equal share of a coalition value is an obvious minimum expectation for the most powerful member of the coalition. This is one of the commonsense arguments underlying the theory of equal division payoff bounds. Moreover, some additional principles enter the picture.

The theory of equal division payoff bounds is restricted to zero-normalized three-person games. For each game in this class the theory specifies three numbers u_1, u_2, and u_3 to be interpreted as lower payoff bounds for the final payoffs of the three players 1, 2, and 3, respectively. The equal division payoff bounds u_1, u_2, and u_3, also shortly called payoff bounds, should be looked upon as the lowest reasonable aspiration levels for players 1, 2, and 3, respectively. This does not rule out the possibility that a player will decide to pursue a higher aspiration level. The theory assumes only that a player's aspiration level will not be below his payoff bound u_i.

The basic ideas of the theory of equal division payoff bounds have been explained in an earlier paper (Selten, 1982). However, that theory should be improved for a number of special cases. Therefore, a new version of the theory is presented here.

For most of the experimental games examined in this chapter it makes no difference whether the theory is applied in its old form or in its new form. The new bounds are different from the old ones only for 2 of the 52 characteristic functions underlying the experiments evaluated here. However, the differences between both versions of the theory may be more important for future experiments on a greater variety of zero-normalized three-person games.

In order to lay the groundwork for the definition of the payoff bounds u_1, u_2, and u_3 it is necessary to introduce some auxiliary notions. All definitions refer to an essential zero-normalized three-person game $G = (N, Q, v)$. We shall continue to use the notation introduced in (3.17) to (3.20). Moreover, it will always be assumed that $Q\backslash123$ is $\{12, 13, 23\}$ or $\{12, 13\}$ or $\{12\}$ or empty. This can be achieved by a suitable numbering of the players. It will also be assumed that the inequalities implied by (3.21) are satisfied for values of permissible coalitions.

3.9.1 The order of strength

Assume that all two-person coalitions are permissible (123 may or may not be permissible). In an intuitively obvious sense player 1 is stronger than player 2 if we have $b > c$, since then player 1's opportunity to form a coalition with player 3 is more profitable than that of player 2. For $b = c$, both are equally strong. Similarly, player 2 is stronger than player 3 for $a > b$, and both are equally strong for $a = b$. We use the symbols $\}$ and $\sim$ to express the relationships "stronger" and "equally strong," respectively. Our conventions of numbering the players permit the following orders of strength:

$$1 \} 2 \} 3 \qquad \text{for} \quad a > b > c \tag{3.55}$$

$$1 \sim 2 \} 3 \qquad \text{for} \quad a > b = c \tag{3.56}$$

$$1 \} 2 \sim 3 \qquad \text{for} \quad a = b > c \tag{3.57}$$

$$1 \sim 2 \sim 3 \qquad \text{for} \quad a = b = c \tag{3.58}$$

A general definition of an order of strength for arbitrary characteristic function games can be found elsewhere (Selten, 1972). For the purpose of this chapter it is sufficient to rely on (3.55) to (3.58). For zero-normalized three-person games in which not all two-person coalitions are permissible, the order of strength is defined as the order of strength of the superadditive cover. Thus the order of strength for the game used by Murnighan and Roth is $1 \} 2 \sim 3$ (see Section 3.8).

3.9.2   Tentative bounds, preliminary bounds, and final bounds

In this section we define three types of bounds for the payoffs of the players. First, however, it will be useful to make an informal remark on the role of these bounds in the theory. "Tentative bounds" are derived from equity considerations combined with the order of strength or from other arguments concerning bounds for more powerful players that must be taken into account by weaker players. Usually player i's highest tentative bound t_i becomes his "preliminary bound" p_i. If the preliminary bound p_i is not sufficiently "round," player i may reduce his aspiration level to the next "round" number below p_i. This yields the "final bound" u_i.

In cases with $g > a$ the players may feel that they should form the three-person coalition in spite of the fact that their highest tentative bounds t_i sum to more than g. In such cases some players may adjust their aspiration levels to preliminary bounds p_i below their highest tentative bounds t_i. Here, too, rounding may result in a further adjustment to the final bound u_i.

3.9.3   Coalition shares and tentative bounds based on them

Coalition shares are equal shares of coalition values. The *coalition shares* of 12, 13, 23, and 123 are $a/2$, $b/2$, $c/2$, and $g/3$, respectively.

Consider a permissible genuine coalition C, where i is one of the strongest members; that is, C has no other members stronger than i. Then

$$v(C)/|C|$$

is a tentative bound of player i.

Interpretation: Since no other member of C is stronger than i, he should receive at least the equal share in $v(C)$, if C is formed. This is an obvious way to combine equity considerations with the order of strength in the derivation of a tentative bound. Suppose that all genuine coalitions are permissible. Then $a/2$ and $g/3$ are tentative bounds of player 1, and $c/2$ is a tentative bound of player 2. For $b > c$ player 3 has no tentative bound of the form (3.59) since in this case there is no coalition in which he is one of the strongest members.

The next share to be defined is relevant only for player 2. Suppose that both 12 and 13 are permissible. Without the help of player 2, player 1 cannot do anything better than to form a coalition with 3, in which case player 1 can get at most b. The increment $a - b$ is available to players 1 and 2 if and only if both of them agree to form 12 instead of 13. Therefore, player 2 should be entitled to obtain at least $(a - b)/2$ if 12 is formed. Of course, 1 is also entitled to this amount, but this is irrelevant due to the fact that player 1's tentative bound $a/2$ is at least as great as $(a - b)/2$. A similar argument cannot be used to establish a tentative bound for player 3, since nothing can be gained if another player is replaced by him.

3.9.4 Player 2's substitution share

Let both 12 and 13 be permissible. Then

$$(a - b)/2$$

called *player 2's substitution share*, is one of the tentative bounds of player 2.

3.9.5 Completion shares

Let i, j, k be the players 1, 2, 3, not necessarily in this order. If both jk and 123 are permissible, then

$$\frac{g - v(jk)}{3}$$

is called player i's *completion share*. Player i's completion share is one of his tentative bounds.

Interpretation: The grand coalition 123 cannot be formed without player i. Players j and k alone cannot get more than $v(jk)$. An agreement of all three players is necessary to obtain the increment $g - v(jk)$. Therefore, player i can claim at least one-third of this increment.

Obviously the completion share is nothing else than player i's value $v_2(i)$ in the power transformation v_2 [see (3.34) in Section 3.5]. However, the theory of equal division payoff bounds does not assert that jk should be able to obtain $v_2(jk)$. Player i's completion share is only one of his tentative bounds and it may not be the highest one. Player 1's completion share is not important for the determination of his payoff bounds u_3 since it cannot be greater than the equal share $g/3$ of the value of the grand coalition.

A further tentative bound that must be introduced concerns only player 3. Before this bound can be discussed, "the highest tentative bounds" of players 1 and 2 must be defined.

3.9.6   Highest tentative bounds of players 1 and 2

Assume that all genuine coalitions are permissible. In this case for $i = 1,2$ *player i's highest tentative bound* t_i is defined as the maximum of player i's tentative bounds introduced in Section 3.9.3, 3.9.4, or 3.9.5. It can be seen immediately that we have

$$t_1 = \max\left[\frac{a}{2}, \frac{g}{3}\right] \tag{3.59}$$

and

$$t_2 = t_1 \qquad \text{for} \quad b = c \tag{3.60}$$

$$t_2 = \max\left[\frac{c}{2}, \frac{a-b}{2}, \frac{g-b}{3}\right] \qquad \text{for} \quad b > c \tag{3.61}$$

If some of the genuine coalitions are not permissible the *highest tentative bounds* t_1 and t_2 are defined in the same way as the maximum of all tentative bounds for the player concerned, which are defined in terms of values of permissible coalitions. The assumptions on G made at the beginning of this section guarantee that for each of the players there is at least one such bound.

3.9.7   Comments on the strategic situation of player 3

Before defining "player 3's competitive bound" in Section 3.9.8, it will
be useful to discuss the strategic situation of player 3 in games with
$a > b$. Assume that all three two-person coalitions are permissible and
that we have $a > b$ and $t_1 + t_2 \leq a$. In view of $a > b$ the coalition 12
is the most attractive two-person coalition. Since both players 1 and 2
can get their highest tentative bounds t_1 and t_2 in 12, player 3 must fear
that 12 will be formed. Player 3 cannot rule out this possibility even if
123 should be permissible with $g > a$. In order to prevent the formation
of 12, player 3 may be willing to make very attractive offers to each of
the other players. Suppose that 1 and 2 do not reduce their aspiration
levels below their highest tentative bounds t_1 and t_2. Then the amounts

$$h_1 = a - t_2 \tag{3.62}$$

and

$$h_2 = a - t_1 \tag{3.63}$$

are upper bounds for the payoffs of 1 and 2 in 12. Therefore, player 3
may be motivated to offer h_1 to player 1 in 13 or alternatively h_2 to
player 2 in 23 in order to prevent the formation of 12. This may induce
player 3 to reduce his aspiration level to the minimum of $b - h_1$ and
$c - h_2$. This leads to the definition given in Section 3.9.8.

3.9.8   Player 3's competitive bound

Assume that all three two-person coalitions are permissible. *Player 3's
competitive bound w* is defined as

$$w = \min[b - h_1, c - h_2] \tag{3.64}$$

where h_1 and h_2 are given by (3.62) and (3.63). The numbers h_1 and h_2
are called *highest competitive offers* to players 1 and 2, respectively.
For $t_1 + t_2 \leq a$ player 3's competitive bound is one of *player 3's
tentative bounds*.

3.9.9   Player 3's highest tentative bound

Assume that all genuine coalitions are permissible; in this case *player
3's highest tentative bound t_3* is the maximum of player 3's tentative

bounds described in Sections 3.9.3, 3.9.5, and 3.9.8. It can be seen immediately that we have

$$t_3 = t_2 \qquad \text{for} \quad a = b \qquad (3.65)$$

$$t_3 = \max\left[\frac{g - a}{3}, w\right] \qquad \text{for} \quad a > b \quad \text{and} \quad t_1 + t_2 \le a \quad (3.66)$$

$$t_3 = \frac{g - a}{3} \qquad \text{for} \quad a > b \quad \text{and} \quad t_1 + t_2 > a \quad (3.67)$$

Now suppose that not all genuine coalitions are permissible. In such cases the definition of *player 3's highest tentative bound* t_3 is as follows: (1) If $2 \sim 3$ holds, we have $t_3 = t_2$. (2) For $2 \nmid 3$, equation (3.67) describes t_3 if $123 \in Q$. (3) For $Q = \{12, 13, 23\}$ with $2 \nmid 3$ and $t_1 + t_2 \le a$, as well as $w > 0$, we have $t_3 = w$. (4) In all other cases where not all genuine coalitions are permissible, t_3 is defined as zero.

Comment: For $t_1 + t_2 > a$ coalition 12 is unattractive and the reasoning that has motivated the definition of player 3's competitive bound cannot be applied. Nevertheless, even in this case the formation of 12 may be a serious threat to player 3. Therefore, it is interesting to consider whether it would make sense for player 3 to reduce his aspiration level to the minimum of $b - h_1$ and $c - h_2$ in spite of $t_1 + t_2 > a$. Assume that all two-person coalitions are permissible and that $t_1 + t_2 > a$ holds. In view of

$$b - h_1 + c - h_2 = a - t_1 - t_2 + c - b < 0 \qquad (3.68)$$

we have

$$\min[b - h_1, c - h_2] < 0 \qquad \text{for} \quad t_1 + t_2 > a \qquad (3.69)$$

Consequently player 3's competitive bound is irrelevant for player 3 even if one extends the reasoning of Section 3.9.7 to the case $t_1 + t_2 > a$.

In view of (3.69) it does not do any harm if (3.66) is also applied to cases with $t_1 + t_2 > a$.

3.9.10 Discussion of the case $t_1 + t_2 + t_3 > g$

The highest tentative bounds t_1, t_2, and t_3 are natural candidates for the preliminary bounds p_1, p_2, and p_3. However, in some cases there may be reasons for lower preliminary bounds. Assume that all genuine coalitions are permissible and that $g > a$ holds. It can happen that we have

$$t_1 + t_2 + t_3 > g \tag{3.70}$$

An example is supplied by one of Medlin's (1976) experimental games. The coalition values for this game are as follows:

$$a = 95; \quad b = 88; \quad c = 81; \quad g = 113 \tag{3.71}$$

Here the highest tentative bounds t_1 and t_2 are $a/2$ and $c/2$, respectively:

$$t_1 = \max\left[\frac{a}{2}, \frac{g}{3}\right] = 47.5 \tag{3.72}$$

$$t_2 = \max\left[\frac{c}{2}, \frac{a-b}{2}, \frac{g-b}{3}\right] = 40.5 \tag{3.73}$$

The highest competitive offers h_1 and h_2 are as follows:

$$h_1 = a - t_2 = 54.5 \tag{3.74}$$

$$h_2 = a - t_1 = 47.5 \tag{3.75}$$

In view of

$$b - h_1 = 88 - 54.5 = 33.5 \tag{3.76}$$

and

$$c - h_2 = 81 - 47.5 = 33.5 \tag{3.77}$$

we have

$$w = 33.5 \tag{3.78}$$

and

$$t_3 = \max\left[\frac{g-a}{3}, w\right] = 33.5 \tag{3.79}$$

Consequently, the highest tentative bounds sum to more than g:

$$t_1 + t_2 + t_3 = 121.5 > g \tag{3.80}$$

However, 123 can distribute 18 points more than the most profitable two-person coalition 12. The players may feel that they should not waste these 18 points. If no one reduces his aspiration level below his highest tentative bound t_i, there is no way to form 123. Therefore, one player has to reduce his aspiration level to below his highest tentative bound in order to make the grand coalition possible. If no one is willing to do this, coalition 12 is the most likely one to be formed. Consequently, player 3 has the strongest reason to reduce his aspiration level to below his highest tentative bound t_3. It is reasonable to expect that he will do this in many cases. Players 1 and 2 probably do not feel a similar pressure.

What is the level to which player 3 should reduce his aspiration level? At first glance, a reduction to $(g - a)/3$ would seem to be required. However, this appears to be an unnecessarily large concession. Medlin's results suggest that a reduction to $g - a = 18$ is sufficient. Players 1 and 2 seem willing to give player 3 the whole increment $g - a$ in order to make 123 possible. Accordingly, player 3's preliminary bound p_3 will be defined as $p_3 = g - a$ in similar cases.

In Medlin's experiment the subjects seem to look at numbers divisible by 5 as "round." This indicates a further reduction of $p_3 = 18$ to the final bound $u_3 = 15$. Medlin's data contain eight plays of the game under consideration. In five of these plays, player 3 was in the final coalition. Player 3 received 16, 18, and 28 in three cases of three-person coalitions and playoffs of 26 and 36 in two cases of final coalitions 23. Among the 52 games in the experiments examined here, there is no other one with $t_1 + t_2 + t_3 > g > a$. Therefore, it must be admitted that for cases of this type the intuition underlying the new version of the theory of equal division playoff bounds rests on meager evidence.

It is not clear how these arguments should be applied to cases with $a = b$ where players 2 and 3 are equally strong. There is no doubt that $t_1 = t_2 = t_3 = g/3$ is reasonable for $g > a = b = c$. However, suppose that $a = b > c$ and

$$a/2 + c > g \tag{3.81}$$

hold. Then in view of $c < a$ we have $a/2 \geq g/3$ and therefore $t_1 = a/2$ and $t_2 = t_3 = c/2$. Consequently, the case $t_1 + t_2 + t_3 > g$ arises here. In this situation player 1 is in a weaker position than in the case discussed above. Two other players rather than only one would have to reduce their aspiration levels below their highest tentative bounds if player 1 were not willing to do so. Therefore, it seems plausible to assume that all three players may feel that they have to be satisfied with lower levels. This suggests

$$p_1 = g/3 \tag{3.82}$$

and

$$p_2 = \tfrac{1}{2}(g - a/2) \tag{3.83}$$

as preliminary levels. One could also consider $p_1 = g - c$ instead of (3.82). However, in view of the lack of experimental evidence, it is perhaps preferable to propose the lower level $p_1 = g/3$.

3.9.11   Preliminary bounds

Assume that all genuine coalitions are permissible. For $i = 1, 2, 3$ *player i's preliminary bound* p_i is defined as follows:

$$\begin{aligned}
&p_i = t_i &&\text{for } i = 1, 2, 3\\
&&&\text{if } g = a \ \text{ or } \ t_1 + t_2 + t_3 \le g
\end{aligned} \tag{3.84}$$

$$\begin{aligned}
&p_i = t_i &&\text{for } i = 1, 2 \ \text{ and } \ p_3 = g - a\\
&&&\text{if } t_1 + t_2 + t_3 > g > a > b \ge c
\end{aligned} \tag{3.85}$$

$$\begin{aligned}
&p_i = \frac{g}{3} &&\text{for } i = 1, 2, 3\\
&&&\text{if } t_1 + t_2 + t_3 > g > a = b = c
\end{aligned} \tag{3.86}$$

$$\begin{aligned}
&p_1 = \frac{g}{3} &&\text{and } \ p_2 = p_3 = g/2 - a/4\\
&&&\text{if } t_1 + t_2 + t_3 > g > a = b > c
\end{aligned} \tag{3.87}$$

If some of the genuine coalitions are not permissible, *player i's preliminary bound* p_i is defined by $p_i = t_i$ for $i = 1, 2, 3$.

3.9.12   Lemma on preliminary bounds

If 12 and 123 are permissible coalitions and $g > a$ holds, we have

$$p_1 + p_2 + p_3 > g \tag{3.88}$$

Proof: First assume that all genuine coalitions are permissible. For $t_1 + t_2 + t_3 \le g$, inequality (3.88) holds in view of (3.84). Assume $t_1 + t_2 + t_3 > g$. It will be shown that this implies $t_1 + t_2 \le a$. Suppose we have $t_1 + t_2 > a$. It can be seen easily that $t_2 \le t_1$ always holds. This yields $t_1 + t_2 \le 2t_1$. Therefore, $t_1 + t_2 \le a$ holds for $t_1 = a/2$. Consider the case $t_1 = g/3$. Equation (3.69) implies $w < 0$. This has the consequence that we must have $t_3 \le g/3$. Hence, $t_1 + t_2 > g$ implies $t_1 + t_2 \le a$, which shows that (3.88) holds for the case covered by (3.85). Obviously, (3.88) also holds for the cases covered by (3.86) and (3.87).

It remains to be shown that (3.88) holds for $Q = \{12, 13, 123\}$ and $Q = \{12, 123\}$. Other cases can be excluded, either by the assumptions of the lemma or by conventions on the numbering of the players. Both cases do not permit $t_3 = w$. In view of $t_2 \le t$, and $t_3 = (g - a)/3$, we have $t_1 + t_2 + t_3 \le g$. Therefore, (3.88) holds.

3.9.13 Smallest money unit

In all experimental games known to the author, payoffs are not infinitely divisible. There is a smallest money unit that cannot be subdivided. The smallest money unit will be denoted by γ. In the experiments of Murnighan and Roth discussed in Section 3.8, the smallest money unit is $\gamma = 0.01$ point. In many other cases the smallest money unit is 1 point. The theory of equal division payoff bounds assumes that a player does not enter a genuine coalition unless he receives at least one smallest money unit. This assumption will enter the definition of the final bounds.

3.9.14 Prominence level

The transition from the preliminary bounds to the final bounds depends on a parameter Δ, called the *prominence level*, which must be adjusted to the data. This parameter is of the form $\Delta = m \, 10^k \gamma$ with $m = 1, 2, 5, 10, 25$ and $k = 0, 1, 2, \ldots$. Ideally the prominence level Δ should be chosen in such a way that a number is perceived as "round" by the experimental subjects if and only if it is divisible by Δ (Albers and Albers, 1983; Tietz, 1984). A new method for the choice of Δ is discussed in Section 3.11. It will be shown that, for the experiments examined here, it is justifiable to work with $\Delta = 5$.

3.9.15 Final bounds

For any real number μ the greatest integer m with $m \le \mu$ will be denoted by int μ. For a fixed prominence level Δ, player i's final bound u_i is defined as

$$u_i = \max \left[\gamma, \Delta \text{ int } \frac{p_i}{\Delta} \right] \tag{3.89}$$

for $i = 1, 2, 3$. This means that player i's preliminary bound p_i is rounded to the next number divisible by Δ not above p_i. The result is the final bound, unless it is zero, in which case the final bound is one smallest money unit.

3.9.16 Predictions of the theory of equal division payoff bounds

The theory of equal division payoff bounds makes the following predictions (A) and (B):

(A) If there is at least one permissible coalition C with

$$\sum_{i \in C} u_i \leq v(C) \tag{3.90}$$

then a coalition C of this kind will be formed.

(B) If a genuine coalition C is formed, the final payoffs x_i of the members of C will not be below their final payoff bounds:

$$x_i \geq u_i \quad \text{for every} \quad i \in C \tag{3.91}$$

The set of all configurations with (A) and (B) is denoted by E_Δ.

3.9.17 Computation of preliminary bounds

In this section we restrict our attention to the case in which all genuine coalitions are permissible. In order to compute the preliminary bounds p_1, p_2, and p_3, one can proceed as follows. One first computes t_1 and t_2 with the help of (3.59) to (3.61). One then determines h_1 and h_2 with the help of (3.62) and (3.63) in order to find w by (3.64). One obtains t_3 with the help of (3.65) to (3.67). Finally p_1, p_2, and p_3 are computed with the help of (3.84) to (3.87).

In order to have a better overview of the implications of the theory of equal division payoff bounds, it is useful to make a case distinction that is sufficiently fine to permit the description of p_1, p_2, and p_3 by closed formulas. This has been done for "cases without symmetries," that is, for $a > b > c$ in Table 3.4 and for "cases with symmetries," that is, for games with $a = b$ or $b = c$ in Table 3.5. It is not necessary to describe in detail how these tables have been derived from the definition of the preliminary bounds, since this has been done in a straightforward way. However, it may be worthwhile to prove the assertions in the footnotes of Table 3.4.

3.9.18 The footnotes of Table 3.4

In order to show that the assertions of the three footnotes hold, we first examine the case $p_1 = g/3$. In this case we have $g/3 \geq a/2$. This yields

$$\frac{g - b}{3} > \frac{a - b}{2} \quad \text{for} \quad p_1 = \frac{g}{3} \tag{3.92}$$

Consequently, the assertion of footnote (1) holds.

Table 3.4. *Preliminary bounds for cases without symmetries*

Conditions	Bounds
$a > b > c^{(1)}$	$p_1 = \max\left[\dfrac{a}{2}, \dfrac{g}{3}\right]$
	$p_2 = \max\left[\dfrac{c}{2}, \dfrac{a-b}{2}, \dfrac{g-b}{3}\right]$
$g = a > b > c^{(2)}$	
$g > a > b > c$ and $p_1 + p_2 + w \le g$	$p_3 = \max\left[w, \dfrac{g-a}{3}\right]$ with $w = \min[b - h_1, c - h_2]$ where $h_1 = a - p_2$ and $h_2 = a - p_1$
$g > a > b > c^{(3)}$ and $p_1 + p_2 + w > g$	$p_3 = g - a$

(1) $a > b > c$ excludes the case $p_1 = g/3$ and $p_2 = (a - b)/2$.
(2) $a > b > c$ has the consequence that $p_3 = w$ implies $p_2 = c/2$.
(3) $g > a > b > c$ and $p_1 + p_2 + w > g$ imply $p_1 = a/2$ and $p_2 = c/2$ and $w > g - a$.

Table 3.5. *Preliminary bounds for cases with symmetries*

Conditions	Bounds
$g = a = b = c$	$p_1 = p_2 = p_3 = a/2$
$g > a = b = c$	$p_1 = p_2 = p_3 = g/3$
$g = a = b > c$	$p_1 = a/2;\quad p_2 = p_3 = c/2$
$g > a = b > c$ and $a/2 + c > g$	$p_1 = g/3$ $p_2 = p_3 = g/2 - a/4$
$g > a = b > c$ and $g \geq a/2 + c$	$p_1 = \max[a/2, g/3]$ $p_2 = p_3 = \max[c/2, (g - a)/3]$
$g = a > b = c$	$p_1 = p_2 = a/2$ $p_3 = \max(0, b - a/2)$
$g > a > b = c$ and $a/2 + b > g$	$p_1 = p_2 = a/2$ $p_3 = g - a$
$g > a > b = c$ and $g \geq a/2 + b$	$p_1 = p_2 = \max[a/2, g/3]$ $p_3 = \max[b - p_1, (g - a)/3]$

We now turn to footnote (2). Assume $p_3 = w$. This implies

$$b - h_1 = b - a + p_2 \geq w \geq \frac{g - a}{3} \tag{3.93}$$

We can conclude

$$p_2 \geq \frac{g - b}{3} + \frac{2}{3}(a - b) > \frac{g - b}{3} \tag{3.94}$$

This excludes $(g - b)/3$ as a possible value of p_2 if $p_3 = w$ holds. Now suppose $p_2 = (a - b)/2$. This implies

$$b - h_1 = b - a + \frac{a - b}{2} = -\frac{a - b}{2} \geq w \tag{3.95}$$

In view of $a > b$ we can conclude that for $p_2 = (a - b)/2$ player 3's competitive bound w is negative. This excludes $(a - b)/2$ as a possible value of p_2 if $p_3 = w$ holds. We must have $p_2 = c/2$ for $p_3 = w$.

Finally, we show the assertion of footnote (3). Assume $p_1 = g/3$. Then we have $p_2 \leq g/3$ and therefore

$$p_1 + p_2 + w \leq p_1 + p_2 + b - a + p_1 \leq g \tag{3.96}$$

Consequently, $p_1 + p_2 + w > g$ implies $p_1 = a/2$. For $p_1 = a/2$ we have $p_2 \leq a/2$ and therefore $p_1 + p_2 \leq a$. Inequality (3.95) shows that for $p_2 = (a - b)/2$ player 3's competitive bound w is negative. Therefore, $p_1 + p_2 + w > g$ excludes $p_2 = (b - a)/2$. Assume $p_1 = a/2$ and $p_2 = (g - b)/3$. Then we have

$$p_1 + p_2 + w \leq a + b - a + p_2 \leq b + \frac{g - b}{3} < g \qquad (3.97)$$

This shows that $p_1 + p_2 + w > g$ excludes $p_2 = (g - b)/3$. We must have $p_1 = a/2$ and $p_2 = c/2$. In view of $p_1 + p_2 < a$ it follows that $p_1 + p_2 + w$ also implies $w > g - a$. Consequently, the assertion of footnote (3) is true.

3.9.19 Limited rationality aspects of the theory

The theory of equal division payoff bounds proceeds from the assumption that the players form aspiration levels on their payoffs in genuine coalitions. The payoff bounds specified by the theory are lower bounds for these aspiration levels. This does not rule out the possibility that players form aspiration levels above these bounds. It is plausible to expect that a player who tries to avoid risks will select a low aspiration level, whereas other players may take the risk involved in a higher aspiration level in order to exploit the chance offered by the low aspiration levels of other players. Atkinson's (1957) theory on the connection between attitudes toward risk and aspiration levels may be relevant here (see also Atkinson and Birch, 1978).

Typically, game-theoretic solution concepts are based on definitions that describe the proposed solution by inner properties. It is then necessary to explore the conditions of existence and to find out how to compute the solution in specific cases. The Aumann–Maschler bargaining set is a typical example. On the basis of a definition of objections and counterobjections, a configuration is described as stable if a counterobjection exists for every objection. It is not immediately clear from this definition how one can find stable configurations, and it is generally not a trivial task to check whether a given configuration is stable.

The theory of equal division payoff bounds has a different character. The payoff bounds are not characterized by inner properties. They are constructively obtained by straightforward commonsense arguments based on easily recognizable features of the strategic situation. The theory does not proceed from stability conditions imposed on the end result of strategic analysis. Instead, it takes the form of a chain of reasoning. Following the order of strength, highest tentative bounds are determined for one player after the other. Coalition shares, completion shares, player 2's substitution share, and player 3's competitive bound are very simple constructs. A final adjustment may be necessary if the highest tentative bounds sum to more than the value of the grand coalition.

Every single step of the chain of reasoning specified by the theory is very simple. However, different arguments apply to different cases, and many case distinctions have to be made if one wants to describe the final result as a function of the parameters. This may create an impression of complexity, which seems to contradict the idea that limited rationality is connected to simplicity. However, in theories of limited rationality one should not look for the simplicity of abstract principles of sweeping generality. A combination of complex case distinctions with very simple decision rules for every single case seems to be very typical for limited rationality decision making.

The subjects involved in a characteristic function game do not try to develop general theories for such games. Their strategic thinking is concentrated on the case at hand. Therefore, one should not expect general properties like monotonicity of payoff bounds as functions of coalition values. In fact, the preliminary payoff bounds p_1, p_2, and p_3 do not increase monotonically with the value g of the grand coalition. Moreover, p_1, p_2, and p_3 do not depend continuously on the parameters of the game. Consider a case with $a > b > c$. If c is increased, the order of strength changes from $1 \mid 2 \mid 3$ to $1 \sim 2 \sim 3$ at $c = b$. This has a profound influence on the arguments relevant to the derivation of payoff bounds; p_2 may jump from $c/2$ to $a/2$ at $c = b$. Owing to such discontinuities it is very important to distinguish between games with symmetries and games without symmetries.

3.9.20 Differences between the old and new versions of equal division payoff bounds

There are two essential differences. In the old version the application of player 3's competitive bound w was restricted to the case $p_1 = a/2$ and $p_2 = c/2$. The results for one of Medlin's games suggest that the competitive bound should also be applied to cases with $p_1 = g/3$ and $p_2 = c/2$. The parameters of this game are $g = 150$, $a = 95$, $b = 88$, and $c = 81$. The old version yields a final payoff bound of 15 for player 3, derived from $(g - b)/3$, whereas the new version arrives at $u_3 = 30$. The grand coalition was formed in seven of eight plays and 12 was formed once. Player 3 received payoffs of at least 40 in all seven cases of three-person coalitions. Four times the players agreed on an even split of 150.

The second essential difference concerns the adjustment of bounds in the case $t_1 + t_2 + t_3 > g > a$. The old version did not postulate this adjustment. The reason for the change is discussed in Section 3.9.10.

3.10   A measure of predictive success

One of the purposes of this chapter is to compare the predictive success of two characteristic function theories: the united bargaining set discussed in Section 3.7 and the new version of the theory of equal division payoff bounds introduced in Section 3.9. Both theories are area theories in the sense explained in the Introduction. An area theory predicts a range of outcomes. In the cases considered here the range of predicted outcomes takes the form of a nonempty subset of the set of all configurations.

In order to compare the predictive success of two area theories for a body of experimental data, it is not sufficient to examine which theory yields more correct predictions. A theory may produce many correct predictions simply because it predicts a very large range. An extreme example is provided by a theory which will be called the *null theory*; the predicted range of the null theory is the set of all configurations.

Obviously, if one wants to compare area theories in a meaningful way, the size of the predicted range must be taken into account. For this purpose W. Krischker and the author have developed a measure of predictive success (Selten and Krischker, 1982). The basic idea underlying the measure of predictive success is quite simple. A measure of the relative size of the predicted range is subtracted from the relative frequency of correct predictions. This yields the measure of predicted success. The term "hit rate" is used for the relative frequency of correct predictions. If the outcomes are randomly distributed over the whole range of outcomes, the hit rate can be expected to be equal to the relative size of the predicted range. The measure of predictive success can be thought of as the surplus of the observed hit rate over the random hit rate.

The informal explanation given above is not yet a definition of the measure of predictive success. In the context of characteristic function game experiments it is by no means obvious how the relative size of the predicted range should be measured. One needs a formal definition of relative size.

3.10.1 Grid games

As explained in Section 3.9.12 characteristic function experiments generally involve a smallest money unity γ. Consequently, the range of possible outcomes is not really a continuum, but rather a finite set of configurations. The formal definition of relative size will take this into account.

A pair (G, γ), where $G = (N, Q, v)$ is a characteristic function game and $\gamma > 0$ is a smallest money unit, is called a *grid game* if the following condition is satisfied for G. The values $v(C)$ of all permissible coalitions are integer multiples of γ. A *grid configuration* $\alpha = (C_1, \ldots, C_m;$ $x_1, \ldots, x_n)$ for a grid game (G, γ) is a configuration for G with the property that the payoffs $x_1, \ldots, x_n$ are integer multiples of the smallest money unit γ. Experimental games should be thought of as grid games. Only grid configurations can be reached as final outcomes, and no other configurations can be predicted for such games.

3.10.2 A problem of dimensions

At first glance the number of predicted grid configurations may appear to be a reasonable measure of the size of a range of predictions. However, this idea must be modified in view of the fact that configurations for different coalition structures are in spaces of different dimensions. In a three-person game a two-person coalition like 12 gives rise to a one-parameter family of configurations of the form

$$\alpha = (12; x_1, a - x_1, 0) \tag{3.98}$$

whereas the grand coalition 123 is connected to a two-parameter family of configurations of the form

$$\alpha = (123; x_1, x_2, g - x_1 - x_2) \tag{3.99}$$

This shows that counting grid configurations in order to determine a measure of size would be similar to adding meters and square meters.

Consider the superadditive zero-normalized three-person game with $a = b = c = g = 100$. This game has 101 grid configurations of the form (3.98) and 5,151 grid configurations of the form (3.99). Obviously, the simplistic measure of size, which counts only grid configurations, gives too much emphasis to the three-person coalition. The game has 5,355 grid configurations. Roughly 94% of these grid configurations are of the form (3.99).

A reasonable definition of relative size should have the property that it admits a sensible interpretation as a random hit rate. This means that something like a null hypothesis on the distribution of experimental results is expressed by a definition of relative size. The assumption that all grid configurations are equally likely does not yield a reasonable null hypothesis. It seems to be more adequate to apply the principle of insufficient reason on two levels: One first assumes that all coalition structures are equally likely and then that all grid configurations with the same coalition structure are equally likely. This null hypothesis is the basis of the definition of relative size.

Of course, to some degree any null hypothesis is arbitrary. However, it should be kept in mind that the null hypothesis is not used as a prior distribution. It serves as a measuring rod that helps to define the kind of predictive success one wants to achieve.

3.10.3   Relative size

Let (G, γ) be a grid game; let J be the number of coalition structures for G and for every coalition structure $C_1, \ldots, C_m$ for G let $I(C_1, \ldots, C_m)$ be the number of grid configurations for G with this coalition structure. For every grid configuration $\alpha = (C_1, \ldots, C_m; x_1, \ldots, x_n)$ for (G, γ) the *weight* $A(\alpha)$ of α is defined as

$$A(\alpha) = 1/JI(C_1, \ldots, C_m) \tag{3.100}$$

Let T be a set of grid configurations for (G, γ). The *area* $A(T)$ of T is the sum of the weights of all grid configurations in T:

$$A(T) = \sum_{\alpha \in T} A(\alpha) \tag{3.101}$$

The area is the measure of relative size used in the definition of the measure of predictive success.

3.10.4   Predictive success

Suppose that a body of experimental data consists of k plays based on m grid games $(G_1, \gamma_1), \ldots, (G_m, \gamma_m)$. For $i = 1, \ldots, m$ let k_i be the number of plays of the grid game (G_i, γ_i). Consider a theory T that predicts a set T_i of grid configurations for each of the grid games (G_i, γ_i). Let A_i be the area of T_i. The *average area* A for the whole body of data is defined as

$$A = \frac{1}{k} \sum_{i=1}^{m} k_i A_i \tag{3.102}$$

Let s be the number of plays correctly predicted by T in the body of data. Then the *hit rate* R for this body of data is

$$R = s/k \qquad (3.103)$$

The *success rate* S of theory T for the body of data is the difference between the hit rate R and the average area A:

$$S = R - A \qquad (3.104)$$

Both R and A are numbers between 0 and 1. Therefore, S has a range between -1 and $+1$.

The null theory that predicts the set of all grid configurations always has the success rate 0 if only grid configurations can occur as possible outcomes.

3.10.5 Difference or quotient

The definition of the success rate S as the difference between R and A may seem arbitrary. The quotient R/A suggests itself as an alternative. However, R/A has serious disadvantages as a measure of predictive success. Consider two theories T and T' with hit rates of $R = .9$ and $R' = .01$ and areas of $A = .3$ and $A' = .001$, respectively. We obtain $R/A = 3$ and $R'/A' = 10$. The quotient measure gives preference to T' in spite of the fact that the predictions of T' are wrong in 99% of all cases. It seems clear that T is preferable.

3.10.6 Area computation

The computation of areas is illustrated by an example in Table 3.6. It is convenient to determine a *subarea* for each coalition structure, which is the number of predicted grid configurations for the coalition structure concerned divided by the number of all grid configurations for this structure. The area is then obtained as the sum of the subareas divided by the number of coalition structures.

If the smallest money unit is very small, one can compute subareas as areas of the geometric figures delineated by the conditions of the theory. If this is done for the example of Table 3.6 one obtains an area of .076127 instead of .082458. The difference is small, but it is doubtful whether it should be looked on as negligible. In this chapter all areas are computed on the basis of numbers of grid configurations.

3.11 Prominence

The idea of prominence was introduced by Schelling, who argued that bargaining results can often be explained by nonstrategic features of

Table 3.6. *Computation of the area of the bargaining set without null structure and with deviations up to 5*

| Coalition structure | Predicted range | Number of grid config- urations for the coali- tion structure | | Subarea |
		Predicted	All	
1, 2, 3	—	0	1	.000000
12, 3	$55 \leq x_1 \leq 65$	11	96	.114583
13, 2	$55 \leq x_1 \leq 65$	11	91	.120879
23, 1	$30 \leq x_2 \leq 40$	11	66	.166667
123	$54 \leq x_1 \leq 63$ $29 \leq x_2 \leq 38$ $24 \leq x_3 \leq 35$	75	7,381	.010161
			Sum:	.412290
			Area:	.082458

Note: The data are for a specific example of a three-person quota game: $v(1) = v(2) = v(3) = 0$, $v(12) = 95$, $v(13) = 90$, $v(23) = 65$, $v(123) = 120$. The smallest money unit was $\gamma = 1$. In 17 of 32 plays the outcome was in the predicted range (Rapoport and Kahan, 1976). This yields a success rate of $.53 - .08 = .45$.

the situation (Schelling, 1960). Cultural traditions and conventions may focus on points in the bargaining range that do not have any special strategic significance. In the context of characteristic function experiments it is important to look at the prominence of round numbers. The phenomenon is known to every researcher in experimental economics, but until recently a theoretical framework was lacking. The pioneering effort of Wulf and Gisela Albers (1983) on the theory of prominence in the decimal system has filled this gap. A very interesting approach to the same question has been taken by Reinhard Tietz (1984), who introduced the idea of a "prominence grid," which will not be explored here.

In this section a new method for determining the prominence level of a set of data is proposed. The concept of a prominence level Δ was introduced in Section 3.9.13. As pointed out in Section 3.7 without making use of the term, one needs a prominence level Δ in order to define a reasonable descriptive bargaining set. The final bounds predicted by the theory of equal division payoff bounds also depend on a prominence level Δ. Therefore, we need a nonarbitrary way to adjust the parameter Δ to the data.

Albers and Albers as well as Tietz examined the question of how to determine the prominence level of a set of numbers. However, the methods proposed by these authors do not seem to be entirely satisfactory tools of statistical analysis, since they depend on judgmental parameters. Thus one of the proposals of Albers and Albers requires that 75% of all data be prominent at least on the level Δ. Undoubtedly this percentage was chosen on the basis of sound empirical judgment guided by a great deal of experience with data sets. Nevertheless, it would be desirable to use a method that eliminates the necessity of referring to sound judgment.

The method proposed here is connected to the measure of predictive success introduced in the previous section. However, an independent justification will be given for the proposed definition of the prominence level of a set of data.

3.11.1 Prominence levels

Let X be the set of all integer multiples of a smallest money unit $\gamma > 0$. A *prominence level* in X is a number Δ of the form $\Delta = \mu \, 10^{\eta} \gamma$ with $\mu = 1, 2, 5, 25$ and $\eta = 1, 2, \ldots$. The set of all prominence levels in X is denoted by X_0. The *prominence level* $\delta(x)$ of a number $x \in X$ is the greatest prominence level $\Delta \in X_0$ such that x is divisible without remainder by Δ.

Comment: The definition of a prominence level follows the work of Albers and Albers, who proposed the idea that the coefficients 1, 2, 5, and 25 occur as the result of increasing or decreasing the step of a "prominence scale" by a factor 2 or in some special cases by a factor 2.5 (Albers and Albers, 1983). Thus a step of 500 may be reduced to a step of 250 in order to make more precise decisions. A further increase in precision would lead to a step of 100 rather than 125.

3.11.2 Description of data sets as frequency distributions

Consider a set of data in which the observations are numbers in the set X introduced in Section 3.11.1. We can think of a data set of this kind as a frequency distribution. Formally, a *frequency distribution over X* is a function k that assigns a positive integer $k(x)$ to every x in a nonempty finite subset Y of X and $k(x) = 0$ to every $x \in X \backslash Y$. The set

Y is the *support* of k. The number $k(x)$ is interpreted as the frequency with which the value x occurs in the data set. The *number of all observations* is given by

$$H = \sum_{x \in X} k(x) \qquad (3.105)$$

For every prominence level $\Delta \in X_0$ let $m(\Delta)$ be the number of values x in Y with $\delta(x) = \Delta$. We call $m(\Delta)$ the *number of values on the prominence level* Δ. For every prominence level $\Delta \in X_0$, let $h(\Delta)$ be the sum of all $k(x)$ with $\delta(x) = \Delta$. We call $h(\Delta)$ the *number of observations* on the prominence level Δ.

For every prominence level $\Delta \in X_0$ let Y_Δ be the set of all $x \in Y$ with $\delta(x) \geq \Delta$. The number of elements of Y_Δ is denoted by $M(\Delta)$. Obviously, $M(\Delta)$ is nothing other than the sum of all $m(\Delta')$ with $\Delta' \geq \Delta$ and $\Delta' \in X_0$. We call $M(\Delta)$ the *number of values at least on the prominence level* Δ. The number of all elements of Y is denoted by M.

The *number H_Δ of observations* at least on the prominence level Δ is defined as

$$H(\Delta) = \sum_{z \in Y_\Delta} k(z) \qquad (3.106)$$

Obviously, $H(\Delta)$ is the sum of all h_Δ, with $\Delta' \geq \Delta$ and $\Delta' \in X_0$.

3.11.3 Intuitive background of the method

Suppose that the data set described by the frequency distribution k has been obtained by experiments in which the subjects are attracted by "round" numbers. Where should we draw the dividing line between "round" numbers and other numbers? It is plausible to assume that subjects perceive a number x as "round" if its prominence level $\delta(x)$ is at least as high as a critical level Δ^*. How should we form an estimate of this critical level Δ^*?

Assume for a moment that, contrary to our expectations, prominence does not influence the subjects' behavior. Under this "null hypothesis," the frequency $k(x)$ of a value $x \in Y$ should not depend on the prominence level $\delta(x)$ of x. This means that for prominence levels Δ with sufficiently larger $M(\Delta)$ one should expect a small difference between the fraction $H(\Delta)/H$ of observations at least on the prominence level Δ and the fraction $M(\Delta)/M$ of values at least on the prominence level Δ.

Now suppose that subjects are attracted to "round" numbers, where roundness of x is defined by $\delta(x) \geq \Delta^*$. Then $k(x)$ should tend to be greater than the overall average frequency H/M for $\delta(x) \geq \Delta^*$ and smaller than H/M for $\delta(x) < \Delta^*$. The expected value of the average frequency $h(\Delta)/m(\Delta)$ for values on the prominence level Δ should be greater than H/M for $\delta(x) \geq \Delta^*$ and smaller than H/M for $\delta(x) < \Delta^*$. If this is true, the expected value of the difference

$$D(\Delta) = \frac{H(\Delta)}{H} - \frac{M(\Delta)}{M} \tag{3.107}$$

is maximal for $\Delta = \Delta^*$. In order to see this, assume that Δ' is the prominence level just below Δ. We have

$$D(\Delta') = \frac{H(\Delta) + h(\Delta')}{H} - \frac{M(\Delta) + m(\Delta')}{M} \tag{3.108}$$

$$D(\Delta') = D(\Delta) + \frac{h(\Delta')}{H} - \frac{m(\Delta')}{M} \tag{3.109}$$

$$D(\Delta') = D(\Delta) + \frac{m(\Delta')}{H}\left(\frac{h(\Delta')}{m(\Delta')} - \frac{H}{M}\right) \tag{3.110}$$

Therefore, the method proposed here estimates the critical value D^* as the maximizer of $D(\Delta)$ or the greatest maximizer of $D(\Delta)$ if several values of Δ maximize D.

3.11.4 Prominence level of a data set

Consider a data set described by a frequency distribution k over X. The *prominence level* Δ^* of k is defined as the greatest maximizer of $D(\Delta)$, where $D(\Delta)$ is given by (3.107).

Example: Table 3.7 illustrates the determination of the prominence level for a data set in the example of player 1's payoffs in two-person coalitions in the game of Murnighan and Roth. The frequency distribution k is shown in Fig. 3.1. There, however, only aggregate frequencies are given for values not divisible by 5. In the experiments by Murnighan and Roth the smallest money unit was $\gamma = 0.01$. The maximum of $D(\Delta)$ is assumed to be $\Delta^* = 5$. This is the prominence level of the data set.

The overall average frequency in the support is $H/M = 412/64 = 6.438$. It is interesting to look at the average frequencies $h(\Delta)/m(\Delta)$. It is no surprise that $h(100)$ is low, since 100 is an extreme value of the range. All other average frequencies $h(\Delta)/m(\Delta)$ with $\Delta \geq 5$ are at least 12. Contrary to this, the highest average frequency for $\Delta < 5$ is

Table 3.7. *Determination of the prominence level of player 1's payoff in two-person coalitions in the game of Murnighan and Roth*

Prominence level Δ	Number of		Cumulative number of		Cumulative distributions		
	Values $m(\Delta)$	Observa-tions $h(\Delta)$	Values $M(\Delta)$	Observa-tions $H(\Delta)$	$\dfrac{M(\Delta)}{M}$	$\dfrac{H(\Delta)}{H}$	Surplus $D(\Delta)$
100	1	3	1	3	.016	.007	.009
50	1	64	2	67	.031	.163	.132
25	2	24	4	91	.062	.221	.159
20	3	79	7	170	.109	.413	.304
10	3	61	10	231	.156	.561	.405
5	5	90	15	321	.234	.779	.545
2.5	11	27	26	348	.406	.845	.439
2	11	24	37	372	.578	.903	.325
1	11	20	48	392	.750	.951	.201
0.5	8	10	56	402	.875	.976	.101
0.25	1	1	57	403	.891	.978	.087
0.2	—	—	57	403	.891	.978	.087
0.1	4	4	61	407	.953	.988	.035
0.05	1	1	62	408	.969	.990	.021
0.02	1	3	63	411	.984	.998	.014
0.01	1	1	64	412	1.000	1.000	000

Note: The game is described in Section 3.8.

$h(0.02)/m(0.02) = 3$. The data show a sharp drop in the average frequency from $\Delta = 5$ to $\Delta = 2.5$. This lends support to the idea that $\Delta^* = 5$ is in fact a critical level that separates "round" numbers from other numbers in the eyes of the subjects. Of course, it is plausible to assume that the most attractive "round" numbers are those that have a higher prominence level, and the least attractive of the other numbers are those that have a lower prominence level. However, this does not rule out the existence of a relatively sharp dividing line between "round" numbers and other numbers.

The data set of Murnighan and Roth consists of an unusually large number of observations on the same game. The same phenomena can also be detected in other data sets, but owing to the smaller number of observations they are rarely as salient as they are here.

3.11.5   Prominence levels of characteristic function experiments

In the choice of a payoff division for a genuine coalition C the players have only $|C| - 1$ degrees of freedom. Therefore, it would be wrong to include all final payoffs in the data set for the determination of the prominence level in a characteristic function experiment. One payoff should be left out in every final coalition. The computations reported here are based on the rule that the smallest payoff in a final coalition is left out, or if there are two or more smallest payoffs, one of the smallest ones is left out. Admittedly, this is an arbitrary convention, but some rule of this kind is necessary. All numbers that are not eliminated by this rule are combined into one sample regardless of the coalition in which they arise. (In Table 3.7 we restricted analysis to one coalition type.)

3.11.6 Connection to the measure of predictive success

The definition of the prominence level of a frequency distribution k over X has a connection to the measure of predictive success discussed in Section 3.8. In order to explain this connection we shall look at fictitious "prominence theories" of the following type. For every nonempty finite set $Y \subseteq X$ of observed values the theory predicts a prominence level $\Delta = \beta(Y)$.

Consider a prominence theory β of this kind. The predicted range of the theory is the set Y_Δ of all $x \in Y$ with $\delta(x) \geq \Delta$. The theory asserts that, apart from some exceptions, observations will tend to be in Y_Δ. The number of elements of Y_Δ is $M(\Delta)$ and the number of elements in Y is M. It is natural to define the *area* of the predicted range Y_Δ as

$$A_\Delta = M(\Delta)/M \tag{3.111}$$

The number of correct predictions is $H(\Delta)$, the number of observations in Y_Δ. This yields the following *hit rate:*

$$R_\Delta = H(\Delta)/H \tag{3.112}$$

The *success rate* $R_\Delta - A_\Delta$ is the difference $D(\Delta)$ of (3.107).

The method for determining the prominence level does not predict Δ, but we can say that it selects the value of Δ that would have been most successful as a prediction if it had been predicted by a prominence theory β.

3.11.7 Statistical tests

The prominence level of a data set has been introduced as a descriptive statistic of a frequency distribution. The point of departure is the idea that the subjects perceive a number as round if its prominence level is at least as great as a critical level Δ^*. This level Δ^* is an unknown behavioral parameter. The method introduced in this section can be thought of as an estimation procedure for this unknown parameter. The question arises as to how one can judge the reliability of the estimate.

A serious difficulty in the application of statistical tests is the lack of independence among observations. The data are generated by groups of interacting subjects and therefore cannot be regarded as independent observations. However, it seems justifiable to make a purely negative use of statistical tests. Wherever no significance can be established even under exaggerated independence assumptions, estimates cannot be taken seriously.

The way in which the prominence level of a data set is defined suggests the application of the Kolmogoroff–Smirnov one-sample test in order to test the presence of prominence effects (see, e.g., Siegel, 1956). For this purpose one can look at $M(\Delta)/M$ as the theoretical cumulative distribution to be compared with the observed cumulative distribution $H(\Delta)/H$. The difference $D(\Delta)$ is nothing other than the Kolmogoroff–Smirnov statistic. For all the samples considered here the null hypothesis can be rejected at the .01 level of significance. However, in view of the lack of independence one cannot interpret this result as a clear indication of the presence of prominence effects.

Even if the independence assumptions of the null hypothesis were satisfied, the Kolmogoroff–Smirnov test would not yet say anything about the reliability of the prominence level as an estimate of the underlying behavioral parameter. In the following we shall look at the possibility of using the binomial test to eliminate unreliable estimates. Suppose that Δ is the prominence level of the frequency distribution k and that Δ' is the next lower level with $m(\Delta') > 0$. The idea that there is a distinct dividing line between "round" numbers and other numbers suggests that the average frequency $h(\Delta')/m(\Delta')$ of Δ' should be significantly lower than the average frequency $h(\Delta)/m(\Delta)$ of Δ. As we have seen, there is in fact a sharp drop in the average frequency from Δ to Δ' in the data of Murnighan and Roth. Another way of posing the same question compares the ratio

$$\lambda(\Delta) = \frac{H(\Delta)}{h(\Delta) + h(\Delta')} \tag{3.113}$$

with the ratio

$$\eta(\Delta) = \frac{m(\Delta)}{m(\Delta) + m(\Delta')} \tag{3.114}$$

Obviously $\lambda(\Delta)$ is greater than $\eta(\Delta)$ if and only if $h(\Delta)/m(\Delta)$ is greater than $h(\Delta')/m(\Delta')$. The binomial test can be used to reject the null hypothesis that $\eta(\Delta)$ is the probability that an observation on one of both prominence levels Δ and Δ' will be on the level Δ.

In Section 3.12 success rates are compared for four samples: Maschler's 27 plays of superadditive games (Maschler, 1978), the data of Murnighan and Roth (1977), 160 plays of five superadditive games of Rapoport and Kahan (1976), and Medlin's 160 plays of 20 superadditive games (Medlin, 1976). In each of the latter three samples the prominence level determined by the method proposed here is $\Delta = 5$. In Maschler's sample one obtains $\Delta = 10$.

The binomial test on $\lambda(\Delta)$ is highly significant for the latter three samples. The two-tailed significance level is smaller than .00001 in all three cases. Even if a cautious interpretation of these results is indicated in view of the lack of independence, one can conclude that the test does not give us any obvious reason to reject $\Delta = 5$ as an unreliable estimate for the three samples. Maschler's sample is relatively small. Therefore, it is not surprising that for this sample the test of $\lambda(\Delta)$ does not yield significance at the .05 level (one-tailed). Therefore, it seems preferable not to trust the result $\Delta = 10$ obtained in this case. Maschler himself, in the discussion of his results, implicitly suggests a prominence level of $\Delta = 5$, even if he does not use the term (Maschler, 1978). In Section 3.12 we follow this recommendation.

3.12   Comparisons of predictive success

This chapter is concerned with the influence of equity considerations on coalition formation in zero-normalized three-person characteristic function games. Two competing theories, the united bargaining set and the new version of equal division payoff bounds, have been discussed in detail. Even if these two theories differ in many respects, both of them involve applications of the equity principle in order to compute equal shares of coalition values and of increments of coalition values. However, as far as the united bargaining set is concerned, equity considerations enter only if the grand coalition is permissible. Therefore, in this chapter we restrict our attention to experiments on zero-normalized three-person characteristic function games in which the grand coalition is permissible.

We shall look at four sets of experimental results taken from studies in which raw data have been published or have been made available to the author (Medlin, 1976; Rapoport and Kahan, 1976; Murnighan and Roth, 1977; Maschler, 1978; Franke, 1980; Kahan and Rapoport, 1984).

Table 3.8. *Hit rates, areas, and success rates for four sets of experimental data*

	$B_0[5]$	$U[5]$	E_5	Experiment
Hit rate	.59	.89	.89	Maschler's 27 plays of 26 super-
Area	.19	.20	.13	additive games
Success rate	.40	.69	.76	
Hit rate	.04	.44	.92	432 plays of $g = a = b = 100$
Area	.03	.12	.31	reported by Murnighan and
Success rate	.01	.32	.61	Roth
Hit rate	.51	.55	.92	160 plays of 5 games reported
Area	.08	.08	.18	by Rapoport and Kahan[1]
Success rate	.43	.47	.74	
Hit rate	.68	.72	.93	Medlin's 160 plays of 20 super-
Area	.09	.09	.20	additive games[2]
Success rate	.59	.63	.73	

Note: Meaning of symbols: $B_0[5]$, bargaining set without null structure and with deviations up to 5; $U[5]$, united bargaining set with deviations up to 5; E_5, equal division payoff bounds with $\Delta = 5$.

[1] In an earlier article the success rate of E_5 was reported as .75 (Selten, 1982). This was due to a small computational mistake, which has been corrected here.

[2] I am grateful to Amnon Rapoport, who sent tables of Medlin's raw data. Obvious misprints in these tables have been corrected with the help of published averages.

The first sample consists of Maschler's 27 plays of various superadditive games. These results are of special interest since Maschler found them in agreement with his thoughts on power transformations and the bargaining set. The second sample consists of the 432 plays of the study of Murnighan and Roth discussed in Section 3.8. The third sample consists of 160 plays of five superadditive games taken from a study of Rapoport and Kahan. These data were obtained by a computerized laboratory procedure. The fourth sample contains 160 plays of 20 superadditive games in the study of Medlin, who used the same laboratory procedures as Rapoport and Kahan. In the experiments by Rapoport and Kahan and by Medlin the players received monetary payoffs.

3.12.1   The predictive success of three theories

Table 3.8 presents hit rates, areas, and success rates for three theories: the bargaining set $B_0[5]$ without null structure and with deviations up to 5, the united bargaining set $U[5]$ with deviations up to 5, and the theory of equal division payoff bounds E_5 with $\Delta = 5$.

The success rates for $U[5]$ are higher than those for $B_0[5]$. This indicates that bargaining set theory is improved if power transformations are taken into account. However, it would be a mistake to neglect the bargaining set of the unmodified characteristic function. In the 160 plays of Rapoport and Kahan, 71 of the 89 outcomes in $U[5]$ belong to $B_0[5]$ but not to $B_1[5]$ or $B_2[5]$.

In the game of Murnighan and Roth the area of $U[5]$ is considerably greater than that of $B_0[5]$. For the other samples there is little difference between the areas of $B_0[5]$ and $U[5]$. This is due to the fact that for $g > a$ the power bargaining sets $B_1[5]$ and $B_2[5]$ are very small. For such games the power bargaining sets increase the hit rate of $U[5]$ without adding more than an insignificant amount to the area. The superiority of $U[5]$ over $B_0[5]$ confirms the impression that the introduction of equity considerations by Maschler's theory of power transformation has succeeded in capturing an important feature of the behavior of experimental subjects. However, it is doubtful whether the bargaining set is the right point of departure.

For all four samples E_5 has considerably higher success rates than $U[5]$. In many cases the area of E_5 is much greater than that of $U[5]$, but this disadvantage of E_5 is more than compensated for by the advantage of a high hit rate. In view of the great variance of experimental results, it seems more important to aim for high hit rates than for small areas in theory construction. In some cases E_5 has a smaller area than $U[5]$. This is true for the average area of Maschler's 27 plays of superadditive games. Maschler's sample contains 14 cases with $a = b$ or $b = c$. Symmetries of this kind tend to decrease the area of E_5. Several other games in Maschler's sample have relatively large cores. In such games the bargaining set can be quite large, since it contains the whole core. Contrary to this, equal division payoff bounds often exclude parts of the core.

3.12.2 Statistical tests

The question arises as to whether the success rates for the three theories are significantly different from one another. We cannot justify applying statistical tests that treat individual plays as independent observations. In a group of interacting subjects shared experiences may lead to group-specific behavioral norms. Even if the data do not show any strong effects of this kind, one cannot rule out this possibility. Suppose that the same behavioral norms are developed by most groups. In this case it would be difficult to detect significant differences among groups. Nevertheless, it would be wrong to look at every play as an independent observation.

Table 3.9. *Level of significance for the two-tailed Wilcoxon Matched-Pairs Signed-Rank Test for the significance of differences between success rates*

	Superiority of $U[5]$ over $B_0[5]$	Superiority of E_5 over $U[5]$
12 triads of Murnighan and Roth	.0001	.0001
8 quartets of Rapoport and Kahan	—	.01
8 quartets of Medlin	—	.05
16 quartets of Rapoport and Kahan and Medlin	.01	.01[1]

Note: Dashes indicate lack of significance at the .05 level.
[1] For the old version of E_5 proposed earlier (Selten, 1982), one obtains the same level of significance.

Luckily, in this section we do not have to succumb to the temptation to follow the widespread regrettable practice of ignoring the lack of independence among observations connected by the interaction of subjects. The experiments of Murnighan and Roth involved 36 triads of subjects. There was no interaction across triads. Similarly, the data of Rapoport and Kahan are from eight quartets of subjects who interacted only within quartets. The same is true for Medlin's experiment, which also involves eight independent quartets. This provides the opportunity to treat aggregate results for triads and quartets as independent observations.

The Wilcoxon Matched-Pairs Signed-Rank Test can be used to test the significance of the difference between the success rates of two theories (see Siegel, 1956; Lehmann, 1975). For this purpose the two success rates for a triad or a quartet are looked upon as a pair of matched observations.

Table 3.9 shows levels of significance for differences in success rates. The difference in the success rates for $U[5]$ and $B_0[5]$ is not significant if one looks separately at the 8 quartets of Rapoport and Kahan and the 8 quartets of Medlin. However, it is not unreasonable to combine these 16 quartets into one sample. Both experiments have used the same computerized procedure and were run in the same laboratory with similar monetary incentives. For the 16 quartets taken together, the difference is significant at the .05 level. The difference in the success rates for E_5 and $U[5]$ is significant at least at the .05 level for all three samples separately. Therefore, it is very unlikely that the better performance of the theory of equal division payoff bounds is due to random fluctuations.

For only 2 of the 52 games used in the four experiments are the predictions of the old version of the theory of equal division payoff bounds different from those of the new version. Both games are among Medlin's 20 superadditive games. The revision of the theory was inspired by the evaluation of Medlin's data. Therefore, it is of interest that for Medlin's experiment the old version has a success rate of .71. This is still a better performance than that of the united bargaining set. However, the difference between the success rates for the old version of E_5 and for $U[5]$ is not significant at the .05 level. In view of the small number of observations, only eight, this is not surprising. The comparison between the old version of $U[5]$ and E_5 yields a significance level of .01 for the 16 quartets of Rapoport and Kahan and of Medlin taken together.

3.12.3   Conclusion

The experimental evidence strongly suggests that equity considerations have an important influence on the behavior of experimental subjects in zero-normalized three-person games. To some extent the united bargaining set takes this influence into account, which explains why its performance is superior to that of the ordinary bargaining set. However, the predictions of the theory of equal division payoff bounds are considerably more successful than those of the united bargaining set.

The success of the theory of equal division payoff bounds confirms the methodological point of view that the limited rationality of human decision behavior must be taken seriously. It is futile to insist on explanations in terms of subjectively expected utility maximization. The optimization approach fails to do justice to the structure of human decision processes. The theory of equal division payoff bounds is based on a combination of simple commonsense arguments derived from easily recognizable features of the strategic situation. It takes the form of a chain of reasoning. On the basis of the order of strength, equity considerations suggest lower bounds for aspiration levels on payoffs in genuine coalitions. Most solution concepts of cooperative game theory are based on stability conditions imposed on the proposed solution. Usually, the question of existence is sufficiently difficult to be investigated and reported in papers accepted by scientific journals. Therefore, it is not surprising that experimental subjects do not even look for such solutions. A thoroughly constructive approach like that of the theory of equal division payoff bounds offers a better chance of predictive success.

In spite of its undeniable predictive success for the data examined here, the theory of equal division payoff bounds in its present form may not yet be the final answer to the problem of finding an adequate area theory for zero-normalized three-person games. Some of the details are not based on strong experimental evidence. Further revisions may be necessary in the face of future experimental evidence. It is not difficult to invent purely speculative extensions of the theory of equal division payoff bounds to more general characteristic function games. However, pure speculation is an unreliable adviser when descriptive theories are concerned. Unfortunately, the development of successful descriptive theories is a slow process that must be guided by experimental evidence. Therefore, no attempt has been made here to apply the basic ideas of the theory of equal division payoff bounds to more general games.

References

Adams, I. Slacy, "Toward an Understanding of Inequity." *Journal of Abnormal and Social Psychology*, 67 (5), 1963, pp. 422–36.

Albers, Wulf, and Gisela Albers, "On the Prominence Structure of the Decimal System," in R. W. Scholz (ed.), *Decision Making under Uncertainty*. Amsterdam: Elsevier, 1983, pp. 271–87.

Atkinson J. W., "Motivational Determinants of Risk-Taking Behavior." *Psychological Review 64*, 1957, pp. 359–72.

Atkinson, J. W., and David Birch, *An Introduction to Motivation*. New York: Van Nostrand, 1978.

Aumann, R. J., and M. Maschler, "The Bargaining Set for Cooperative Games," in M. Dresher, L. S. Shapley, and A. W. Tucker (eds.), *Advances in Game Theory*. Princeton, N.J.: Princeton University Press, 1964, pp. 443–76.

Crott, H. W., and W. Albers, "The Equal Division Kernel: An Equity Approach to Coalition Formation and Payoff Distribution in *N*-Person Games." *European Journal of Social Psychology*, 77, 1981, pp. 285–305.

Franke, G., "Ein Ueberblick über Experimente auf der Basis von charakteristischen Funktionsspielen," Diplomarbeit (unpublished master's thesis). Universität Bielefeld, Fakultät für Wirtschaftswissenschaften, 1980.

Harris, R. J., "Handling Negative Inputs in Equity Theory: On the Plausible Equity Formulae." *Journal of Experimental Social Psychology*, 12, 1976, pp. 194–209.

Homans, G. C., *Social Behavior: Its Elementary Forms*. New York: Harcourt Brace & World, 1961.

Huber, O., *Entscheiden als Problemlösen*. Berlin: Verlag Hans Huber, 1982.

Kahan, J. P., and A. Rapoport, "Test of the Bargaining Set and Kernel Models in Three-Person Games," in A. Rapoport (ed.), *Game Theory as a Theory of Conflict Resolution*. Dordrecht: Reidel, 1974, pp. 119–59.

Theories of Coalition Formation. Hillsdale, N.J.: Erlbaum, 1984.

Kalish, G. K., S. W. Milnor, J. F. Nash, and E. D. Nering, "Some Experimental *N*-Person Games," in R. M. Thrall, C. H. Coombs, and R. L. Davis (eds.), *Decision Processes*. New York: Wiley, 1954, pp. 301–27.

Kastl, L. (ed.), *Kartelle in der Wirklichkeit, Festschrift für Max Metzner.* Cologne: Carl-Heymans-Verlag, 1963.

Komorita, S. S., "An Equal Excess Model of Coalition Formation." *Behavioral Science, 24,* 1979, pp. 369–81.

"Coalition Bargaining," in L. Berkowitz (ed.), *Advances in Experimental Social Psychology,* Vol. 18. New York: Academic Press, 1984, pp. 183–245.

Komorita, S. S., and J. M. Cherkhoff, "A Bargaining Theory of Coalition Formation." *Psychological Review, 80,* May 1973, pp. 149–62.

Lehmann, E. L., *Nonparametrics: Statistical Methods Based on Ranks.* New York: McGraw-Hill, 1975.

Leventhal, G. S., and J. W. Michaels, "Extending the Equity Model: Perception of Inputs and Allocation of Rewards as a Function of Duration and Quantity of Performance." *Journal of Personality and Social Psychology 12,* 1969, pp. 303–9.

Maschler, M., "The Power of a Coalition." *Management Science, 10,* 1963, pp. 8–29.

"Playing an *N*-Person Game: An Experiment," in H. Sauermann (ed.), *Coalition Forming Behavior,* Contributions to Experimental Economics, Vol. 8. Tübingen: Mohr, 1978, pp. 231–328.

Medlin, S. M., "Effects of Grand Coalition Payoffs on Coalition Formation in Three-Person Games." *Behavioral Science, 21,* 1976, pp. 48–61.

Mikula, G. (ed.), *Gerechtigkeit und soziale Interaktion.* Berlin: Verlag Hans Huber, 1980.

Murnighan, J. K., and A. E. Roth, "The Effects of Communication and Information Availability in an Experimental Study of a Three-Person Game." *Management Science, 23,* 1977, pp. 1336–48.

Nydegger, R. V., and G. Owen, "Two-Person Bargaining: An Experimental Test of the Nash Axioms." *International Journal of Game Theory, 3,* 1974, pp. 239–50.

Owen, G., *Game Theory,* 2d ed. New York: Academic Press, 1982.

Rapoport, A., and J. P. Kahan, "When Three Is Not Always Two against One: Coalitions in Experimental Three-Person Cooperative Games." *Journal of Experimental Social Psychology, 12,* 1976, pp. 253–73.

Rosenmüller, J., *The Theory of Games and Markets.* Amsterdam: North Holland, 1981.

Sauermann, H., and R. Selten, "Anspruchsanpassungstheorie der Unternehmung." *Zeitschrift für die gesamte Staatswissenschaft, 118,* 1962, pp. 577–97.

Schelling, T. C., *The Strategy of Conflict.* Cambridge, Mass: Harvard University Press, 1960.

Selten, R., "Equal Share Analysis of Characteristic Function Experiments," in H. Sauermann (ed.), *Contributions to Experimental Economics,* Vol. 3. Tübingen: Mohr, 1972, pp. 130–65.

"The Equity Principle in Economic Behavior," in H. W. Gottinger and W. Leinfellner (eds.), *Decision Theory and Social Ethics: Issues in Social Choice.* Dordrecht: Reidel, 1978, pp. 289–301.

"Equal Division Payoff Bounds for 3-Person Characteristic Function Experiments," in R. Tietz (ed.), *Aspiration Levels in Bargaining and Economic Decision Making,* Springer Lecture Notes in Economics and Mathematical Systems, No. 213. Berlin: Springer-Verlag, 1982, pp. 265–75.

Selten, R., and W. Krischker, "Comparison of Two Theories for Characteristic Function

Experiments," in R. Tietz (ed.), *Aspiration Levels in Bargaining and Economic Decision Making*, Springer Lecture Notes in Economic and Mathematical Systems No. 213. Berlin: Springer-Verlag, 1982, pp. 259–64.

Simon, H. A., *Models of Man*. New York: Wiley, 1957.

Siegel, S., *Nonparametric Statistics for the Behavioral Sciences*. New York: McGraw-Hill, 1956.

Tietz, R., "The Prominence Standard: Part 1. Discussion Paper A18." Professur für Volkswirtschaftslehre, insbesondere Verhaltensforschung, Fachbereich Wirtschaftswissenschaften, Johann-Wolfgang-Goethe-Universität, D-6000 Frankfurt/M., 1984.

von Neumann, J., and O. Morgenstern, *Theory of Games and Economic Behavior*. Princeton, N.J.: Princeton University Press, 1944.

Walster, E., G. E. Walster, and E. Berscheid, *Equity: Theory and Research*. Allyn & Bacon, 1978.

CHAPTER 4

The psychology of choice and the assumptions of economics

RICHARD THALER

4.1 Introduction

Neoclassical economics is based on the premise that models that characterize rational, optimizing behavior also characterize actual human behavior. The same model is used as a normative definition of rational choice and a descriptive predictor of observed choice. Many of the advances in economic theory in the past 50 years have constituted clarifications of the normative model. One of the most significant of these advances was the normative theory of choice under uncertainty, expected utility theory, formulated by John von Neumann and Oskar Morgenstern (1947). Expected utility theory defined rational choice in the context of uncertainty. Because of the dual role economic theories are expected to play, expected utility theory also provided the basis for a new style of research pioneered by Maurice Allais (1953) and Daniel Ellsberg (1961). Allais and Ellsberg exploited the precision of the theory to construct crisp counterexamples of its descriptive predictions. The methods they used to demonstrate the force of their counterexamples were similar. Some prominent economists and statisticians were presented with problems to which most gave answers inconsistent with the theory. The fact that Savage was induced to violate one of his own axioms was taken to be sufficient proof that a genuine effect had been discovered. When Savage was confronted with the inconsistency of his choices and his axioms, he responded that he had made a mistake and wished to change his choices! This reaction is very instructive. Savage readily admitted that the choices he had made

This chapter was to have been written in collaboration with Daniel Kahneman and Amos Tversky. Indeed, I had discussions with both during the writing process. Unfortunately, Tversky was unable to attend the conference, and time limitations prevented us from completing the paper as a threesome. However, I owe them both more than the usual thanks. I also thank the Alfred P. Sloan Foundation's program in behavioral economics for financial support.

were intuitively attractive but not so attractive that he wished to abandon his axioms as the appropriate standard against which to characterize rational choice.

Although this original work was done by economists, the continuing research on individual decision making has been conducted primarily by psychologists. In the past two decades a new field has emerged that can perhaps be called behavioral decision research (BDR).[1] This research has combined the tradition of Allais and Ellsberg's counterexamples with Savage's respect for the normative theory. The BDR approach to the study of human decision making has been similar to (and strongly influenced by) the psychological approach to the study of perception. Much can be learned about visual processes by studying powerful optical illusions. Counterexamples such as those of Allais and Ellsberg have the force of an illusion to many and have provided similar insights into decision processes. It goes without saying that the existence of an optical illusion that causes us to see one of two equal lines as longer than the other should not reduce the value we place on accurate measurement. On the contrary, illusions demonstrate the need for rulers! Similarly, a demonstration that human choices often violate the axioms of rationality does not necessarily imply any criticism of the axioms of rational choice *as* a normative ideal. Rather, the research is simply intended to show that, for descriptive purposes, alternative models are sometimes necessary.

Expected utility theory has not been the only source of counterexamples in BDR. Other aspects of the normative theory of rational choice have been exploited to construct insightful counterexamples. The hypotheses that individuals make choices and judgments that are consistent with the principles of optimization and the laws of probability yield additional predictions that can be tested. In summarizing the research in this area I have selected 15 principles of rationality that economists use to describe actual choices. Each of these tenets is widely accepted as a normative principle; yet there is evidence that each is descriptively inappropriate. (Although each tenet makes a somewhat different point about actual behavior, the tenets are not meant to be independent.)

The plan of the chapter is as follows. Section 4.2 offers a brief and selective review of the studies of individual decision making and the observed conflicts with the tenets of rational choice. Section 4.3 discusses some methodological issues, specifically the role of learning

---

[1] A more common term for the field is behavioral decision theory (BDT). Behavioral decision research seems more accurate for two reasons: The field is as much empirical as it is theoretical, and there is more than one theory.

and incentives. And Section 4.4 concerns some of the implications of BDR for economics.

4.2   Choice

4.2.1   Decision weights

The following principle, formalized as the substitution axiom by von Neumann and Morgenstern (1947), the extended sure-thing principle by Savage (1954), and the independence axiom by Luce and Krantz (1971), can be informally stated as Tenet 4.1:

> **Tenet 4.1. Cancellation.** *The choice between two options depends only on the states in which those options yield different outcomes.*

Various techniques are used to construct counterexamples. One is to devise a pair of problems to which subjects give inconsistent answers. Allais (1953) used this technique to demonstrate a violation of the independence axiom:

Problem 4.1. Choose between

A. $1 million with certainty
B. $5 million with probability .1, $1 million with probability .89, and $0 with probability .01

Problem 4.2. Choose between

C. $1 million with probability .11 and $0 with probability .89
D. $5 million with probability .10 and $0 with probability .90

The common responses, including those of Allais's famous subjects, are A and D. These violate the independence axiom. More recently, Kahneman and Tversky (1979) replicated Allais's findings with another problem pair. This pair demonstrates that the enormous amounts of money in the original formulation are not essential.

Problem 4.3. Choose between

A. 2,500 with probability   .33   [18%]
    2,400 with probability   .66
    0 with probability   .01
B. 2,400 with certainty   [82%]

Problem 4.4. Choose between

A. 2,500 with probability   .33   [83%]
    0 with probability   .67
B. 2,400 with probability   .34   [17%]
    0 with probability   .66
[*Source:* Kahneman and Tversky, 1979]

The percentage of subjects who chose each option is indicated in brackets. Since Problem 4.4 is obtained from Problem 4.3 by eliminating a .66 chance of winning 2,400, the combined choices violate the independence axiom. Problems 4.3 and 4.4 illustrate what Kahneman and Tversky call the *certainty effect*. The reversals in both Allais's problem and this pair are explained by the apparent overweighting of certainty relative to probabilities less than unity.

Allais's paradox has stimulated numerous attempts to provide alternative theories that are consistent with the observed choices. One class of alternative models (e.g., Machina, 1982; Chew, 1983; Fishburn, 1983) are attempts to make the theory more descriptively valid by relaxing the cancellation principle in minimal fashion; so, for example, the Allais parodox can be handled by replacing the independence axiom with a more general representation. In prospect theory Kahneman and Tversky (1979) have taken a different approach. Prospect theory is explicitly a *descriptive* theory, with no normative pretensions. As such, it was developed inductively, starting with the results of experimental research, rather than deductively from a set of axioms. It is an attempt to make sense of many different kinds of anomalies, some, as we shall see, even more damaging to the rational modeling tradition than the counterexamples discussed so far.

There are two central features of prospect theory: a decision weighting function $\pi(p)$, which translates subjective probabilities into decision weight, and a value function $v(\cdot)$, which serves the role of the traditional utility function and which is discussed in Section 4.2.2. The π function is a monotonic function of p but is not a probability; π does not satisfy either Tenet 4.1 or 4.2. It has the following properties. First, although the scale is normalized so that $\pi(0) = 0$ and $\pi(1) = 1$, the function is not well behaved near the end points. Second, for low probabilities $\pi(p) > p$, but $\pi(p) + \pi(1 - p) \leq 1$. Thus low probabilities are overweighted, moderate and high probabilities are underweighted, and the latter effect is less pronounced than the former. Third, $\pi(pr)/\pi(p) < \pi(prq)/\pi(pq)$ for all $0 < p, q, r \leq 1$. That is, for any fixed probability ratio q, the ratio of decision weights is closer to unity when the probabilities are lower than when they are higher, for

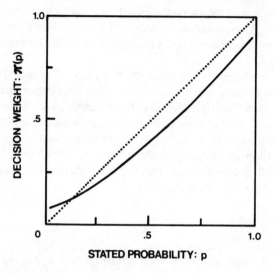

Figure 4.1. A π function.

example, $\pi(.1)/\pi(.2) > \pi(.4)/\pi(.8)$. An illustrative π function is shown in Figure 4.1.

> **Tenet 4.2. Expectation.** *The utility of an outcome is weighted by its probability. Decision weights do not depend on the origin of the uncertainty.*

Another way to create a violation of rational choice is to induce subjects to exhibit a strict preference for one of two alternatives that are normatively equivalent. Ellsberg discovered that people are sensitive to attributes of prospects that are not captured in the standard formulation. The simplest version of Ellsberg's problem is as follows:

Problem 4.5. There are two urns containing a large number of red and black balls. Urn A is known to have 50% red balls and 50% black balls. Urn B has red and black balls in unknown proportions. You will win $100 if you draw the color ball of your choice from an urn. From which urn would you rather choose a ball?

Most subjects express a strict preference for urn A with the known proportion rather than "ambiguous" urn B. Subjects readily admit that they would be indifferent about trying for a red or black ball from the ambiguous urn, thereby indicating that their subjective probabilities of each are the same and presumably equal to $\frac{1}{2}$, which is the known proportion in urn A. Nevertheless, most subjects feel that the ambiguous urn is in some sense riskier. This preference for the known urn violates Tenet 4.2.

Dealing with ambiguity in a theoretical model of choice is more complicated than dealing with violations of the cancellation principle. The prospect theory decision weights, for example, are defined over stated probabilities and are thus undefined in ambiguous situations. A further complication is that preferences about ambiguity appear to depend on both the sign and magnitude of the outcomes, so a complete description would necessitate abandoning the independence between the decision weights and the outcomes.[2]

4.2.2   Values

> **Tenet 4.3. Risk aversion.** *The utility function for wealth is concave (risk averse).*

Although risk aversion is neither an axiom of rationality nor a necessary component of economic analysis, the assumption of diminishing marginal utility has a tradition in the study of choice behavior that dates back to Bernoulli and is widely used in economics today. The popularity of gambling has long been recognized as a potential problem for the assumption of risk aversion, but gambling is (reasonably, I think) generally considered to be a special case explained in large part by the utility of the activity rather than the utility of the outcomes. (It is also explained, in part, by the overweighting of small probabilities.) Problem 4.6 demonstrates a violation of risk aversion that is more troubling than the popularity of gambling.

Problem 4.6. Choose between

    A. An 80% chance to lose $4,000   [92%]
    B. A certain loss of $3,000   [8%]

[*Source:* Kahneman and Tversky, 1979]

Problem 4.6 illustrates a common preference for risk seeking in the domain of losses that is generally observed and opposite to the usual preference in the domain of gains. This suggests a reformulation of the

---

[2] For example, ambiguity may be preferred for small gains or for losses. For one approach to the study of ambiguity see Einhorn and Hogarth (1985).

utility function that depends on the sign of the perceived changes in wealth, in violation of the following tenet:

> **Tenet 4.4. Asset integration.** *The domain of the utility function is final states.*

In expected utility theory wealth is the carrier of value. To describe behavior successfully, Tenet 4.4 must be relaxed. Consider the following pair of problems:

Problem 4.7. Assume yourself richer by $300 than you are today. You are offered a choice between

A.	A sure gain of $100	[72%]
B.	A 50% chance to gain $200 and a 50% chance to gain nothing	[64%]

Problem 4.8. Assume yourself richer by $500 than you are today. You are offered a choice between

A.	A sure loss of $100	[36%]
B.	A 50% chance to lose $200 and a 50% chance to lose nothing	[64%]

[*Source:* Tversky and Kahneman, 1986]

Since the problems are identical in terms of final asset positions, the inconsistency between the choices demonstrates that subjects tend to evaluate prospects in terms of *gains and losses* relative to some reference point, rather than final states. As in Problem 4.6, subjects choose the risky choice in Problem 4.8 (which is characterized in terms of losses) while selecting the risk-averse choice in Problem 4.7 (which is described in terms of gains). Both of these phenomena (attention to gains and losses and risk seeking in the domain of losses) are captured in the *value function* in Kahneman and Tversky's (1979) prospect theory.

The formulation of the value function was intended to incorporate three important behavioral regularities observed in the study of both perception and choice. First, people seem to respond to perceived gains or losses rather than to their hypothetical end states (wealth positions) as assumed by expected utility theory. Second, there is diminishing marginal sensitivity to changes, irrespective of the sign of the change. Third, losses loom larger than gains. The corresponding features of the value function are as follows. (1) The value function

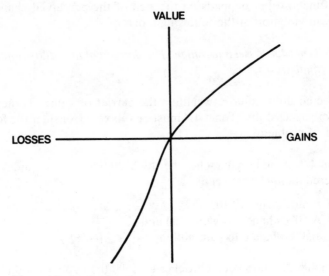

Figure 4.2. A value function.

explicitly adopts *changes* as the carriers of value. (2) The value function is assumed to be concave for gains and convex for losses, $v''(X) < 0, x > 0; v''(x) > 0, x < 0$. (3) The function is steeper for losses than gains, that is, $v(x) < -v(-x), x > 0$. The last feature is called *loss aversion*. A typical value function is illustrated in Figure 4.2.

In many contexts, the concept of loss aversion, the sharp disutility associated with perceived losses, is more useful than the concept of risk aversion. Behavior often considered motivated by risk aversion, such as an unwillingness to accept low-stakes gambles at better than fair odds, is more accurately characterized as loss aversion.

4.2.3   Framing

> **Tenet 4.5. Preference ordering.** *Preferences are independent of the method used to elicit them.*

The existence of a well-defined preference ordering is one of many assumptions that are often taken for granted. If a preference ordering exists, it should be recoverable in any number of alternative elicitation procedures. Dramatic violations of Tenet 4.5 were discovered in a series of experiments conducted by psychologists Sarah Lichtenstein and Paul Slovic (1971). Lichtenstein and Slovic asked subjects first to choose between two bets. One bet, called the "*p* bet," offered a high probability of winning a small amount of money (e.g., a $\frac{35}{36}$ chance to win \$4). The other bet, called the "\$ bet," offered a smaller chance of winning a larger amount of money (e.g., an $\frac{11}{36}$ chance to win \$16). The expected value of the two bets was about the same. Subjects were also asked to value each bet by stating the minimum amount they would accept to sell each of the bets if they owned the right to play them (or, alternatively, the maximum amount they would pay to buy the gamble). Surprisingly, a large proportion of the subjects who preferred the *p* bet in the choice task assigned a larger value to the \$ bet in the judgment task. Thus in violation of Tenet 4.5, preferences depend on the method of elicitation. This result, called the *preference reversal effect*, has been replicated with real money on the floor of a Las Vegas casino (Lichtenstein and Slovic, 1973) and by economists David Grether and Charles Plott (1979).[3]

> *Tenet 4.6. Invariance. Choices between options are independent of their representation or description.*

Like the existence of a preference ordering, the invariance principle is so basic to rational choice that it is usually tacitly assumed in the characterization of options rather than explicitly assumed as an axiom of choice. Moreover, whereas cancellation and expectation may be considered by some to be expendable features of rational choice, invariance is essential. Nevertheless, numerous experiments have shown that choice depends on the way a problem is formulated or *framed*. One example of this is the problem pair 4.7 and 4.8, in which reframing the outcomes altered choices. The following three problems demonstrate that the framing of contingencies can also influence choice:

Problem 4.9. Which of the following options do you prefer?

    A.   A sure win of \$30   [78%]
    B.   An 80% chance to win \$45   [22%]

Problem 4.10. Consider the following two-stage game. In the first stage, there is a 75% chance to end the game without winning anything and a 25% chance to move into the second stage. If you reach the second stage you have a choice between

    C.   A sure win of \$30   [74%]
    D.   An 80% chance to win \$45   [26%]

[3] For a review see Slovic and Lichtenstein (1983).

Your choice must be made before the game starts, that is, before the outcome of the first-stage game is known. Please indicate the option you prefer.

Problem 4.11. Which of the following options do you prefer?
    E.   A 25% chance to win $30   [42%]
    F.   A 20% chance to win $45   [58%]
[*Source:* Tversky and Kahneman, 1981]

Since Problems 4.10 and 4.11 are identical in terms of probabilities and outcomes, they should produce consistent responses. However, subjects appear to treat Problem 4.10 as equivalent to Problem 4.9 rather than Problem 4.11. The attraction of option A in Problem 4.9 is explained by the certainty effect. In Problem 4.10, the attractiveness of option C is due to the illusion of certainty created by the two-stage formulation. Tversky and Kahneman (1981) call this the *pseudocertainty effect*. When the framing of a contingency suggests certainty, the option will acquire the same attractiveness accorded to a genuinely certain event.

Another essential principle of rational choice is dominance.

> **Tenet 4.7. Dominance.** *If option A is better than option B in every respect, then A is preferred to B.*

The following set of problems illustrates how both invariance and dominance can be violated:

Problem 4.12. Imagine that you face the following pair of concurrent decisions. First examine both decisions; then indicate the options you prefer:

Decision (i). Choose between
    A.   A sure gain of $240   [84%]
    B.   25% chance to gain $1,000
          and 75% chance to gain nothing   [16%]

Decision (ii). Choose between
    C.   A sure loss of $750   [13%]
    D.   75% chance to lose $1,000
          and 25% chance to lose nothing   [87%]
[*Source*: Tversky and Kahneman, 1981]

The majority choices indicate the usual pattern of risk aversion in the domain of gains and risk seeking in the domain of losses. A total of 75% of the subjects chose the portfolio A&D, whereas only 3% picked the combination B&C. This pattern is of interest because the combination B&C actually dominates A&D. This becomes obvious when the problem is reformulated.

Problem 4.13. Choose between

E (= A&D). 25% chance to win $240
and 75% chance to lose $760   [0%]
F (= B&C). 25% chance to win $250
and 75% chance to lose $750   [100%]

[*Source:* Tversky and Kahneman, 1981]

The violations of invariance and dominance illustrated by Problems 4.12 and 4.13 raise two important points. First, since invariance and dominance are fundamental to any rational model of choice, no hybrid, nearly rational model can possibly capture this type of behavior. Second, the problems illustrate the useful distinction between *transparent* and opaque choices. All subjects choose the dominant option in Problem 4.13 because the dominance is so easy to detect. In contrast, the dominance is not transparent in Problem 4.12, and so most subjects go astray. If all real-life problems were transparent, BDR would have much less relevance to economics. Expected utility theory is often an accurate representation of choices in transparent problems. Alas, the world appears to be opaque.

4.2.4 Deterministic choice

The psychology of choice applies to deterministic choice as well as decisions under uncertainty. Here the basic principles of economic analysis provide the tenets that can be questioned by counterexamples. One of the first lessons in Economics 101 is the concept of opportunity costs.

> **Tenet 4.8. Opportunity costs.** *Willingness to pay equals willingness to sell (disregarding income effects and transactions costs); opportunity costs and out-of-pocket costs are equivalent.*

Willingness to pay and willingness to accept compensation are two measures of the value a person places on something. In the absence of transactions costs these two measures should differ only by an income effect, which in most cases is small. I first noticed a large discrepancy between these measures when doing research on the value of saving lives. Subjects were asked two questions: (1) How much would you pay to reduce your risk of death by .001? (2) How much would you have to be paid to take a risk of death of .001? The amounts indicated in response to question (2) typically exceeded those in response to question (1) by more than an order of magnitude![4] In less dramatic contexts, people often act as if they would not sell an item in their endowment for x, but if the item were lost or stolen, they would not replace it at a cost of less than $x. In Thaler (1980), I called this the *endowment effect* and pointed out that the behavior is partly explained by loss aversion.

The disparity between buying and selling prices has been demonstrated in an elegantly simple experiment by Knetsch and Sinden (1984). Knetsch and Sinden gave half their subjects tickets to a lottery and the other half of the subjects $3. Then the first group was given the opportunity to sell their tickets for $3 and the second group was permitted to buy tickets for $3. Again, a large disparity was observed. Of the people given a ticket, 82% (31/38) kept them, whereas only 38% of the other group (15 of 39) opted to buy a ticket. Notice that this experiment used real stakes and had no income effects confounding the results. This disparity between buying and selling prices raises serious problems for practitioners of cost–benefit analysis who must try to put monetary values on goods that are not traded in markets.

Another basic principle of microeconomics is that of marginal analysis.

Tenet 4.9. Marginal analysis. Choices are made to equate marginal costs with marginal benefits.

One application of marginal analysis is optimal search. Search for the lowest price should continue until the expected marginal gain equals the value of the search costs. This is likely to be violated if the context of the search influences the perception of the value of the savings. In Thaler (1980), I argued that individuals were more likely to spend 20 minutes to save $5 on the purchase of a clock radio than to save the

---

[4] Although the disparity is in the same direction as a potential income effect, the disparity is much too large to be plausibly explained in this way.

same amount on the purchase of a $500 television.[5] This intuition was confirmed in the following example:

Problem 4.14. Imagine that you are about to purchase a jacket for ($125)[$15] and a calculator for ($15)[$125]. The calculator salesman informs you that the calculator you wish to buy is on sale for ($10)[$120] at the other branch of the store, a 20-minute drive away. Would you make the trip to the other store?
[*Source:* Tversky and Kahneman, 1981]

The responses to the two versions of this problem (one with the numbers in parentheses, the other with the numbers in brackets) were quite different. When the calculator cost $125, only 29% of the subjects said they would make the trip, whereas 68% said they would go when the calculator cost only $15.

Economics students often make mistakes in applying Tenet 4.9 by confusing average and marginal costs. An experiment by Gottfries and Hylton (1983) showed that even MIT students are not immune to this error. Students on the MIT dining plan pay for meals according to a schedule in which the price per meal falls considerably after a certain number of meals have been purchased. Gottfries and Hylton asked students on this meal plan whether they would switch to another dining hall or restaurant for two weeks. The price of the alternative was above the marginal cost of the meal plan but below the average cost. Among those students for whom the lower marginal cost was relevant, 68% said they would switch and gave as their reason "to save money."

Of the tenets presented in this chapter, the following may be violated most often:

> **Tenet 4.10. Sunk costs.** *Fixed, historical, and other sunk costs do not influence decisions.*

A classic sunk cost situation is illustrated by the following example:

[5] Savage commented on the same behavioral regularity: "A man buying a car for $2,134.56 is tempted to order it with a radio installed, which will bring the total price to $2,228.41, feeling that the difference is trifling. But, when he reflects that, if he already had the car, he certainly would not spend $93.85 for a radio for it, he realizes that he has made an error" (Savage, 1954, p. 103). Of course, many people may not do the second part of Savage's analysis, or even if they do, they may nevertheless believe that the purchase of the radio hurts less when bought with the car.

Problem 4.15. You have tickets to a basketball game in a city 60 miles from your home. On the day of the game there is a major snow storm, and the roads are very bad. Holding constant the value you place on going to the game, are you more likely to go to the game (1) if you paid $20 each for the tickets or (2) if you got the tickets for free?
[*Source:* Thaler, 1980]

The lure of the sunk cost is so strong in this problem that, when it is presented to subjects untrained in economics, substantial explanations must be given to convince subjects that the economic analysis is sensible.

Numerous studies have documented the failure of subjects to ignore sunk costs, (e.g. Staw, 1976; Teger, 1980; Laughhunn and Payne, 1984; Thaler and Johnson, 1986), but one particularly clean demonstration in a natural setting was performed by Arkes and Blumer (1985). In their experiment, customers who purchased season tickets to a campus theater group were assigned randomly to either one of two experimental groups or a control group. The experimental groups received refunds of $2 or $7 from the normal $15 price of the tickets, whereas the control group received no refund. The season consisted of 10 plays. The authors analyzed the attendance to the first 5 plays separately from the last 5. Over the first 5 plays, the sunk cost had a significant effect. Those who paid full price attended significantly more plays than those who received a discount. This effect was not significant for the second half of the season, suggesting that sunk costs may become less relevant with time.

Households and individuals behave as if they had an implicit mental accounting system. One reason sunk costs are not ignored is that costs that have not been "mentally amortized" are coded as losses. Mental accounting also influences choices when either sources or uses of funds are placed in particular accounts. Choices influenced in this way violate Tenet 4.11.

> *Tenet 4.11. Fungibility. Money is spent on its highest valued use. Money has no labels.*

The following problems show how the relevance of sunk costs can be influenced by the mental accounting system:

Problem 4.16. Imagine that you have decided to see a play, admission to which is $10 per ticket. As you enter the theater you discover that you have lost a $10 bill. Would you still pay $10 for the ticket to the play?

Yes: 88%   No: 12%

Problem 4.17. Imagine that you have decided to see a play and paid the admission price of $10 per ticket. As you enter the theater you discover that you have lost your ticket. The seat was not marked and the ticket cannot be recovered. Would you pay $10 for another ticket?

Yes: 46%   No: 54%

[*Source:* Tversky and Kahneman, 1981]

In Problems 4.16 and 4.17 the loss of the $10 affects the choice of whether to buy a ticket only when it is coded in the same account.

A key question in the investigation of mental accounting systems is the relationship between costs and losses. In the context of the prospect theory loss function, when is a cost a loss? A portion of a cost may be coded as a loss if the cost is considered to be excessive by the customer. This coding can lead to violations of the following tenet:

> **Tenet 4.12. Domain of utility.** *Willingness to pay for a good depends only on the characteristics of the good and not on the perceived merits of the deal.*

The potential importance of the reference price (the price a consumer expects to have to pay in a particular context) is illustrated by the following pair of questionnaires (one group of subjects received the information in parentheses and the other received the information in brackets):

Problem 4.18. You are lying on the beach on a hot day. All you have to drink is ice water. For the past hour you have been thinking about how much you would enjoy a nice cold bottle of your favorite brand of beer. A companion gets up to make a phone call and offers to bring back a beer from the only nearby place where beer is sold (a fancy resort hotel) [a small, rundown grocery store]. He says that the beer may be expensive and so asks how much you are willing to pay for it. He says that he will buy the beer if it costs as much as or less than the price you state, but if it costs more than the price you state he will not buy it. You trust your friend and there is no possibility of bargaining with (the bartender) [the store owner].

[*Source:* Thaler, 1985]

When this questionnaire was administered to the participants in an executive education program, the median reponses were $2.65 in the hotel version and $1.50 in the grocery store version. This disparity occurs even though the question is incentive compatible, and there is no "atmosphere" consumed in either version. This result violates Tenet 4.12.

In contrast to Tenet 4.12, I have suggested that consumers consider the value of the "deal" (a function of the difference between the price paid and the reference price), as well as the utility of the item being purchased, in evaluating a potential transaction (Thaler, 1985). The beer on the beach example illustrates that, when consumers feel that they are being treated unfairly, they will be unwilling to make a purchase that would otherwise make them better off. There is probably an effect in the opposite direction as well. That is, if a good is perceived to be a sufficiently attractive bargain, it may be purchased even if its value is less than its price.

The last tenet of this section is implicit in most economic analyses:

> *Tenet 4.13. Economic opportunities. All legal economic opportunities for gains will be exploited.*

Although Tenet 4.13 may seem reasonable at first, clearly there are some limits to what constitutes an economic opportunity. If you observe someone drop his wallet on the bus, does this constitute an economic opportunity? To what extent is behavior governed by social norms? A related question concerns implicit contracts. To what extent is enforceability necessary for implicit contracts to operate? In collaboration with Daniel Kahneman and Jack Knetsch, I have been involved in a research project investigating these issues with a new (to BDR) methodology (Kahneman, Knetsch, and Thaler, 1986). Residents of Toronto and Vancouver were contacted by telephone and asked questions regarding their perceptions of fairness. I report here the responses to a question about an unenforceable implicit contract, namely tipping in strange restaurants.

Problem 4.19. If the service is satisfactory, how much of a tip do you think most people leave after ordering a meal costing $10 in a restaurant that they visit frequently?

Mean response: $1.28

Problem 4.20. If the service is satisfactory, how much of a tip do you think most people leave after ordering a meal costing $10 in a restaurant that they do not expect to visit again?

Mean response: $1.27

Our panel evidently does not treat the possibility of enforcement as a significant factor in the control of tipping.

4.2.5 Judgment

The principles of rationality and maximization are used by economists to describe not only people's choices but also their judgments. Thus the following tenet, though associated with a specific modern branch of macroeconomics, is really in keeping with, rather than a radical departure from, the general principles of economic theory:

> **Tenet 4.14. Rational expectations.** *Probabilistic judgments are consistent and unbiased.*

When John Muth (1961) coined the term "rational expectations" he believed he was merely applying standard techniques to the problem of expectations. This is clear from his definition of rational expectations: ". . . the same as the predictions of the relevant economic theory" (p. 316). It is instructive that in Steven Sheffrin's (1983) review of the rational expectations literature he found little empirical support for the notion that actual expectations satisfy the criteria that define rational expectations. In reviewing several studies using the Livingstone data set (a collection of published professional inflation forecasts), Sheffrin concludes: "The results of the extensive research on the Livingstone data are, at best, mixed. The verdict on Muth rationality for the aggregate series depends on the time period examined, the econometric techniques, and the aggregation procedure. The one study on the individual responses clearly rejected the rationality hypothesis" (p. 21). Since rational expectations models are intended to be positive theories, one might think that the lack of empirical support for the hypothesis would be considered damaging. However, some advocates of the hypothesis have continued to use it apparently on the grounds that there is no alternative:

The rational expectations assumption may be excessively strong . . . but it is a more persuasive starting point than the alternative of using a rule of thumb for expectations formation that is independent of the stochastic properties of the time path of the variable about which expectations are formed. A fundamental difficulty with theories of expectations that are not based on the predictions of the relevant economic model . . . is that they require a theory of systematic mistakes. (Barro and Fisher, 1976, p. 163)

To provide a theory of systematic mistakes, one must become more concerned with the actual processes used to make judgments (and choices). This point was stressed in the pioneering work of Herbert

Simon (e.g., 1955). Simon's interest in artificial intelligence gave him not only great respect for the human mind, but also a considerable appreciation for the mind's limitations. He stressed that, because of the mind's limited information-processing and storage capabilities, humans must use simple rules of thumb and heuristics to help make decisions and solve problems. Simon coined the terms "bounded rationality" and "satisficing" to describe humans' limited mental abilities and decision-making strategies, respectively.

Kahneman and Tversky took the next step in developing a theory of systematic mistakes by identifying three specific heuristics people use in making judgments of magnitudes, frequencies, or probabilities: the *availability, representativeness,* and *anchoring and adjustment* heuristics. Each of the heuristics is a useful way of making judgments, but the use of each leads to predictable, systematic errors. When using the availability heuristic (Tversky and Kahneman, 1973), people estimate the frequency of a class by the ease with which they can recall specific instances in that class. Thus "John" is judged to be a common name (by English speakers) since it is easy to think of many people with that name. Biases are generated when the frequency of an event is not perfectly correlated with its ease of recall. This is illustrated by the following problems:

Problem 4.21. In four pages of a novel (about 2,000 words), how many words would you expect to find that have the form _ _ _ _ing (seven-letter words that end with "ing")? Indicate your best estimate by circling one of the values below:

0   1–2   3–4   5–7   8–10   11–15   16+   median = 13.4

Problem 4.22. In four pages of a novel (about 2,000 words), how many words would you expect to find that have the form _ _ _ _ _ n _ (seven-letter words that have the letter *n* in the sixth position)? Indicate your best estimate by circling one of the values below:

0   1–2   3–4   5–7   8–10   11–15   16+   median = 4.7

[*Source:* Tversky and Kahneman, 1983]

Subjects here estimate that there are many more words ending with "ing" because it is easier to retrieve instances of that type. This judgment violates the conjunction rule of probability: The probability of a conjunction $p(A\&B)$ cannot exceed the probability of either of its constituents, $p(A)$ and $p(B)$.

The bias in Problems 4.21 and 4.22 is caused by the nature of the memory retrieval system. In other cases a bias can be induced by external factors. When asked whether suicide or homicide is more common, most people guess homicide since it receives greater press coverage, although in fact suicide is more common. Slovic, Fischhoff, and Lichtenstein (1979) found that generally people overestimate the frequency of highly publicized causes of death (e.g., accidents and floods) and underestimate the frequencies of quieter fatalities (e.g., diabetes and stroke).

The representativeness heuristic (Kahneman and Tversky, 1972, 1973) is used to estimate the likelihood that a particular event or case belongs to a certain class. This heuristic judges such a frequency by comparing the similarity of the case with the image or stereotype of the class. Here a bias is generated when frequency and similarity are not well correlated. This is illustrated by the next problem.

Problem 4.23. Consider a regular six-sided die with four green faces and two red faces. The die will be rolled 20 times and the sequence of greens (G) and reds (R) will be recorded. You are asked to select one sequence, from a set of three, and you will win $25 if the sequence you choose appears on successive rolls of the die. Please check the sequence of greens and reds on which you prefer to bet:

A. RGRRR
B. GRGRRR
C. GRRRRR

[*Source:* Tversky and Kahneman, 1983]

Notice that sequence A is simply sequence B with the first G deleted. Thus A must be more probable than B. However, sequence B may appear more "representative" of the die than sequence A because it has two Gs rather than one. The latter consideration is evidently quite powerful since about 63% of the subjects chose B, whereas only 35% chose A (the rest taking C). Once again the use of a heuristic leads to a violation of the conjunction rule and thus Tenet 13. In this case the majority choice also violates stochastic dominance.

The final tenet is a common assumption in both theoretical and applied economics research:

> **Tenet 4.15. Bayesian learning.** *Probabilistic judgments are updated by the appropriate use of Bayes's rule.*

One of the biases that can be introduced by use of the representativeness heuristic is the violation of Bayes's rule. Empirical research (Kahneman and Tversky, 1972, 1973) indicates that subjects tend to give too little weight to prior or base-rate information and too much weight to new information. For example, in one experiment subjects were given a description of a man and were asked to guess whether he was a lawyer or an engineer. The subjects' answers were insensitive to whether they had been told that the descriptions came from a sample containing 70% lawyers or 30% lawyers (Kahneman and Tversky, 1973).

Perhaps because Tenet 4.15 is so commonly used in economics research, David Grether (1980) replicated the Kahneman and Tversky findings with a clever new experimental design. The subjects were shown two bingo cages, one of which (cage X) had three balls marked "N" and three marked "G" and the other of which (cage Y) had four N's and two G's. One of the cages was selected by a random process (a draw from a third bingo cage). The prior probabilities of selecting either cage were transparent to the subjects. A sample of six draws with replacement was taken from the selected cage, and the subjects' task was to guess which cage had been selected.

Grether's design allowed him to estimate a logit model in which the dependent variable was the judgment of which cage had been selected, and the independent variables were the prior odds and likelihood ratio (in multiplicative form). If subjects made judgments as if they were using Bayes's rule, the estimated coefficients for the two independent variables would both be 1.0. Instead, the estimated coefficient for the likelihood ratio was significantly higher than the coefficient for the prior, indicating that subjects were giving insufficient weight to the prior, as predicted by the representativeness heuristic. Significantly, and of considerable surprise to Grether, subjects who were given financial incentives to respond accurately did no better than those without financial incentives.

One manifestation of the use of the representativeness heuristic is that predictions tend to be nonregressive. For example, when one group of subjects are asked to *evaluate* a high school student's record and another group is asked to *predict* (on the basis of the same record) how well the student will do in college, the groups tend to give equally extreme judgments, whereas, of course, the latter judgments should be much less extreme. In a dynamic world, such behavior will produce *overreaction* to new information. As noted by Kenneth Arrow (1982), the price movements in financial markets seem to display precisely this type of behavior. Arrow cites the work of Shiller (1981), which shows that stock prices are excessively volatile. Dreman (1982) uses the same argument to explain the observed excess return to firms with low price–earnings ratios, and De Bondt and Thaler (1985) were able to predict similar excess returns to firms that have previously had large negative excess returns. Arrow concludes:

I hope to have made a case for the proposition that an important class of intertemporal markets shows systematic deviations from individual rational behavior and that these deviations are consonant with evidence from very different sources collected by psychologists. (Arrow, 1982, p. 8)

4.3   Methodological issues

The research described in the preceding sections is characterized by three general traits: (1) short questions appealing to subjects' intuitions, (2) few or no monetary incentives, (3) no opportunity for learning. The latter two have received some criticism and, therefore, deserve attention.

4.3.1   Incentives

The issue of monetary incentives can be addressed at two levels. (1) Is the purely hypothetical nature of many of the experiments a matter of concern? Would even small monetary incentives eliminate the observed anomalies? (2) Are the differences between the stakes in the laboratory and the real world sufficiently large that *all* laboratory experiments are of questionable value in assessing actual choice behavior? I shall discuss each point in turn.

For some kinds of problems it is a simple matter to make the payments to subjects depend on the quality of their decisions. To determine whether the addition of monetary incentives would improve decision making, numerous researchers, both psychologists and economists, have run parallel experiments with and without incentives (e.g., Lichtenstein and Slovic, 1971, 1973; Lichtenstein, Fischhoff, and Phillips, 1977; Grether and Plott, 1979; Grether, 1980; Tversky and Kahneman, 1981, 1983; Pommerehne, Schneider, and Zweifel, 1982; Reilly, 1982; Knetsch and Sinden, 1984). These methodological experiments have produced two basic conclusions. First, monetary incentives do induce subjects to pay a little more attention, so the data generated with incentives tend to have less noise. Second, the violations of rationality observed tend to be somewhat *stronger* in the incentive condition (see, e.g., Grether and Plott, 1979). This result, although of considerable surprise to the economists who have obtained it, is not really counterintuitive. If the effects under study are real, the presence of monetary incentives simply magnifies the effect by inducing the subjects to be attentive.

The expectations of some economists on this issue have been that, without incentives, subjects will lie about their true preferences and beliefs, perhaps using some clever strategic ploy, and/or subjects will not bother to think carefully about the problems posed and will respond in an offhand fashion. Subjects are portrayed as devious, cognitive misers. There is little, if any, empirical evidence for this characterization. Nevertheless, I do not wish to give the impression that the studies cited validate the use of hypothetical questions in all types of research. Hypothetical questions appear to work well when subjects have access to their intuitions and have no particular incentive to lie. When strangers are asked for the time of day, few intentionally lie. However, it would be naïve to expect truthful answers to questions about cheating on exams or income taxes.

That monetary incentives have proved to be irrelevant in many cases should be considered good news. Asking purely hypothetical questions is inexpensive, fast, and convenient. This means that many more experiments can be run with much larger samples than is possible in a monetary-incentives methodology. (The experiments described in this chapter have often used more than a hundred subjects to answer each of several versions of the questions.) Also, in some cases the use of real money is impossible. It is not practical to use real stakes to investigate subjects' preferences regarding large amounts of money, and it is difficult to expose subjects to actual losses of even moderate amounts.[6]

Since even real-money experiments are played for relatively small stakes, a different sort of critique is that the incentives in the real world are greater and thus rationality may obtain "when it counts."[7] This

---

[6] Thaler and Johnson (1986) ran some real-money choice experiments involving losses by allowing subjects to choose whether to participate under real-money or under hypothetical conditions. This procedure has some potential merit, but the problem is that the real-money subjects tend to be much more risk seeking than those in the hypothetical condition, making comparisons across conditions difficult.

[7] This critique applies with equal force to any experimental markets that fail to obtain a rational equilibrium (e.g., Plott and Sunder, 1983). A true believer can interpret an experiment that does obtain a rational equilibrium (see, e.g., Plott and Sunder's earlier article, 1982) as evidence that markets work, while dismissing the latter article as irrelevant because the stakes are too small or the traders too inexperienced. Such a bias, if reflected in the choice of papers to be published, could distort considerably the impression generated by experimental economics about the robustness of the predictions of economic theory.

critique is related to the "cognitive miser" hypothesis: The failings that have been observed are rational reactions to the "cost of thinking." I find the hypothesis implausible. There is no evidence to suggest that thinking longer or harder about cognitive illusions makes them go away, any more than there is reason to think that staring more intently at mirages makes them disappear. Furthermore, people do not appear to be particularly rational in making the most important decisions in life. The high failure rate of new businesses is a case in point. It is difficult to reconcile this datum with both rational expectations and risk aversion. Furthermore, although it would be possible for people to hire consultants to help them overcome their cognitive failings in important situations, this is rarely observed. Even for the purchase of a house, the largest financial decision most people make, few people get any decision-making help, aside from that received from a real estate agent, a person more likely to initiate biases than to eliminate them.

4.3.2 Learning

When a subject is given a single opportunity to make a particular choice or judgment and makes a mistake, it is natural to ask whether the subject would not do better if there were opportunities for learning. Although it is indisputable that people can and do learn, it is not clear what is the best way of finding out how people make choices outside the laboratory. Suppose a subject is given a problem to solve, and the subject makes a mistake. Suppose the subject is then given considerable practice in performing the same task with highly structured, constructive feedback. What should we conclude if the subject eventually learns to avoid the mistake? Should we conclude that the mistake will not be made in the real world? Not necessarily.

What do we mean when we say that a subject has learned a task? All teachers are familiar with the frustration of seeing how badly students can perform on last month's concept when incorporated into this month's test. Does any statistics teacher suffer the delusion that the students who successfully answered a problem on Bayes's rule in June will apply the concept correctly, out of context, in July, much less several years later? The reason for conducting one-shot decision-making experiments is to try to discover the intuitions that subjects bring with them to the laboratory. Those intuitions do not include the proper use of Bayes's rule or the proper use of the (implicit) concepts of sunk costs and opportunity costs. There is every reason to believe that an initial response in the laboratory will most likely be the one a subject will make in a similar real-life problem. The response after several learning trials may be no more general than the response students give on exam questions.

Although the subjects in BDR experiments may not have learned to solve the problems posed by the experimenters, perhaps they have learned to deal with their own problems successfully. Is there any reason to believe that the real world teaches people to choose and judge rationally? Unfortunately, one must be skeptical about this prospect. First, many decisions are made infrequently. Particularly when major decisions are involved, most people get too few trials to receive much training. We marry, choose careers, and take jobs a few times at most.

Second, even for repeated decisions, the quality of the learning depends crucially on the quality of the feedback. As Einhorn and Hogarth (1978) have shown, many routine situations are structured in such a way that the feedback is not conducive to learning. In some tasks, confidence in one's judgment ability can increase with experience, regardless of the actual quality of the judgments being made (e.g., admissions directors at selective colleges with a low dropout rate). Feedback is often delayed, and even when failure is recognized there are usually multiple explanations for it. Hindsight biases (Fischhoff, 1975) also interfere with proper ex post evaluations. Particularly in stochastic environments, learning about the quality of the decisions being made simply from the outcomes being observed is very difficult.

Third, even studies of expert decision making have revealed numerous biases. A study by McNeil et al. (1982) illustrates this point in a dramatic (and disturbing) fashion. Three large groups of subjects were given a question regarding a choice between surgery and radiation treatments for lung cancer. The subjects were patients, physicians, and graduate students of business. Two versions of the problem were given, one with the outcomes framed as survival probabilities, the other with the outcomes framed as mortality probabilities. There was a large discrepancy between the answers to this problem across the two frames for all three groups of subjects. (The attractiveness of surgery increased when the data were presented as probabilities of living.) Of interest here is the fact that the framing manipulation had the greatest effect on the sample of physicians. Thus rather than being immune to framing, the doctors turned out to be particularly susceptible. This result was obtained despite the fact that the decision they faced was quite realistic and one with which they had considerable experience.

In at least one case, a class of experts has learned to avoid a bias that most other individuals exhibit, namely overconfidence. In studies of *calibration* (see Lichtenstein, et al., 1977) subjects are given a factual statement (e.g., Albany is the capital of New York State) and are then asked to state the probability they assign to the statement's being true. The general result of overconfidence is reflected in the finding that when subjects say they are "sure" the statement is true (i.e., $p = 1.0$), the statement is false about 20% of the time. The one group of experts studied that does not exhibit overconfidence (and, in fact, is nearly perfectly calibrated) is meteorologists. When the weather reporter says that there is an 80% chance of rain, it will rain about 80% of the time. This high degree of calibration is to be expected (in spite of a bad reputation) since practicing meteorologists receive quick, precise, and repeated feedback, exactly the conditions that facilitate learning. Since most people do not get this type of feedback on the job, or in life generally, this result would seem to be the exception rather than the rule.

4.3.3   Markets, evolution, and ecological validity

One way in which both learning and incentives can sometimes be brought into the analysis is to argue that competitive markets will somehow force individuals to behave rationally. The question to ask is how? The evolutionary analogy has been used to argue that firms that fail to maximize profits will be driven out of business by firms that get things right (Alchian, 1950; Friedman, 1953; Winter, 1964). This argument has some merit, and we would certainly expect the decisions of General Motors and IBM to be more in keeping with economic theory than the decisions of some of their less successful competitors. (Even in these cases, however, one must be careful. Evolutionary processes tend to be fairly slow.) It is quite another matter to apply this argument to individuals in their roles as employees, consumers, savers, and investors. Violations of transitivity or dominance are rarely life threatening. Since such concepts as rational expectations, life-cycle saving, and optimal search are used to model individuals as well as firms, these assumptions should be confirmed empirically rather than on the basis of some evolutionary argument.

It is true that some highly efficient markets can render irrationality irrelevant. Someone who believes that pesos are better than dollars (since more is better than less) is generally protected by the efficiency of foreign exchange markets. In other markets, however, there is ample opportunity for bad decision making to have an impact (Russell and Thaler, 1985). The market does not automatically protect a consumer who buys an inefficient product because its advertisement was worded (framed) cleverly, nor is there protection for an unemployed worker who turns down job offers because she mistakenly thinks that she can find another job at her old wage rate.

All the issues raised in this section are related to the questions of ecological validity, an issue of concern to all experimentalists. Many experimental economics studies use repeated trials and monetary incentives on the grounds that these factors make the experiments resemble situations encountered in real markets. The validity of this assertion is less obvious than it seems. Individuals interact with other market participants in many ways. Some markets offer opportunities for learning, but few if any offer the instantaneous feedback used in most market experiments. A provocative and useful illustration of these issues is provided by Coursey, Hovis, and Schulze (forthcoming). These investigators studied the disparity between willingness to pay (WTP) and willingness to accept (WTA) as demonstrated by Knetsch and Sinden (1984). They noted that Knetsch and Sinden's methodology "ignores much of the tradition and procedures developed in experimental economics" (p. 1). By employing a market mechanism, Coursey, Hovis, and Schulze hoped to obtain what they regard as "true" values for WTP and WTA.

The commodity they studied was SOA, a foul-tasting but harmless liquid. Subjects either offered to taste one ounce of the stuff for 20 seconds for a fee (WTA) or agreed to pay to avoid tasting the liquid (WTP). A three-stage process was used to solicit WTP and WTA. In the first stage subjects made purely hypothetical, uninformed offers without knowing how bad SOA tasted. In the second stage subjects tasted a few drops of SOA and then made new hypothetical bids. At this point the usual disparity was observed, namely WTA exceeded WTP by more than a plausible income effect. The experimenter then tried systematically to lower the WTAs and raise the WTPs. The method by which this was accomplished was not described. In the third stage, the subjects participated in groups of eight in a Vickrey auction. Four of the members of the group would have to taste the liquid. The results of this auction, however, were not binding unless, after the market clearing price was announced, the "winners" unanimously agreed to accept the outcome. Furthermore, even if unanimity was obtained in one of the first four trials, the process continued until the fifth trial. The authors commented on their procedure as follows: "Both the unanimity requirement and the nonbinding practice trials have been shown to be helpful in promoting learning, and, as a result, in revealing true values in induced value experiments. In particular, the unanimity requirement allows a 'winner' who has made a mistake to reject the outcome and force another auction trial" (p. 6).

The most striking result of the experiment was that the disparity between WTP and WTA was substantially reduced (such that it was no longer significant) in the latter trials of the auction, all of the adjustment occurring in the WTAs. Taking this result at face value, what conclusions should be reached? One reasonable conclusion is that intensive practice and repetition can help subjects learn to equate opportunity costs and out-of-pocket costs. However, just as it would be a mistake to conclude from the earlier studies that there is always a buying–selling discrepancy, it would also be a mistake to conclude that these results[8] imply that there will be no discrepancy in market contexts.[8] It remains an open question what market contexts are similar to the conditions in the experiments of Coursey, Hovis, and Schulze.

4.4 Implications: how much rationality is appropriate?

Consider the following problem and decide what answer you would give before going on:

In the following exercise, you will represent Company A (the acquirer) which is currently considering acquiring Company T (the target) by means of a tender offer. You plan to tender in cash for 100% of Company T's shares but are unsure how high a price to offer. The main complication is this: the value of the company depends directly on the outcome of a major oil exploration project it is currently undertaking.

The very viability of Company T depends on the exploration outcome. In the worst case (if the exploration fails completely), the company under current management will be worth nothing – $0/share. In the best case (a complete success), the value under current management could be as high as $100/share. Given the range of exploration outcomes, *all share values between $0 and $100 per share are considered equally likely*. By all estimates the company will be worth considerably more in the hands of Company A than under current management. In fact, whatever the value under current management, *the company will be worth 50% more under the management of Company A than under Company T*.

The board of directors of Company A has asked you to determine the price they should offer for Company T's shares. This offer must be made *now, before* the outcome of the drilling project is known. . . . *Thus, you (Company A) will not know the results of the exploration project when submitting your offer, but*

---

[8] Both my work (Thaler, 1980, 1985) and that of Kahneman and Tversky (1984) have stressed the difference between costs and losses. The buying–selling discrepancy, to the extent that it is caused by loss aversion rather than issues of legitimacy, will not occur for those who consider themselves "traders." A grocer does not consider the sale of a loaf of bread a loss. Even nontraders will behave differently when there is an active resale market. See Kahneman, Knetsch, and Thaler (1986).

Company T will know the results when deciding whether or not to accept your offer. In addition, Company T is expected to accept any offer by Company A that is greater than or equal to the (per share) value of the company under its own management.

As the representative of Company A, you are deliberating over price offers in the range $0/share to $150/share. What offer per share would you tender? (Samuelson and Bazerman, 1985)

A typical subject's analysis of this problem is as follows. The expected value of the firm to the current owner is $50. It is worth 50% more to me. Therefore, I should bid something in the interval between $50 and $75. Nearly all subjects (114 of 123) made positive bids, mostly in the $50–$75 range.

Nevertheless, it is fairly straightforward to show that the optimal bid in this problem is zero. The key to the correct analysis is that there is asymmetric information. Since the owner knows the firm's true value, she will sell only if you bid more than that amount. Thus if you bid, say, $60, she will accept only if the value to her is less than $60. The expected value of the firm to her, contingent on her acceptance of your bid, is therefore just $30, or only $45 to you. So a bid of $60 has a negative expected gain, as does any positive bid.

As the results of Samuelson and Bazerman's experiment demonstrated, the above analysis is far from transparent. (Daniel Kahneman and I replicated their results with a group of faculty members and doctoral students: 20 of 24 subjects made positive bids, and two of those who bid zero later admitted that they did the right thing only out of cowardice.) To get the right answers requires appreciating the role of asymmetric information, a subtle point. Now suppose a firm were being sold under the conditions specified in the problem. What should we predict will be the winning bid? The standard economic prediction of the winning bid would be $0. Since optimal behavior requires only zero bids, that is what the theory must predict. Notice that the theory implicitly assumes that the problem is transparent *to every potential bidder*. If even one person fails to get the analysis right, then the winning bid will be positive.

The characterization of the relevant economic theory for this problem is not simply hypothetical. Samuelson and Bazerman's problem corresponds exactly to George Akerlof's (1970) classic model of the market for lemons in which there is no equilibrium at a positive price. Again, his analysis depends on the implicit assumption that all potential used-car buyers understand the implications of the asymmetry in information. If some potential buyers do not appreciate the lemons problem, there is a positive equilibrium price. There is a paradox here.

Akerlof's analysis assumes that an idea that had not been previously understood by other economists is nevertheless transparent to all the participants in his model.

The obvious question to resolve is how best to try to describe the behavior of economic agents in complex environments. Perhaps in the market for used cars a healthy dose of skepticism on the part of buyers would lead them to behave as if they understood the subtleties of asymmetric information. Whether this happens is an empirical question. In the absence of empirical evidence it might be sensible to extend Akerlof's analysis by investigating the operation of models with both asymmetric information and limited rationality.

4.5   Conclusion

Most economists believe that their subject is the strongest of the social sciences because it has a theoretical foundation, making it closer to the acknowledged king of sciences, physics. The theory, they believe, is a tool that gives them an inherent advantage over their weaker social science cousins in explaining human behavior. Although the power of economic theory is surely unsurpassed in social science, I believe that in some cases this tool becomes a handicap, weighting economists down rather than giving them an edge. It becomes a handicap when economists restrict their investigations to those explanations consistent with the paradigm, to the exclusion of simpler and more reasonable hypotheses. For example, in the introduction to an issue devoted to the size effect anomaly in financial markets (small firms appear to earn excess returns, most of which occur the first week in January), an editor of the *Journal of Financial Economics* commented; "To successfully explain the 'size effect', new theory must be developed that is consistent with rational maximizing behavior on the part of *all* actors in the model" (Schwert, 1983, p. 10, emphasis added). Is it not possible that the explanation for the excess return to small firms in January is based, at least in part, on some of the agents behaving less than fully rationally some of the time?

Many economists continue to assume rationality because they think they have no alternative. Robert Lucas has said this explicitly:

The attempt to discover a competitive equilibrium account of the business cycle may appear merely eccentric, or at best, an aesthetically motivated theoretical exercise. On the contrary, it is in fact motivated entirely by practical considerations. The problem of quantitatively assessing hypothetical countercyclical policies (say, a monetary growth rule or a fiscal stabilizer) involves imagining how agents will behave in a situation which has never been observed. To do this successfully, one must have some understanding of the way agents' decisions have been made in the past *and* some method of determining how these decisions would be altered by the hypothetical change in policy. In so far as our descriptions of past behavior rely on arbitrary mechanical rules of thumb, adjustment rules, illusions, and unspecified institutional barriers, this task will be made difficult, or impossible. Who knows how "illusions" will be affected by an investment tax credit? (Lucas, 1981, p. 180)

Two comments seem in order. First, there is no guarantee that the models based solely on rational behavior are correct. This is an empirical question to be addressed by macroeconomists. Certainly not everyone shares Lucas's explanation for apparent involuntary unemployment. Second, although the task of incorporating less than fully rational agents into economic models may be difficult, as Lucas states, the research summarized in this chapter suggests that the task of producing a theory of systematic error is not impossible.

References

Akerlof, George A., "The Market for 'Lemons': Quality Uncertainty and the Market Mechanism." *Quarterly Journal of Economics, 84,* August 1970, 488–500.

Alchian, Armen A., "Uncertainty, Evolution and Economic Theory." *Journal of Political Economy, 58,* June 1950, 211–21.

Allais, Maurice, "Le comportement de l'homme rationnel devant le risque: Critique des postulats et axiomes de l'école americaine." *Econometrica, 21,* October 1953, 503–46.

Arkes, Hal R., and Blumer, Catherine, "The Psychology of Sunk Cost." *Organizational Behavior and Human Decision Processes, 35,* 1985, 124–40.

Arrow, Kenneth J., "Risk Perception in Psychology and Economics." *Economic Inquiry, 20,* January 1982, 1–9.

Barro, Robert, and Fisher, Stanley, "Recent Developments in Monetary Theory." *Journal of Monetary Economics, 2,* 1976, 13–76.

Chew, Soo Hong, "A Generalization of the Quasilinear Mean with Applications to the Measurement of Income Inequality and Decision Theory Resolving the Allais Paradox." *Econometrica, 51,* July 1983, 1065–92.

Coursey, Donald L., Hovis, John J., and Schulze, William D, "On the Supposed Disparity Between Willingness to Accept and Willingness to Pay Measures of Value." *Quarterly Journal of Economics,* forthcoming.

De Bondt, Werner F. M., and Thaler, Richard, "Does the Stock Market Overreact?" *Journal of Finance, 60,* July 1985, 793–805.

Dreman, David, *The New Contrarian Investment Strategy* (New York: Random House), 1982.

Einhorn, Hillel J., and Hogarth, Robin M., "Confidence in Judgment: Persistence of the Illusion of Validity." *Psychological Review, 85,* September 1978, 395–416.

"Ambiguity and Uncertainty in Probabilistic Inference." *Psychological Review, 92,* October 1985, 433–61.

Ellsberg, Daniel, "Risk, ambiguity and the Savage Axioms." *Quarterly Journal of Economics, 75,* November 1961, 643–69.

Fischhoff, Baruch, "Hindsight $\neq$ Foresight: The Effect of Outcome Knowledge on

Judgment Under Uncertainty." *Journal of Experimental Psychology: Human Perception and Performance, 1,* 1975, 288–99.

Fishburn, Peter C., "Transitive Measurable Utility." *Journal of Economic Theory, 31,* December 1983, 293–317.

Friedman, Milton, "The Methodology of Positive Economics." in Milton Friedman (Ed.), *Essays in Positive Economics* (University of Chicago Press), 1953, pp. 3–46.

Gottfries, Nils, and Hylton, Keith, "Are MIT Students Rational?" Unpublished manuscript, Massachusetts Institute of Technology, Cambridge, March 1983.

Grether, David M., "Bayes' Rule as a Descriptive Model: The Representativeness Heuristic." *Quarterly Journal of Economics, 95,* November 1980, 537–57.

Grether, David M., and Plott, Charles R., "Economic Theory of Choice and the Preference Reversal Phenomenon." *American Economic Review, 69,* September 1979, 623–38.

Kahneman, Daniel, Knetsch, Jack, and Thaler, Richard, "Fairness as a Constraint of Profit Seeking: Entitlements in the Market." *American Economic Review, 76,* September 1986, 728–41.

"Fairness and the Assumptions of Economics." *Journal of Business, 59,* 1986, S285–300.

Kahneman, Daniel, and Tversky, Amos, "Subjective Probability: A Judgment of Representativeness." *Cognitive Psychology, 3,* 1972, 430–54.

"On the Psychology of Prediction." *Psychological Review, 80,* 1973, 237–51.

"Prospect Theory: An Analysis of Decision Under Risk." *Econometrica, 47,* March 1979, 263–91.

"Choices, Values and Frames." *American Psychologist, 39,* April 1984, 341–50.

Knetsch, Jack L., and Sinden, John A., "Willingness to Pay and Compensation Demanded: Experimental Evidence of an Unexpected Disparity in Measures of Value." *Quarterly Journal of Economics, 99,* August 1984, 507–21.

Laughhunn, D. J., and Payne, John. W. "The Impact of Sunk Outcomes on Risky Choice Behavior." *INFOR (Canadian Journal of Operations Research and Information Processing), 22,* 1984, 151–81.

Lichtenstein, Sarah, and Slovic, Paul, 'Reversals of Preference Between Bids and Choices in Gambling Decisions." *Journal of Experimental Psychology, 89,* January 1971, 46–55.

"Response-Induced Reversals of Preference in Gambling: An Extended Replication in Las Vegas." *Journal of Experimental Psychology, 101,* November 1973, 16–20.

Lichtenstein, Sarah, Fischhoff, Baruch, and Phillips, Lawrence D,. "Calibration of Probabilities: The State of the Art," in H. Jungerman and G. deZeeuw (Eds.), *Decision Making and Change in Human Affairs* (Amsterdam: Reidel) 1977, pp. 275–324.

Lucas, Robert E., *Studies in Business-Cycle Theory* (Cambridge, Mass: MIT Press), 1981.

Luce, R. Duncan, and Krantz, David H., "Conditional Expected Utility." *Econometrica, 39,* March 1971, 253–71.

Machina, Mark J., "'Expected Utility' Analysis without the Independence Axiom." *Econometrica, 50,* March 1982, 277–323.

McNeil, Barbara J., Pauker, Stephen G., Sox, Harold C., and Tversky, Amos, "On the Elicitation of Preferences for Alternative Therapies." *New England Journal of Medicine, 306,* 1982, 1259–62.

Muth, John F. "Rational Expectations and the Theory of Price Movements." *Econometrica, 29,* 1961, 315–35.

Plott, Charles, and Sunder, Shyam, "Efficiency of Experimental Security Markets with

Insider Information: An Application of Rational Expectation Models." *Journal of Political Economy, 90,* August 1982, 663–98.

"Rational Expectations and the Aggregation of Diverse Information in Laboratory Security Markets," Working Paper No. 934, California Institue of Technology, Department of Social Sciences, 1983.

Pommerehne, Werner W., Schneider, Friedrich, and Zweifel, Peter, "Economic Theory of Choice and the Preference Reversal Phenomenon: A Reexamination," *American Economic Review, 72,* June 1982, 569–74.

Reilly, Robert J., "Preference Reversal: Further Evidence and Some Suggested Modifications in Experimental Design." *American Economic Review, 72,* June 1982, 576–84.

Russell, Thomas, and Thaler, Richard H., "The Relevance of Quasi Rationality in Competitive Markets." *American Economic Review, 75,* December 1985, 1071–82.

Samuelson, William F., and Bazerman, Max H., "The Winner's Curse in Bilateral Negotiations," in Vernon L. Smith (Ed.), *Research in Experimental Economics,* Vol. 3 (Greenwich, Conn.: JAI Press), 1985, pp. 105–37.

Savage, Leonard J., *The Foundations of Statistics* (New York: Wiley), 1954.

Schwert, George W., "Size and Stock Returns, and Other Empirical Regularities." *Journal of Financial Economics, 12,* July 1983, 3–12.

Sheffrin, Steven M., *Rational Expectations* (Cambridge University Press), 1983.

Shiller, Robert J., "Do Stock Prices Move Too Much to Be Justified by Subsequent Changes in Dividends?" *American Economic Review, 71,* June 1981, 421–36.

Simon, Herbert A., "A Behavioral Model of Rational Choice." *Quarterly Journal of Economics, 69,* February 1955, 99–118.

Slovic, Paul, Fischhoff, Baruch, and Lichtenstein, Sarah, "Rating the Risks." *Environment, 21,* 1979, 14–20, 36–39.

Slovic, Paul and Lichtenstein, Sarah, "Preference Reversals: A Broader Perspective." *American Economic Review, 73,* September 1983, 596–605.

Staw, Barry M., "Knee-deep in the Big Muddy; A Study of Escalating Commitment to a Chosen Course of Action." *Organizational Behavior and Human Performance, 16,* 1976, 27–44.

Teger, A. I., *Too Much Invested to Quit* (New York: Pergamon), 1980.

Thaler, Richard H., "Toward a Positive Theory of Consumer Choice." *Journal of Economic Behavior and Organization, 1,* March 1980, 39–60.

"Mental Accounting and Consumer Choice," *Marketing Science, 4,* Summer 1985, 199–214.

Thaler, Richard, and Johnson, Eric, "Hedonic Framing and the Break-Even Effect." Cornell University, Johnson Graduate School of Management Working Paper, 1986.

Tversky, Amos, and Kahneman, Daniel, "Availability: A Heuristic for Judging Frequency and Probability." *Cognitive Psychology, 5,* 1973, 207–32.

"The Framing of Decisions and the Psychology of Choice." *Science,* January 30, 1981, pp. 453–58.

"Extensional versus Intuitive Reasoning: The Conjunction Fallacy in Probability Judgment." *Psychological Review, 90,* October 1983, 293–315.

"Rational Choice and the Framing of Decisions." *Journal of Business, 59,* 1986, S251–278.

von Neumann, John, and Morgenstern, Oskar, *Theory of Games and Economic Behavior* (Princeton, N.J.: Princeton University Press), 1947.

Winter, Jr., Sidney G., "Economic 'Natural Selection' and the Theory of the Firm." *Yale Economic Essays, 4,* Spring 1964, 225–72.

CHAPTER 5

Hypothetical valuations and preference reversals in the context of asset trading

MARC KNEZ AND VERNON L. SMITH

5.1 Background and setting

Several studies soliciting willingness-to-pay (WTP) and willingness-to-accept (WTA) responses for a variety of goods have found a large disparity between these "buying price" and "selling price" measures of value (see Knetsch and Sinden, 1984, for a summary of these studies). Although utility theory is consistent with some disparity between them, scholars generally have argued that the empirical disparity in these responses is much larger than is expected from the theory. Indeed, the mean WTA values obtained in this way are frequently several times greater than the mean WTP values so obtained. These empirical results are very robust under investigations designed to determine the effect of monetary incentives, experience, and other factors on the disparity. These results cast serious doubt on the validity of utility (or demand) theory as a calculating, cognitive model of individual decision behavior.

Another related series of experimental results have established what is commonly referred to as the preference reversal phenomenon (see the survey by Slovic and Lichtenstein, 1983). This refers to the large proportion of subjects who report that they prefer item A to item B (or B to A) but whose WTP or WTA is smaller for A than for B (or larger for A than for B if they said they preferred B to A). Often A and B are prospects or gambles, but they can be any items of value to the individual. Again, these preference reversal results are robust under careful controls designed to provide good incentives for reporting "true" subjective preferences. Although such preference reversals have been interpreted as violating transitivity, Karni and Safra (1985) show that they may violate independence rather than transitivity and are not inconsistent with non-expected utility models of decision making. However, the preference reversal phenomenon clearly violates expected utility theory (EUT).

131

However, other experimental studies based on choices in repetitive, revealed demand, market, or marketlike settings have shown high consistency with standard demand utility theory. Thus the consumption–leisure revealed demand behavior of mice, rats, monkeys, pigeons, and people in repeat-purchase environments yields steady-state results consistent with the Slutsky–Hicks demand model of maximizing behavior. Similarly, many studies of individual and market behavior based on expected utility models of market decision making yield results consistent with these models (for references see Smith, 1985; Knez, Smith, and Williams, 1985).

Coursey, Hovis, and Schulze (forthcoming) have challenged the conventional interpretation of this WTA–WTP disparity by allowing individuals to bid in a repetitive series of second price auctions for entitlements to an item. The resulting bids provide revealed measures of WTP (or WTA), which are then compared with hypothetical measures of WTA and WTP. Coursey, Hovis and Schulze found that the WTA–WTP disparity in hypothetical measures is also observed in an initial auction market but that it tends to disappear after a series of such auctions.

All these studies taken together appear to support the proposition that utility theory and demand theory do very poorly as cognitive calculating models of single-choice decision behavior but relatively well in the learning-feedback environment of a repetitive market. Why is it important to study the theory of individual choice in the context of markets in particular and institutions in general? We suggest three reasons:

1. Markets are the distinguishing forte of the economist. Indeed, professional economics was born in the context of the attempt by Adam Smith and his forerunners to understand the broad social significance of the universal human "propensity to truck, barter and exchange." Only later, after articulating the demand (supply) theory of market price, did economists turn to the derivation of demand from hypotheses about individual behavior and the additivity of this behavior across individuals.

2. The efficiency and social significance of markets does not depend on the validity of any particular theory of individual demand. Theory asserts that markets are efficient if they yield market clearing prices under the appropriate property right arrangements, even if the given demand behavior is inconsistent with individual "rationality" in the sense of utility theory. Hence, the empirical validity or falsity of efficient markets theory is a proposition that is entirely distinct from

the empirical validity or falsity of theories of individual demand in markets. The economic theory of market behavior may be empirically sound, whereas the economic theory of individual behavior is not, or vice versa. Distinguishing between individual choice behavior and individual behavior in markets is justified for the same reason that distinguishing between the psychology and sociology of individual behavior is justified.

3. The institutions in which individuals function can directly, and may indirectly, impinge on individual rationality in the sense of demand theory. Thus in the Treasury bill auction and on the New York Stock Exchange, individuals may want to submit a multiple bid order, for example, a maximum of 20,000 units at price 96 and a maximum of an additional 20,000 units at price 97. Demand theory hypothesizes that the individual's ordering of these bids should be reversed, that is, up to 20,000 at 97, and 20,000 more at 96. But these trading institutions operate under rules *requiring* any bid stating a higher price to have exchange priority over any other bid stating a lower price. In effect, the market rules impose diminishing returns on the submitted multiple bids of any individual. Indirectly, markets may impinge on individual rationality because of emulative behavior and/or learning.

This chapter reports the results of a series of six experiments. In each experiment the objects of value are two assets (gambles), each conveying the right to a dividend drawn from each of two distinct probability distributions. In the next section we discuss briefly some related earlier experiments that conditioned the designs we chose for the new series of experiments reported here.

5.2 Related earlier experiments

This study was directly motivated by an earlier article (Knez et al., 1985) that was confined to the study of WTP–WTA responses and trading behavior for units of an asset with a given dividend structure. Figure 5.1 charts the detailed results of one of these earlier experiments (reported in very abbreviated form as experiment 37, series II, in Knez et al., 1985).

In this experiment, nine subjects were given the opportunity to trade an asset in a sequence of trading periods in which all individual endowments of cash and shares are *reinitialized* at the beginning of each period. Thus except for individual learning, these trading periods represent pure replications under the same treatment conditions. In particular, this design controls for trading effects due to capital gains

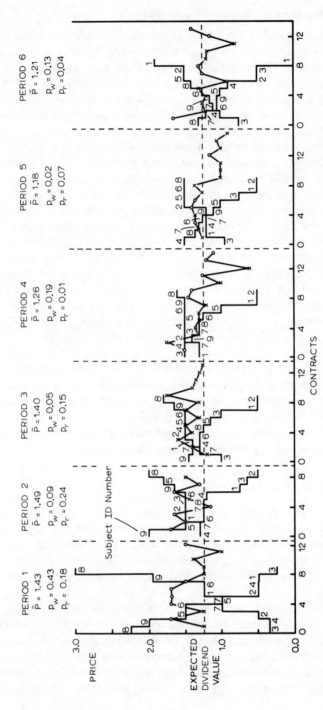

Figure 5.1. Experiment 37. Key: $\bar{P}$, mean price; P_w, hypothetical competitive price; $P_w = |P_w - \bar{P}|$; x, accepted offer. $p_r = |1.25 - \bar{P}|$; ○, accepted bid; x, accepted offer.

expectations across periods, although not, of course, for such expectations within a period. A single draw at the end of each trading period is made from a binary probability distribution of dividends $(p_1, d_1; p_2, d_2) = (\frac{1}{2}, \$0.50; \frac{1}{2}, \$2.00)$. The expected holding value of the asset is therefore \$1.25. Letting E_i = (cash, shares) be the endowment vector for subject i, each experiment has three agent classes, $E_1 = (\$4.50, 1)$, $E_2 = (\$3.25, 2)$, and $E_3 = (\$2.00, 3)$, with three subjects assigned randomly to each class (nine subject traders). Note that the expected value of each agent's endowment is \$5.75 in each of the independently initialized trading periods of an experiment. The instructions fully inform the subjects about the dividend distribution and state that this dividend structure means that "on average" a share has a "holding value" of \$1.25. Each subject is informed only of her own endowment vector. After completing the instructions (which are devoted largely to explaining the rules of double-auction trading) but before the countdown to the first (timed) period of trading, the following two questions are put to each of the subjects (the blanks are filled in with the applicable numbers):

(1) Given your endowment of \$_____ cash (i.e., working capital) and _____ asset units, what would be the minimum price you would be willing to accept in order to sell one unit of your inventory in the trading period about to begin? (2) Given your endowment of \$_____ cash (i.e., working capital) and _____ asset units, what would be the maximum price that you would be willing to pay in order to buy one unit of this asset in the trading period about to begin?_____

After each trading period, each subject is logged into a new one-period asset trading experiment identical to the one described above. Before the countdown to the opening of trade, the questionnaire is filled in again. This cycle of endowment initialization, questionnaire administration, followed by trading was conducted six times, as shown in Figure 5.1.

Each of the six panels in Figure 5.1 graphs the hypothetical demand represented by the individual WTP_i responses arrayed from highest to lowest and the hypothetical supply represented by the WTA_i arrayed from lowest to highest. For example in period 1, before trading, subject 8 reported $WTP_8 = \$2.25$ and $WTA_8 = \$3.00$. Subject 9 reported $WTP_9 = \$2.00$ and $WTA_9 = \$1.95$. Since the maximum possible dividend was \$2.00, neither of these responses can be described as inspiring confidence in any known concept of individual rationality. However, before trading in period 2, subject 8 is providing responses that are not inconsistent with EUT, and by period 3, subject 9 is no longer claiming to be willing to pay \$2.00 for a 50–50 chance of receiving $0.50 or $2.00. In each period note that the hypothetical demand and supply schedules yield a competitive market clearing price P_w (= $1, e.g., in period 1). We can think of this price as the *market's* hypothetical value for the asset. Each panel also plots the contract prices in the sequential order in which the exchanges occurred. In period 1 the first contract occurred when some seller accepted the standing bid (shown as an x) of some buyer at $1.25. In the second contract a buyer accepted a standing offer (shown as a circle) at $1.70, and so on.

Several features of the results illustrated in Figure 5.1 should be emphasized. Although there are numerous instances of individually "irrational" reported values for the asset, the social valuation represented by the hypothetical market price P_w is not inconsistent with EUT. In period 1, although two subjects (8 and 9) report WTPs equal to or larger than maximum payoff, and three (2, 3, and 4) report WTAs less than or equal to the minimum payoff, the market value based on these WTP–WTA schedules is P_w = $1.00, which is a reasonable risk-averse adjusted value for a one-shot draw with a 50–50 chance of yielding $0.50 or $2.00. "Irrationally" high WTPs (or low WTAs) do not imply irrational market clearing prices since the latter are determined by the marginal WTP–WTA valuations. To be sure, this hypothetical market value rises to $1.40 in period 2, but that is a reasonable response to the observation that 11 of the 12 trades in period 1 were at prices at least as high as $1.25. Subjects' stated WTPs or WTAs are not independent of what they think the market price will be. Although in the first three periods prices are at levels consistent with risk-preferring behavior, there is a general downtrend, with the frequency of risk-averse (or neutral) valuations predominating in the last two periods.

Individual traders repeatedly reveal selling prices below their reported WTA and buying prices above their reported WTP. For example, in period 2 the fourth contract occurred at a price below the stated WTA of any seller, and in period 3, the third, fifth, seventh, and ninth contracts occurred at prices in excess of the stated WTP of any buyer. Across all three experiments of this type, Knez et al. (1985) reported that for 34% of the subjects the lowest offer made was below their stated WTA_i, whereas for 47% the highest submitted bid exceeded the reported WTP_i. The impunity with which subjects violate their own reported values suggests that these responses may serve (at best) only as pretrade bargaining objectives from which deviations are made contingent on events experienced in the trading process.

Capital gains expectations may not have been controlled sufficiently by restricting the trading horizon to a single period. This is suggested in Figure 5.1 by the observance of multiple trades by individuals and a trading volume in every period that was many times larger than the hypothetical volume based on single-unit (per subject) buying and selling prices. Also, the downtrend of prices within each period and across successive periods may be due to the failure of initial capital gains expectations to be realized, leading to a sell-off.

5.3   Preferences, valuation, and double-auction asset trading

A new series, consisting of six experiments, was designed with the following features. Several groups of subjects who participated in other double-auction market experiments unrelated to the six reported in this section were asked to respond to a questionnaire before leaving the laboratory but after completing the experiment for which they had been recruited. This questionnaire described two gambles (situations) using the pie charts (Grether and Plott, 1979) that are standard in this research: Asset A provides a probability distribution of dividends given by $(p_1, d_1; p_2, d_2) = (\frac{1}{36}, -\$1.00; \frac{35}{36}, +\$4.00)$. Asset B provides a probability distribution of dividends given by $(p_1, d_1; p_2) = (\frac{25}{36}, -\$1.50; \frac{11}{36}, +\$16.00)$. If the individual had been a seller in the experiment in which she had just participated she was asked which situation, A, B, or "don't care," she preferred. Then she was asked, if she were in situation A, "What is the lowest price that you would accept for one unit of that particular asset?" Similarly, she reported her WTA for asset B. If the individual had been a buyer, his preference was solicited in the same manner, and he was asked to state the highest price that he would pay for each of the two assets A and B. These responses were used to classify subject sellers and buyers as to whether they were preference reversers [e.g., A preferred or indifferent to B, but WTP_A $(WTA_A) < WTP_B (WTA_B)$] or nonreversers. Because of the difficulty of getting a large pool of preference-reversing subjects in this way, we supplemented the pool with questionnaires given to individuals who were on our sign-up lists for participation in experiments. Our total pool of 118 subjects consisted of 66 nonreversers and 52 reversers (44%).

From this subject pool we recruited groups of buyers and groups of sellers to return for our asset-trading experiment. The subjects were logged into an asset-trading experiment describing the rules of trading and the characteristics of the asset to be traded, which was asset A as just described. They were also informed that, when the trading period for asset A was completed, they would be logged into an experiment in which they would have the opportunity to trade asset B for one period. Those subjects who had been buyers in their original double-auction experiment and who responded to the questionnaire for buyers were constrained to be buyers only in the new experiment for assets A and B. These buyer subjects were given the endowment vector E_A^B = (cash, shares) = ($5.50, 0) for asset A and E_B^B = (cash, shares) = ($5.50, 0) for asset B. In the trading period for asset A, each buyer could buy no more than a single unit of A. Similarly, in trading asset B, each buyer was constrained to buy no more than a single unit of asset B. Those subjects who originally had been sellers and responded to the seller questionnaire were constrained to be sellers only in the new experiment. These sellers were given the endowment E_A^S = (cash, shares) = ($1.65, 1) for asset A and the endowment E_B^S = (cash, shares) = ($1.65, 1) for asset B. Note that the expected value of all the endowments for both buyers and sellers and for both asset A and B is $5.50. All trading was constrained to one unit per buyer (seller) for the purpose of controlling for expectations of capital gains from resale within a trading period.

After the subjects completed the instruction for asset trading and were assigned their endowments, but before the commencement of the first trading period for asset A, the buyers and sellers were given questionnaires similar to the original screening questionnaire. However, in this case the questionnaires were endowment specific (see appendixes A and B): that is, situations A and B not only specified the (dividend) outcomes and probabilities, but also specified the endowments in each situation. Both preferences and the WTP for buyers (WTA for sellers) were therefore "framed" in terms of the endowments that would constrain actual trading.

Each experiment (except experiment 60) consisted of questionnaire response 1, trading 1 (asset A, then asset B); response 2, trading 2; response 3, trading 3; response 4. Thus the questionnaire was administered before and after each two-period trading sequence in asset A followed by B.

5.3.1   *Hypothetical supply and demand, and trade realizations over time*

Figures 5.2 and 5.3 chart the market results from experiments 73 and 87, respectively. In each figure the hypothetical supply and demand schedules, based on subject WTA–WTP responses, are drawn for each interrogation, and the contract realizations from trade are plotted for the subsequent markets in asset A and asset B.

As in Figure 5.1 we note several obvious violations of simple dominance; in Figure 5.2, response 1, buyer 1 claims to be willing to pay $5 for asset A, which cannot possibly yield more than $4, whereas buyers 2 and 5 state WTPs of $4, an outcome that is probable but not certain. In the subsequent market we observe two trades at "reasonable" prices below expected value ($3.85). As in Figure 5.1, the line connecting x's (accepted bids) or O's (accepted offers) represents contracts. An x or O at the end of a period indicates the closing bid and offer when they existed. Over time in markets A.1 through A.3 the price of asset A rises, with all contracts reflecting slight risk-preferring behavior in period 3. Similarly, the market price of asset B rises over time, except that in period 1 the contracts are near the risk-neutral level and rise to modest risk-preferring levels. However, a comparison of the hypothetical supply and demand schedules with price realizations reveals that, except for period 1, prices tend frequently to be outside the predicted WTA–WTP bounds.

In Figure 5.3 we see more violations of simple dominance in WTP responses: buyer 3 in responses A.1 and A.2, and buyer 4 in response A.2. As in Figure 5.2 the price of asset A rises but hovers near expected value in periods 2 and 3. Except for the first trade in asset B, the price of B is fairly steady, near expected value, across all three trading periods. As in Figure 5.2, several of the trades are outside the bounds predicted by the hypothetical supply and demand schedules. These schedules do not appear to be reliable predictors of the range of contract prices.

Figure 5.4 charts only the contracts for experiments 60, 70, 98, and 101. Across all six experiments we count 3 in 76 contracts (4%) that represent clear violations of EUT. In each case a buyer purchased a unit of asset A at a price of $4 or more. This contrasts with 14 instances in which a buyer's *reported* WTP was $4 or more. In experiment 101, involving experienced subjects, contract prices for both A and B are more stable than in any of the other experiments. Prices are consistent with risk aversion in both markets. Prices for A tend to exceed prices for B, revealing an overall preference for A over B.

5.3.2 Effect of trading experience on reported preference reversals

Figure 5.5 plots the percentage of all subject buyers and sellers who exhibit preference reversals. The results of the initial screening response questionnaire is recorded as response 0: 63% reversals for buyers, 52% for sellers. After subjects return for the asset market experiment, buyer reversals fall to 42% whereas seller reversals remain

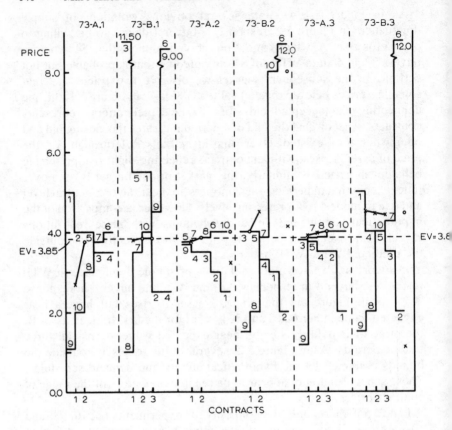

Figure 5.2. Experiment 73. Key: x, bid; o, offer. Subjects: 1–5, buyers; 6–10, sellers.

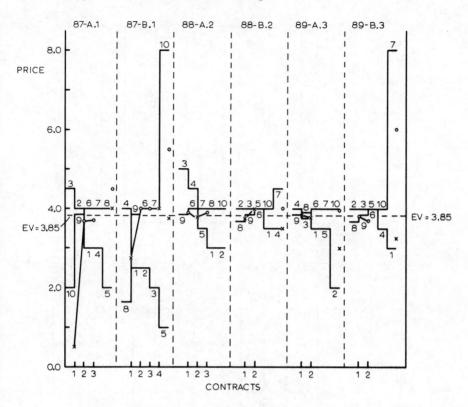

Figure 5.3. Experiment 87. Key: x, bid; o, offer. Subjects: 1–5, buyers; 6–10, sellers.

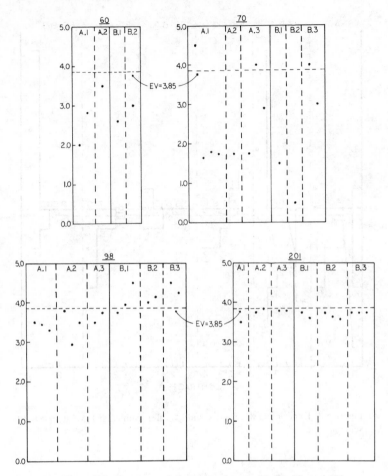

Figure 5.4. Contract prices in experiments 60, 70, 98, and 101.

at 52%. After three trading periods, each followed by a new interrogation, reversals decline to 38% for sellers and 35% for buyers, but the decline is not monotonic. Also plotted in Figure 5.5 are the results for the small sample (nine) of buyers and sellers who repeated the experimental sequence a second time. It seems clear that there is a hard core of 35 to 38% reversals that continue to be exhibited by the reported preferences and values of these subjects.

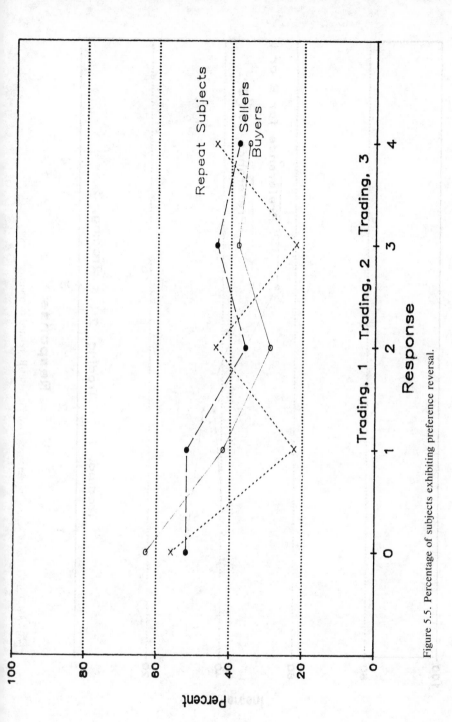

Figure 5.5. Percentage of subjects exhibiting preference reversal.

143

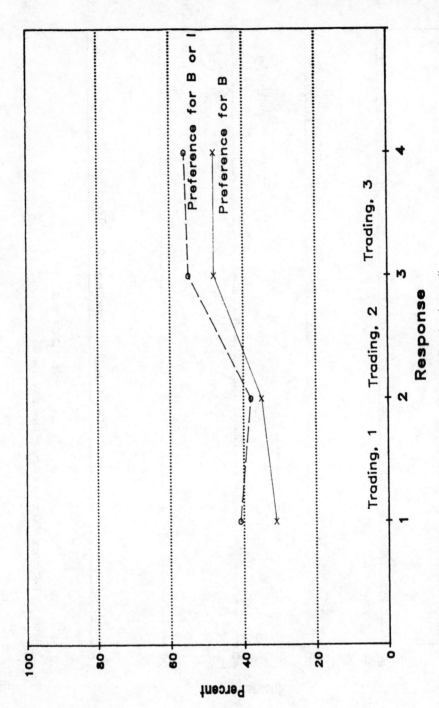

Figure 5.6. Percentage of sellers' preferences favoring asset B, related to trading.

144

145

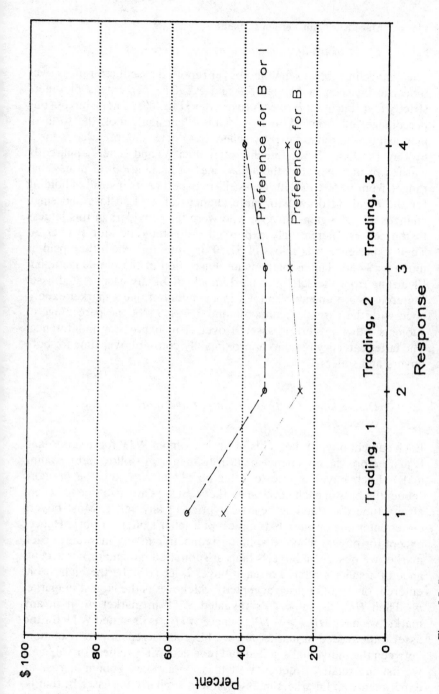

Figure 5.7. Percentage of buyers' preferences favoring asset B, related to trading.

5.3.3   Effect of trading on stated asset preferences

The change in subject seller and buyer reported asset preferences over time can be seen in Figures 5.6 and 5.7. The percentage of sellers strictly favoring asset B over A rose from 31 to 48%; among buyers this percentage fell from 45 to 28%. Thus "learning" took the form of increasing preference for B by sellers but decreasing preference for B by buyers. Asset B was much riskier than A, and sellers apparently learned from experience the advantages of cashing out at prices that ranged from $0.50 to $4.50 across all six experiments instead of holding for the dividend draw with large chances of a $1.50 loss and small chances of a $16 gain. Buyers, who were the providers of this largess to the sellers, increasingly expressed a dispreference for B over A. Their experience was a loss of $1.50 on units for which they paid as much as $4.50. This is perhaps an illustration of the old adage about "learning from the school of hard knocks." In any case, stated asset preferences are unstable and not independent of one's market experience with the assets. Figures 5.6 and 5.7 also plot the percentage of subjects either preferring asset B over A or expressing indifference. The latter category remains approximately constant over time for both buyers and sellers.

5.3.4   Discrepancies between reported and market-revealed asset values

Each subject buyer reports his or her maximum WTP for assets A and B just before the commencement of trading in A (followed by trading in B). Each buyer is free to enter no bid or to enter one or more sequential bids in each of these markets. Buyers are also free to accept at any time the standing best offer price of any seller. Most buyers either enter one or more bids or accept a seller's offer, or both. Hence, except for buyers who are voluntarily inactive in any market, in each market we observe a buyer's highest submitted bid and/or her acceptance of a seller's offer. For each buyer i, let HB_{im} be the highest bid entered, or the offer price accepted, whichever is the largest in market m. Then HB_{im} is subject i's revealed WTP in market m. If in any market we have $HB_{im} > WTP_{im}$ (where WTP_{im} is i's stated WTP for the asset to be traded in market m), we have a discrepancy (or violation) between the individual's stated and revealed WTP values. In Table 5.1 we list the relative frequency of these violations, pooling across all experiments and markets in asset A, and similarly for asset B; that is, $N(HB_{im} > WTP_{im})$ is the number of such discrepancies for each asset.

Table 5.1. *Incidence of discrepancy between reported and market-revealed asset value, all experiments*

Subjects	Asset		
	A	B	A and B
Buyers			
$\dfrac{N\,(HB_{im} > WTP_{im})}{\text{trade opportunities}}$	$\dfrac{30}{83} = 36\%$	$\dfrac{37}{83} = 45\%$	$\dfrac{67}{166} = 40\%$
Sellers			
$\dfrac{N\,(WTA_{im} > LO_{im})}{\text{trade opportunities}}$	$\dfrac{28}{83} = 34\%$	$\dfrac{28}{83} = 34\%$	$\dfrac{56}{166} = 34\%$
Buyers and sellers	$\dfrac{58}{166} = 35\%$	$\dfrac{65}{166} = 39\%$	$\dfrac{123}{332} = 37\%$

For sellers we have a violation if $WTA_{im} > LO_{im}$; that is, a seller's lowest offer (or acceptance price of a buyer's standing bid) is below his prior stated lowest WTA.

From Table 5.1 we see that the incidence of these discrepancies exceeds one-third under all four classifications. Seller violations are the same (34%) for both A and B, but buyer violations are more frequent for B (45%) than for A (36%).

Table 5.2 answers a different question: How large are these violations? To answer this we sum over all instances in which $HB_i - WTP_i > 0$ for buyers and over all the $(WTA_i - LO_i) > 0$ cases for sellers. We see that the dollar magnitude of seller discrepancies is larger than it is for buyers, especially for asset B, in which seller discrepancies are 50% larger than buyer discrepancies. The magnitude of these discrepancies is also larger for asset B than asset A for both buyers and sellers and roughly two-thirds larger for buyers and sellers combined. Clearly, both buyers and sellers have more difficulty living up to their valuation estimates for asset B than for A, and sellers exhibit more such difficulty than buyers for both assets. This is consistent with the results reported by Coursey et al. (1984) in which sellers' hypothetical valuations are much larger relative to revealed value than is the case for buyers.

5.3.5 Examples of individual responses to discrepancies between hypothetical and revealed valuations

The high incidence with which subjects' bid (offer) behavior violates their previous WTP (WTA) responses raises the following question.

Table 5.2. *Magnitude ($) of discrepancy between reported and market-revealed asset value, all experiments*

	Asset		
Agent	A	B	A and B
Buyers $\Sigma_{i\in P}$ ($HB_i - WTP_i$)	28.44	40.22	68.66
Sellers $\Sigma_{i\in P}$ ($WTA_i - LO_i$)	30.15	60.53	90.68
Total, buyers and sellers	58.59	100.75	159.34

Note: Here P is the set of subjects for whom $HB_i - WTP_i$ or $WTA_i - LO_i$ is positive; i.e., the WTP_i or WTA_i limits are violated by the subsequent revealed measures.

How do subjects respond to these discrepancies? There are many types of responses – too many, we think, to suggest a useful classification scheme, and in any case such a scheme would contain subjective elements of judgment. However, we can identify three types of behavior that illustrate the polar cases. One type of subject never bids (offers) in violation of her stated WTP (WTA). Of the subjects who exhibit such a discrepancy in an earlier trading period (for either asset A or B or both), there are two polar response cases: Those who show a persistent discrepancy across market replications and those who respond to the discrepancy either by correcting their market behavior or by correcting their stated valuations.

In Figure 5.8, seller 5 in experiment 70 entered slight upward adjustments in reported WTA after each trading period, but the lowest offer made in each period was never below the previously stated WTA. In Figure 5.9 buyer 3 in experiment 87 always entered highest bids below the previously stated WTP. The latter rose from response 1 to response 2, then stabilized in the third and fourth responses. Seller 3 in experiment 98 and buyer 2 in experiment 73 provide examples of subjects who repeatedly violated their own WTA–WTP by factors of 2 or more. Their behavior suggests that they attach no value whatsoever to consistency between their actions and their statements. Seller 2 (Figure 5.8) offered less than WTA(1) in period 1, drastically lowered the WTA(2), then submitted a higher LO(2), adjusted WTA(3) upward, again made a consistent offer, and finally raised WTA(4) to a level consistent with the offers in periods 2 and 3. Buyer 3 (Figure 5.9) performed in a similar manner after exhibiting discrepancies in the first two trading periods.

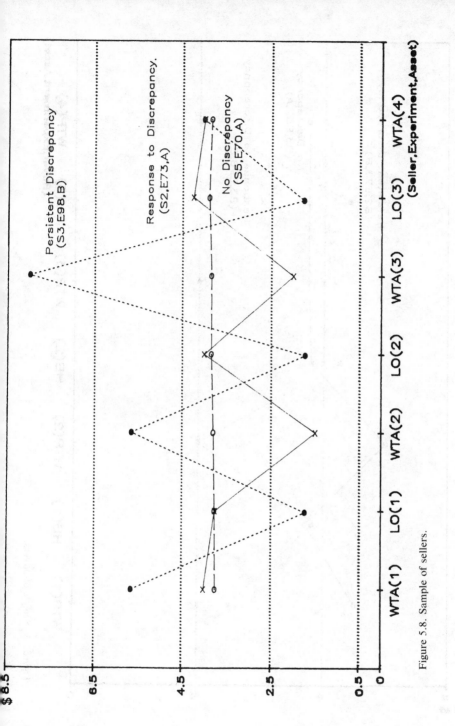

Figure 5.8. Sample of sellers.

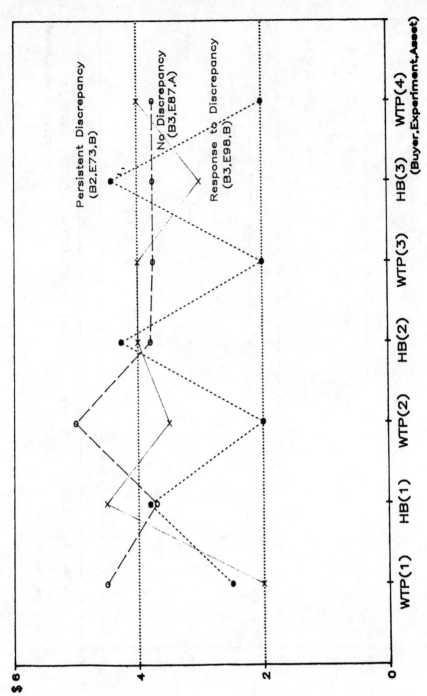

Figure 5.9. Sample of buyers.

5.3.6   Summary

Our results and conclusions can be summarized briefly as follows. From a pool of 118 subjects, buyers, 63% of whom were preference reversers, and sellers, 52% consisting of preference reversers, were recruited to engage in markets for the two assets A and B used in the initial questionnaire instrument to partition the subjects into four categories (buyer, seller), (reverser, nonreverser). Subjects who were asked for their WTP responses for A and B would be buyers; those asked for their WTA responses would be sellers.

After arriving for the market experiments, reading the instructions for double-auction asset trading, and learning their (cash, shares) endowments, each subject was again asked for his or her preference for A and B and corresponding WTP or WTA responses. Buyer reversals decline to 42%, whereas seller reversals remain at 52%.

Pooling the hypothetical response data and trading data across all markets, we find 14 instances in which a buyer's reported WTP violates dominance, but only 3 cases in which contracts occur at *prices* that violate dominance. Some 73 contracts (96%) are consistent with EUT. "Rationality," in the expected utility sense, as revealed in repeat-experience market outcomes is clearly greater than rationality as revealed in individual response measures.

Reported preference for asset A or B changes across trading periods 1 through 3. At the end of period 3 the percentage of buyers strictly favoring asset B over A falls from 45 to 28%, but among sellers this percentage rises from 31 to 48%. Since asset B was much riskier than A, sellers apparently learned from trading the advantages of cashing out at positive prices (from \$0.50 to \$4.50) instead of risking the dividend draw with high probability of a \$1.50 loss, whereas the buyers who paid these prices and risked the loss learned the disadvantages of incurring this gamble. These data illustrate how market experience may produce a socializing effect on individual values as measured by the response questionnaire.

Reported WTP and WTA measures of asset value are frequently violated by individual subjects' subsequent highest bid or lowest offer in double-auction trading. The incidence of such buyer or seller discrepancies across the two assets varies from 34% (for sellers of both A and B) to 45% (for buyers of B). However, the size of these discrepancies is larger for sellers across A and B [$\Sigma(WTA_i - LO_i) =$ \$91] than for buyers [$\Sigma(HB_i - WTP_i) =$ \$69].

How are subjects' hypothetical WTP–WTA responses altered by these discrepancies? There are three polar cases: (1) the subject who never bids or offers in violation of her reported WTP or WTA, (2) the subject who persists in this discrepancy across repeated interrogations and market trading periods, and (3) the subject who responds to the discrepancy either by correcting his market behavior or correcting his stated valuations. These results show the great variability in the importance that individual subjects attach to maintaining consistency between reported and revealed valuation behavior.

The results of this study call into question the interpretation, reliability, and robustness of preference reversal phenomena in the joint context of repetitive responses and market trading. However, we would not suggest that the phenomena have significance only in such contexts. They are obviously of potential importance in interpreting the rationality of nonmarket or nonrepetitive market decision making. However, even in these contexts there are institutional elements that may impinge on the phenomena, such as the use of "expert advice," in the case of large infrequent transactions and the use of committees and other social processes in nonmarket decision making.

Appendix A: seller questionnaire

Seller _____

Suppose you are confronted with the following two situations:

A. You are given a cash endowment of $1.65 and one asset unit, which you may sell. This particular asset unit will pay a dividend of either $-$1.00 (a loss) with probability $\frac{1}{36}$ or $4.00 (a gain) with probability $\frac{35}{36}$.

B. You are given a cash endowment of $1.65 and one asset unit, which you may sell. This particular asset will pay a dividend of either $-$1.50 (a loss) with probability $\frac{25}{36}$ or $+$16.00 (a gain) with probability $\frac{11}{36}$.

Note that in both A and B the only source of reward from holding a unit of the asset is the prospective dividend it will pay. So your decision in both A and B is made up of the following two choices: (1) Hold onto your cash endowment and keep your one asset unit and collect whatever dividend you receive from it. (2) Hold onto your cash endowment and sell your one asset unit, and keep all the money you receive from the sale.

Please answer the following questions:

1. Suppose you have the opportunity to be in situation A or B; which would you prefer? Check one:

A_____
B_____
Don't care_____

2. (a) Suppose now you are in situation A. What is the lowest price that you would accept for one unit of that particular asset?_____
   (b) Suppose now you are in situation B. What is the lowest price that you would accept for one unit of that particular asset?_____

Appendix B: buyer questionnaire

Buyer_____

Suppose you are confronted with the following two situations:

A. You are given a cash endowment of $5.50, which you may use to buy one asset unit. This particular asset unit will pay a dividend of either −$1.00 (a loss) with probability $\frac{1}{36}$ or $4.00 (a gain) with probability $\frac{35}{36}$.

B. You are given a cash endowment of $5.50, which you may use to buy one asset unit. This particular asset unit will pay a dividend of either −$1.50 (a loss) with probability $\frac{25}{36}$ or $16.00 (a gain) with probability $\frac{11}{36}$.

Note that in both A and B the only source of reward from holding a unit of the asset is the prospective dividend it will pay. So your decision in both A and B is made up of the following two choices: (1) Hold onto your cash endowment and not buy an asset unit. (2) Use some part of your cash endowment to buy a unit of the asset and keep whatever is left of your cash endowment after adjustment for the dividend you receive.

Please answer the following questions:

1. Suppose you have the opportunity to be in situation A or B; which would you prefer? Check one:

   A_____
   B_____
   Don't care_____

2. (a) Suppose now you are in situation A. What is the highest

price that you would pay for one unit of that particular asset?_____

(b) Suppose now you are in situation B. What is the highest price that you would pay for one unit of that particular asset?_____

References

Coursey, Don, Hovis, John, and Schulze, William, "On the Supposed Disparity Between Willingness-to-Accept and Willingness-to-Pay Measures of Value." *Quarterly Journal of Economics*, forthcoming.

Grether, David, and Plott, Charles, "Economic Theory of Choice and the Preference Reversal Phenomenon," *American Economic Review*, 69, September 1979, 623–38.

Karni, Edi, and Safra, Svi, "Preference Reversal and the Observability of Preferences by Experimental Methods." Johns Hopkins University, Department of Political Economy, November 1985.

Knetsch, Jack, and Sinden, J. A., "Willingness to Pay and Compensation Demanded: Experimental Evidence of an Unexpected Disparity in Measures of Value," *Quarterly Journal of Economics*, 99, August 1984, 507–21.

Knez, Peter, Smith, Vernon, and Williams, Arlington, "Individual Rationality, Market Rationality, and Value Estimation." *American Economic Review*, 75, May 1985, 397–402.

Slovic, Paul, and Lichtenstein, Sarah, "Preference Reversals: A Broader Perspective." *American Economic Review*, 73, September 1983, 596–605.

Smith, Vernon L., "Experimental Economics: Reply." *American Economic Review*, 75, March 1985, 265–72.

CHAPTER 6

Economics according to the rats (and pigeons too): what have we learned and what can we hope to learn?

JOHN H. KAGEL

6.1 Introduction

It has been more than 10 years since we published our first experimental test of economic choice theory using animal subjects (Kagel et al., 1975) and even longer since we began conducting economic choice experiments with animal subjects (1971). We continue to be engaged in experimental studies with animal subjects, extending our inquiries beyond static models of consumer choice and labor supply behavior under certainty to choices among risky alternatives (Battalio, Kagel, and MacDonald, 1985) and intertemporal choice behavior (Kagel, Green, and Caraco, 1986). Although no other economists we know of have undertaken experimental studies of animal choice behavior (i.e., with their own laboratories), there is a growing dialogue between economists and psychologists concerned with investigating economic choice theories using animal subjects, as judged by the expanding number of research proposals and working papers involving such collaborative efforts. In addition, efforts by psychologists to design and analyze animal choice experiments with economic models (e.g., Lea, 1981; Hursh, 1984) have increased, as has the use of optimization theories in biology, borrowed more or less directly from economics and operations research, to analyze the ecological behavior of animals (Maynard-Smith, 1978). At the same time there has been a virtual explosion in economics of experimental studies of market behavior using human subjects (for reviews see Smith, 1982a; Plott, 1982) and a

This research was supported by grants from the National Science Foundation and an Earhart Foundation Fellowship. The chapter has benefited from the comments of the conference participants and my associates, especially Tom Caraco, Len Green, and Dan Levin, all of whom will undoubtedly still disagree sharply with a number of points in the text but who have helped clarify my views on the issues.

155

smaller number of studies investigating individual choice behavior with human subjects.

The developments in biology and psychology suggest a secure place in these disciplines for experimental studies of economic choice theory involving animal subjects. Indeed, this work has always been rather well received in psychology and biology. Furthermore, most economists readily acknowledge the benefits these *other* disciplines are bound to receive from a little economic theory – economic imperialism at its finest!

The role of animal experiments in economics is on somewhat less certain footing, however. In commenting on an earlier methodological article summarizing research results to date (Kagel and Battalio, 1980), Cross (1980, p. 405) states that "Kagel and Battalio confine their discussion to more elementary economic phenomena than does Smith. . . . However they pay a price for this conservatism in that their conclusions reflect phenomena which are already extremely well documented in wider (and more relevant) market environments." Furthermore, there is always present the overriding issue of generalizability. Again, Cross (1980, p. 403) writes, "Both of these papers stress the principle that behavioral laws which apply in experimental settings can be expected to apply with equal force to less limited 'real world' circumstances. Smith treats this 'parallelism' virtually as an axiom, while Kagel and Battalio go even farther and extend the principle not only beyond the limits of the laboratory but across the boundaries of the human species as well." Cross's (1980) concerns regarding the role of animal experiments in economics are shared by considerably more sympathetic commentators and even those of us doing "animal economics" (e.g., Lea, 1981).[1]

---

[1] To quote from correspondence with a friendly colleague: "It seems to me that much of your research has been directed at the objective of verifying existing economic theory. For example in the paper you sent me you found downward sloping demand curves. In other work you have produced Giffen goods under the conditions dictated by the Slutsky equation. Research of that sort is well suited to establishing the relevancy of animal experiments to economics. For your purposes, that objective is a worthy objective in itself. However I am a "true believer" in microeconomic theory, and as a result I am perfectly willing to accept mathematical proofs without experimental verification." On the question of generalizability we cite Vernon Smith (1982b, p. xi), clearly one of the strongest supporters of animal experimentation among economists: "The unanswered question is how important it is, and what differences it makes, for an organism to be able to think about its decision."

The present chapter addresses the issue of what economists have learned from experimental studies of animal behavior and what they can hope to learn through continued study. We begin with methodological issues, discussing some of the advantages and limitations of animal experimentation as a research tool in experimental economics and their implications for the choice of questions to be studied and the means of studying them. Along with Lea (1981) we argue that, although the limitations are real, the advantages are great enough to make the small-scale use of animal experimentation well worthwhile. We argue that animal research has an important role to play in demonstrating "extremely well documented" economic phenomena and in contesting economic models with psychological and biological (and other behavioral) models accounting for these phenomena.

We also argue that animal experiments have an important role to play in sorting out competing hypotheses all of which are sustainable within mainstream economics. That maximization theory in conjunction with convex indifference curves rarely makes unambiguous predictions regarding behavior is hardly surprising to those familiar with economic theory. That different parameter specifications regarding the structures of preferences can result in markedly different predictions, a number of which have important public policy implications, is also well recognized. What we argue here is that animal experiments have a role to play in sorting out, and clarifying the issues involved in, these competing formulations. We support this argument by example as we enumerate the results of recent research along these lines.

6.2   Advantages and limitations of animal experiments

There is little doubt that physiological continuity exists across species – that there is not one set of theories of physiology and medicine for humans and another, nonoverlapping set of theories for other animal species. Our experimental studies of the economics of animal behavior take as their starting point the premise that there is behavioral as well as physiological continuity across species. This notion of behavioral continuity is seemingly well accepted in psychology and behavioral biology, both of which have well-developed subdisciplines that make extensive use of animal experimentation. Thus principles of economic behavior would be unique if they did not apply, with some variation, of course, across species as well.

In this section we elaborate some of the methodological issues involved in animal experiments aimed at testing and developing laws of economic behavior applicable to both animals and humans, with emphasis on the issues involved in going from animals to humans and vice versa.

6.2.1   Limitations of animal experiments: with answers to some often asked and unasked questions

The species extrapolation problem: The fundamental limitation inherent in animal experiments is the possibility that results obtained with animal species are not applicable to humans (Lea, 1981). In studying consumer demand and labor supply behavior of rats, we are not studying the behavior of simplified humans. The behavior of a given species is constrained by its psychological and biological characteristics, its ecological niche, which is peculiar to that species. As such there can be no general answer to the species extrapolation problem. Rather our presumption is that a theory that works well across species has a greater likelihood of being valid than one that works well with only one species or a limited set of species.

One practical implication of the fact that an animal's behavior is constrained by its ecological niche is that we design job tasks and choice problems that are compatible with the organisms' biological characteristics: Job tasks for rats are defined in terms of lever pressing, for pigeons in terms of key pecking; choice commodities are typically edibles, "luxury" goods being determined on the basis of the organisms' revealed preferences; for example, rats clearly prefer root beer to water at equal effort price. A second implication is that we conduct comparable experiments across different species and under a variety of experimental conditions in an effort to identify responses that are species specific and/or dependent on the particular institutional structure employed. (Efforts along this second line are endemic to the experimental process in general.) In this enterprise we look for qualitative, not quantitative, similarities and differences in response patterns. Furthermore, we do not expect to find similarities in all possible dimensions of behavior across species. Rather it is those differences in observed behavior relative to the predictions of a theory or hypothesis, as opposed to incidental differences, that provide cause for immediate concern. It is only when observed differences are codified in terms of a theoretical framework that we are able to determine whether new behavioral principles are required to account for these differences or whether the differences result from different constraints on choice or different initial conditions underlying the observations.[2]

Cognition and behavior: In reviewing the species extrapolation argument, I am struck by the fact that it is qualitatively indistinguishable from arguments regarding the limitations of extrapolating results from human economic experiments involving college sophomores and M.B.A. students to the target population of experienced economic agents operating under market conditions within national economic systems (see Smith, 1982a). After all, one can readily imagine a number of differences in overall economic and environmental conditions facing college students participating in an auction market experiment and those facing a target population consisting of seasoned executives bidding on offshore oil leases or Treasury bill auctions, and that these differences might have important implications for bidding behavior. Many would undoubtedly argue, however, that extrapolation from animals to humans is substantially different than extrapolation from M.B.A.s to experienced business people. Part, if not all, of the reason for this most likely rests on the assumed similarities in cognitive processes between M.B.A.s and "real" business people and dissimilarities in cognitive processes between humans and animals. This, in conjunction with the fact that the underlying optimization process implicit in most economic models involves rational forethought, would seem to make for significant differences in the likelihood of successful generalizability from laboratory to "real" world.

---

[2] Lea (1981) cites a paper by Lowe (1979) in which he details considerable differences between human and animal performance on some schedules of reinforcement in order to demonstrate that the generalizability of animal results to humans in these cases clearly breaks down. I object to Lowe's (1979) and Lea's (1981) conclusions on two grounds. First, some of the differences reported are open to interpretation; see Matthews et al.'s (1977) interpretation of performance on fixed interval schedules compared with Lowe's and our (Kagel and Battalio, 1980) interpretation of performance on ratio schedules compared with Lowe's. Second, I suspect that the principles of labor supply theory we have employed to interpret a number of performance characteristics under various schedules of reinforcement can explain the differences Lowe identifies between humans and animals, and it is certain that none of the differences identified contradict predictions of the labor supply model employed. As noted in the text, it is only when behavioral differences are codified in terms of a theoretical framework that we can determine whether any new behavioral principles are required to account for observed differences, and this is what we continue to look for.

Two aspects of cognition and behavior are of immediate relevance here. First, most economists are probably unaware of recent research on animal cognition that suggests the existence of parallel cognitive processes between humans and subhuman organisms. I briefly elaborate this research in this section. Second, and more important, it is not clear that conscious optimization has anything to do with the mechanism underlying human agents' economic performance or that economic agents have to optimize consciously in order to satisfy the predictive implications of economic theory. I deal with this issue in the next section.

Psychologists and biologists are now looking at animal cognition much more seriously than they have for several decades and finding evidence for similarities in cognitive processes across species, as a review of Donald Griffin's (1984) book, *Animal Thinking*, demonstrates:

He leaves the reader in no doubt that the minds of behavioral scientists have been unjustifiably closed to considerations of animal consciousness, even when a particular animal action would imply intention, knowledge, or thought if performed by a human being. For Griffin, the inescapable logic leading us to believe in the existence of other people's minds (opposed to the solipsist's argument that the only mind we can know to exist for sure is our own) extends to the minds of animals as well. Moreover, turning Ockam's razor against Lloyd Morgan's canon, he argues that attributing mentality to animals is a more economical way of accounting for their flexible and adaptive actions than postulating countless reflexive stimulus–response connections to explain the same phenomena. Finally, he suggests, the efficiency and economy of conscious thinking would favor its natural selection in cases where it is a conceivable option to a built-in or conditioned mechanism. He also questions the assumption that instincts are always exercised unconsciously. (Beer, 1984, p. 30)

In the same vein Anthony Wright and his associates have been studying the effects on memory recall of the serial position of an item in a list of items. The importance of serial position function in testing theories of human memory processing makes it a natural choice for testing animal memory. Wright et al. (1985) show that the shape of serial position functions obtained from pigeons, monkeys, and humans is affected in the same manner by the interval of time between the display of the last item in the list and the recall probe. These similarities in serial position function across species implicate similar memory mechanisms across species.

I am not arguing here that cognitive capacities of humans and rats or pigeons are the same, only that to the extent that one can derive observable analogs to cognitive performance across species, the evidence does not support a presumption of sudden discontinuities. Granted that pigeons and rats have more limited cognitive and information-processing capacities in a number of respects than humans, we pose choice situations that are simpler than, but qualitatively and theoretically similar to, those we would wish to employ, if we had the opportunity, for humans. The process here is not unlike some recent common-value auction experiments we have been conducting with human subjects in which we simplify the auction structure and information flows so that students without Ph.D.s in statistics and operations research can make contact with the environmental contingencies (Kagel and Levin, 1986). In both human and animal experiments the challenge is to employ a simplified environment that captures all the essential characteristics of the process in question but does not lie beyond the subject's capacity to "understand" in the time allotted to conduct the experiment.

Conscious optimization as description or as mechanism

. . . . it is possible to formulate our conditions of equilibrium as those of an extremum problem, even though it is admittedly not a case of an individual's behaving in a maximizing manner, just as it is often possible in classical dynamics to express the path of a particle as one which maximizes (minimizes) some quantity despite the fact that the particle is obviously not acting consciously or purposively. (Samuelson, 1947, p. 23)

The issue posed by Samuelson is whether conscious optimization – conscious previewing in the imagination (Lea, 1981) – is a descriptive device or the mechanism underlying economic choice processes, be they human or animal. The way we teach choice and demand theory, by an appeal to both introspection and reason, deeply ingrains in students of economics the belief that the economizing behavior of individuals is brought about through a process of conscious optimization. As Samuelson (1947) notes and as Armen Alchian (1950) so clearly demonstrated in the case of the theory of the firm, this need not be the case. Indeed, the abundant laboratory demonstrations that nonhumans typically have negatively sloped demand curves (Lea, 1978; Allison, 1979; Kagel et al., 1981) and behave "correctly" in response to Slutsky compensated price and wage changes (Kagel et al., 1975; Battalio, Green, and Kagel, 1981) must be taken as evidence either that animals can engage in conscious forethought or that this need not be the mechanism underlying economizing behavior. The receptiveness of the economics profession to these results (and they are now almost a staple of elementary and intermediate price theory textbooks) rests in large measure on the latter, and this is substantially more convincing evidence regarding the validity of the theory, to the uninitiated at least, than repeated appeals to conscious optimization.

Optimization accounts in animal psychology and biology: Animal psychologists and ecologists accept optimality accounts as explanations in terms of final causes, not as mechanisms actually guiding choice (Lea, 1981; Staddon and Hinson, 1983). The argument depends on natural selection. Individuals showing the best adaptation to their environment will leave a disproportionate number of descendants, so that optimal behavior (or the best available strategy) will tend to predominate. The evolutionary imperative for optimality provides only an ultimate cause of behavior. Within the life span of individual organisms one must look for proximate mechanisms to explain how the organism copes given its genetic endowment and the set of environment constraints it faces, and these mechanisms may vary across species. From this perspective the basis for both physiological and behavioral continuity across species rests on shared evolutionary histories. In the evolutionary process all species have had to solve similar constrained optimization problems, and common selection forces are likely to have favored similar solutions.

One finds objections to this argument when applied to humans on the following grounds. Although this shared response to evolutionary pressure is very clear when it is being applied to nonhuman species, where the maximand fitness is directly related to the evolutionary selective survival mechanism, it is less compelling when applied to modern human behavior, which in many parts of the world is largely free from evolutionary pressures (see, e.g., Ben-Portah, 1982). What this argument ignores, however, is the fact that modern humans have lived under surplus conditions for a relatively short period of time, from an evolutionary perspective, which is hardly sufficiently long for a new set of behavioral mechanisms to have evolved. One might argue along the same lines, as some have, that the laboratory rat, or laboratory pigeon, is not even a suitable experimental model for its wild brethren on the grounds that it is not subject to normal evolutionary pressures, being bred and maintained strictly for laboratory use. (In fact, its period of release from these pressures might well be longer, in terms of number of generations, than that of humans.) Nevertheless, a majority of experimental psychologists and biologists continue to use domesticated rats and pigeons in favor of wild pigeons and rats, precisely because behavioral processes where investigated have been shown to be qualitatively similar across wild and domesticated variants of the same species (see, e.g., Baum, 1974; Galef, 1977).

In this context Schwartz and Lacey (1982) offer the following interesting argument concerning the generalizability of behavioral principles developed on the basis of controlled laboratory experimentation (operant conditioning experiments of the sort we conduct). Schwartz and Lacey tend to agree with ethologists' criticism that principles of behavior developed on the basis of laboratory experiments are likely to be of limited use in understanding animal behavior in natural habitats, on the grounds that the artificiality of the experimental environment suppresses the Pavlovian (reflex-based) and genetically rooted influences on behavior that dominate in the natural habitat. Although this obviates the generality of results with laboratory animals for animals in their natural habitat, they argue that it does not do so for humans since it makes little sense to talk of the "natural" environment of human beings. Human environments change from generation to generation and in marked ways from age to age. Furthermore, unlike animals in their natural environments, we would expect the behavior of humans to be quite free of biological and Pavlovian influences. As such, contexts that may be artificial for animals may be quite "natural" for humans.

Schwartz and Lacey (1982) go on to argue that the human environment in which Pavlovian and genetically rooted influences is most suppressed is the modern industrialized economy with its emphasis on factory production and highly specialized, interdependent economic agents. In effect, it is this environment that can be most faithfully reproduced in the animal experimental chamber. As such, the behavioral principles developed in the laboratory are most likely to generalize to just such environments. Although I do not agree with all the particulars of the Schwartz and Lacey argument, I certainly find it an interesting one to consider.

6.2.2   Advantages of animal experiments: with answers to some often asked and unasked questions

The only way to answer some questions: The fundamental advantage of animal experimentation is that we can carry out experiments that at times cannot be done in any other way. The common complaint among economists, that economics is not an experimental discipline, is fast slipping by the wayside. However, there are some experiments that, literally, can be performed only with animals, because comparable manipulations with humans are simply not technically feasible and/or run up against clear ethical constraints. One example of this is the cycle of poverty experiments reported in Section 6.3.2. Irving Fisher (1907) conjectured that one element of persistent poverty is an inverse variation of the subjective rate of time discount with family income or wealth. The impact on savings rates and human capital investment helps perpetuate poverty. Disentangling time discount factors from the host of other factors potentially responsible for poverty cycles is a hopeless econometric task based on natural phenomena. Nor is it clear how, even ignoring costs for the moment, one might conduct a social experiment to test Fisher's conjecture. Designing an appropriate experiment with animals, however, is a relatively straightforward task.

Once we leave the realm of experiments that are impossible to perform with humans, there are a large number of economic issues that, practically speaking (costs vs. benefits), are most appropriately studied with animals. I have in mind here the study of individual choice behavior that has provided the focus for our research. Tests of predictions of the Slutsky–Hicks theory of consumer choice and labor supply using aggregate per capita time series and/or cross-sectional data drawn from national economic systems have serious shortcomings: (1) Predictions of the model break down when applied to aggregates or across individuals except with the most stringent aggregation requirements, which we have shown not to hold even for animal consumers (Battalio, Dwyer, and Kagel, 1987; Kagel, Battalio, and Green, 1987); (2) tests of the theories' predictions are conditional on the validity of the functional form of the estimating equations, which are typically subject to considerable controversy in their own right.[3] We have overcome these problems in our experiments with pigeons and rats by using individual subject data as the primary observation unit and using experimental manipulations instead of statistical estimation to control for confounding influences on behavior, thereby obviating the need to specify functional forms for estimating equations in testing the theory.

The clever idea of using household records of purchases (budget panel data) to study these issues (Koo, 1963; Koo and Hasenkamp, 1972) is flawed because of serious errors of observation underlying the budget accounts; this has important implications regarding the reliability of the test outcomes (see Battalio et al., 1973, for elaboration). Further confounds result from the inability to control such simple exogenous influences as weather variation on type and quantity of beverage consumption. The study of these issues by means of social experiments suffers from a similar inability to control exogenous changes in important economic variables. For example, the New Jersey negative income tax experiments were confounded by wide

---

[3] See Kagel and Battalio (1980) for further discussion of these issues.

swings in state welfare and aid to dependent children benefits, involving, at times, greater benefits (for some subjects) and at times worse benefits than in the experiment. In addition, the cost of social experiments is sufficiently high that limiting the research agenda to a couple of experiments per year would alone absorb virtually all of the federal government's funds for economic research.

The method of asking individual humans questions about choices over hypothetical outcomes, a common tactic in tests of expected utility theory and earlier tests of consumer choice theory (May, 1954), suffers from the problem that subjects' responses frequently do not match their behavior.[4] Although responses to these questions may be suggestive, it is almost impossible to identify on a priori grounds when responses to hypothetical choices will match responses to actual choices. Animal experiments have a potentially important role to play in identifying classes of choice problems in which actual behavior matches hypothetical responses via the construction of real choice situations analogous to the hypothetical situations of interest and actually observing behavior (see Section 6.3.3). Finally, commodity choice and labor supply experiments in which subjects make choices among a number of outcomes and are required to experience one, or a small subset, of their choices (McCrimmon and Toda, 1969, and references cited there) suffer from potentially trivial induced valuations on the experiments' outcomes. In our experiments with animals the technologies employed result in the commodities and/or jobs in the choice set being an integral part of the ongoing activities of subjects for reasonably long periods of time. This automatically induces nontrivial values on the outcomes of individual responses to the experimental contingencies, an important element in designing effective economic experiments (Siegel, 1961; Smith, 1976).

The downside of this criticism of alternative technologies is the difficulty of conducting direct experimental evaluations of the generalizability of behavior across species. Practically speaking, direct tests

---

[4] For instance, Ebbeson and Konecni (1975) could not predict the bail set by judges in a courtroom from their choices when faced with hypothetical bail-setting problems in the laboratory. Nisbett and Wilson (1977) found that verbal reports were often inconsistent with other measures of behavior, and Siegel (1961) found that the phenomena of probability matching, which is at odds with choosing on the basis of a first-degree stochastic dominance criteria, was highly dependent on the absence of financial payoffs. The literature is far from completely one-sided on this matter, however (Bem and Allen,1974; Grether and Plott, 1979), indicating the need for testing propositions with real payoffs wherever possible.

of generalizability are limited. The best tactic here would seem to involve tests of accessible predictive consequences of the theory or process in question using experimental technologies that resemble, as closely as possible, those employed with the animals (see, e.g., Matthews et al., 1977). An alternative strategy is to look for similarities and differences in results between econometric and animal investigations where appropriate (see Section 6.3.1). When results from the two methods of inquiry match qualitatively, there is heightened confidence in the results. When they differ, the question clearly calls for further investigation using both experimental and econometric procedures.

Why study what we already know? One of the key criticisms of animal experimentation in economics is that the "conclusions reflect phenomena which are already extremely well documented in wider (and more relevant) market environments" (Cross, 1980, p. 405). In investigating a particular area of economic behavior there are two basic reasons for our initially examining "well-documented" phenomena. The first as an exchange in the *American Economic Review* points out, is that, in some circles of respectable economic thought at least, the phenomena are much less well documented than Cross (1980) and others would have us believe:

Laboratory experiments [of market and small-group behavior] in economics have been structured around the assumption of fully determinate preference orderings, usually in the form of prespecified demand and supply value schedules. This assumption is basic to standard choice theory, but it is nevertheless a theoretically created rather than an empirically discovered feature. (Heiner, 1985, p. 263)

. . . the evidence for a bedrock assumption of economic theory – the existence of well-defined individual preferences – is not very compelling in nonexperimental market settings. (Friedman, 1985, p. 264)

In pursuing a particular line of inquiry, say commodity choice behavior, our results documenting "well-known" phenomena – for example, the "law of demand" for normal goods (Kagel et al., 1981) – provides a modest contribution to the reexamination of the roots of our discipline that we as experimentalists are engaged in (Smith, 1982a).

The second objective of establishing what we "already know," or think we know, is strictly practical. It provides a starting point for attacking issues for which there is far less professional consensus concerning our common knowledge.[5] Would it make any sense to

---

[5] One thing is certain: There will always be some economists who will claim that the observed behavior, no matter how poorly documented it is, is "well

identify experimental conditions promoting the existence of inferior goods and trying to establish the existence of Giffen goods (an enterprise we are currently engaged in) if we had not first found negatively sloped demand curves, with reasonably stable preferences, in the case of normal goods, especially when working with animal consumers? The answer is clearly no. Few members of our professional fraternity would take the results seriously, and virtually no one (including ourselves) would know how to interpret them.

Having established "well-known" principles of economic behavior with a particular species and a particular research protocol, one must take much more seriously the outcomes of similar experiments when directed to more contentious issues. The argument (raised by some of the conference participants) that we can use animal experiments to support principles of economic behavior but not to cast doubt on them is simply scientifically untenable. I agree that finding, for example, that presumably dumb animals consistently reduce labor supply and consumption in response to compensated wage increases buttresses our faith in this principle of static labor supply theory, and suggests its prevalence under much more general conditions than most economists had imagined (for the results of these experiments see Battalio et al., 1981; Battalio and Kagel, 1985). I also agree with critics that findings on more contentious issues with animals – for example, results relating dynamic responses to unearned income and the existence and importance of a "welfare trap" (see Section 6.3.1) – do not necessarily imply that the same results will be found with humans. However, the burden is on those who would continue to support a hypothesis that the animal experiments falsified to provide data of comparable quality in support of their position or to cite weaknesses in the experimental design that we know, from empirically validated theory, to obviate the results as they apply to the human condition.

documented." There are two reasons for this. First, it is reasonably well established that individual recall of subjective probabilities of uncertain events shifts systematically in favor of ex post observed outcomes. This is the old Monday morning quarterback problem (Fischoff, 1975). Second, for an alarming number of economists, theoretical demonstration eliminates the need for observation (recall the comments of our friendly critic in footnote 1). To borrow Vernon Smith's (1982a) terminology for these economists, knowledge of what we have created (theory as hypothesis) is indistinguishable from what we have discovered (hypothesis that, to date, is or is not falsified by observation).

Using animal experiments to test competing explanatory paradigms

What the empirical data do confirm is that demand curves generally have negative slopes. . . . But negatively sloping demand curves could result from a wide range of behaviors. (Simon, 1979, p. 496)

This quotation from Herbert Simon's Nobel lecture points out that mainstream economic theory provides only one of several possible theoretical explanations for commonly accepted empirical laws of economic behavior. Not surprisingly, psychologists and biologists, and some particularly free thinking (or quixotic) economists, have alternative theoretical explanations for these empirical laws of behavior. As Cross (1980) correctly noted in his commentary on our earlier article (Kagel and Battalio, 1980), although psychological models typically have something to say about human and animal behavior, the explanation rarely matches that of mainstream neoclassical economic theory, and these models can also explain "commonly observed" empirical regularities. (The latter is an elementary survival property of most extant theories.) Experiments whose outcomes reflect "well-documented" phenomena rarely distinguish the process underlying the phenomena.

Animal experiments have an important role to play in sorting out competing explanations of "well-established" principles of economic behavior. First, they provide readily available observations of individual subject behavior, often the necessary unit of observation required to distinguish among explanations. Second, they provide a readily available laboratory for conducting the manipulations essential to the sorting out process. For example, a demonstration of the existence of Giffen goods would rule out a number of competing explanations of consumer choice behavior offered both from within economics (e.g., Heiner, 1983, vs. standard Slutsky–Hicks) and from without. Nevertheless, there are a number of cogent reasons one would not expect, using market data, to observe the positively sloped portion of the demand curve for a Giffen good, should one actually exist (Dwyer and Lindsay, 1984). Since these factors are readily overcome in the laboratory, with its capacity to enforce completely elastic supply curves and the "small-country" conditions required to observe Giffen goods, it would seem that this is the only place where reliable sightings are likely to be obtained. Until they are, we must be prepared to accept a number of alternative explanations of the processes underlying negatively sloped demand curves.

A considerable amount of our recent research efforts have been devoted to contesting alternative explanations of the processes underlying animals' behavior. With respect to commodity choice and labor supply behavior, we have investigated random-behavior models, the matching law (the leading quantitative choice model employed by animal psychologists), and psychological and biological models based on minimizing the distance to a "bliss point" in the choice space (Rachlin, Kagel, Battalio, 1980; Green, Kagel, Battalio, 1982; Kagel, Dwyer, and Battalio, 1987; Kagel, Battalio, and Green, 1985). The most interesting battles have been with psychologists contesting matching-based explanations with economic explanations based on commodity choice and labor supply behavior (Prelec, 1982; Kagel, Battalio, and Green, 1983; Rachlin, 1983). It is beyond the scope of this chapter to review these arguments here. What we can say with some confidence is that the static commodity choice and labor supply models have held up quite credibly in these arguments, identifying a number of anomalous behaviors that the matching adherents have yet to come to grips with (Kagel et al., 1983; Rachlin, 1983). The debate has led matchers to perform new kinds of experiments whose results one can explain only by resorting to dynamic choice concepts that fully account for animals' tendency to discount delayed rewards (Vaughan, 1981; Silberberg and Ziriax, 1985) and/or search behavior under uncertainty.

What we have not been able to do in these debates is to provide a once and for all test of optimizing versus nonoptimizing accounts of behavior. I doubt that such tests exist. What we can do is test particular optimizing versus nonoptimizing accounts. In this way we gain insight into the processes underlying the choice regularities observed.

If you see it in an animal, it must be real: To the extent that we establish empirical laws of economic behavior with animals, irrespective of how well documented they are elsewhere or how contentious the explanation of the process generating the behavior, the results suggest the basic nature of the behavior. For one thing, the results cannot be attributed to a particular element in the animals' upbringing, or if they are, these elements are readily manipulated to determine their relevance. For another thing, they cannot be attributed to the particular political, economic, and cultural context in which the animals grew up or operate. (This is not to argue that the political, economic, and cultural context in which behavior takes place is irrelevant to the promotion of one type of behavioral outcome or another.) Finally, the results cannot be attributed to the animals not being adequately motivated or "playing games" with the experimenter, for these variables are readily controlled as well. This provides the ultimate scientific and personal satisfaction in searching for, and confirming, a particular economic proposition with animals.

6.3   Some recent and ongoing experimental results

In the Introduction I argued that animal experiments have a potentially important role to play in sorting out competing hypotheses all of which are sustainable or have been maintained within mainstream economics. In Section 6.3.2 I argued that one practical reason for establishing what economists "already know," or think they know, is to provide a starting point for attacking issues for which there is less professional consensus concerning our common knowledge. In this section I summarize some of our current research that is related to this topic. The point here is not to astound the reader with a dazzling series of counterintuitive (countermainstream) results (see footnote 5). Rather, I argue that our results shed light on contentious issues in economics, some of which have potentially important public policy implications. In the process of reporting them I elaborate some of the methodological issues raised in Section 6.3.

6.3.1   Dynamic responses to guaranteed-income programs: the welfare trap hypothesis

The research hypothesis: The standard static utility representation of labor supply predicts that the introduction of a welfare program (e.g., a negative income tax program) will have a disincentive effect on the labor supply of those eligible to receive benefits from the program. Although there is little dispute among economists regarding these short-run disincentive effects, there has been considerable interest in the longer-run dynamic responses to such programs. Two distinctly different points of view are expressed in the literature. On the one hand, Conlisk (1986) conjectures (or can imagine) a world in which delivery of unearned income, since it tends to increase total consumption, may, contrary to the static model, enhance labor supply in the long run as the unearned income generates a taste for increased consumption ("getting hooked" on income). On the other hand, some have expressed concern that the income transfers inherent in welfare programs will result in taste changes in the opposite direction ("getting hooked" on leisure?), creating even greater dependency and contributing to poverty cycles.[6] This is sometimes referred to as the "welfare trap hypothesis" (see, e.g., Plant, 1984).

In the context of an experimental analysis of labor supply behavior, the question of dynamic responses to unearned income reduces to a question of the repeat reliability of the labor supply data. After periods involving the delivery of high levels of unearned income, do we observe systematic deviations in the replication of labor supply behavior at lower levels of unearned income? What is the relative magnitude and direction of any deviations observed, and what are the forces underlying them?

Experimental procedures: We have studied the labor supply of animal workers using what psychologists refer to as a ratio schedule of reinforcement. Under ratio schedules of reinforcement, one induces value on a job task by making performance of the task a prerequisite of obtaining access to preferred activities. Commonly used job tasks consist of key pecking and treadle running for pigeons, lever pressing and wheel running for rats. Preferred activities typically consist of eating or drinking for food- or water-deprived animals, although a substantially wider variety of reinforcers have been used.

Under a ratio schedule of reinforcement the job task must be performed a prescribed number of times β, on average, to obtain a prescribed amount α of the preferred commodity. This experimentally induced constraint on behavior can be written as

$$x_c = wx_h; \qquad w = \alpha/\beta \tag{6.1}$$

where x_h is the total number of times the job task is performed and x_c the total consumption of the preferred commodity. Equation (6.1) characterizes job-related earnings under a piecework pay schedule in a barter economy, where w is the real wage rate, x_h the total number of pieces produced, and x_c the total consumption derived from working.

Our experimental studies of labor supply behavior have employed two different sets of procedures – which we refer to as closed- and

---

[6] Some will object to the use of the term "taste change" here, preferring to model any shifts in consumption patterns in terms of changes in the production technology for transforming physical inputs into outputs (Stigler and Becker, 1977) or other endogenous change processes (e.g., Phlips, 1974). I do not know how to distinguish observationally between taste changes and these alternative formulations. Furthermore, the distinction seems irrelevant to the issue at hand, namely the direction and magnitude of shifts in consumption–leisure choices following the delivery of unearned income.

open-economy conditions – each with its own method of delivering unearned consumption. Under closed-economy conditions, rats have two levers on which to respond, one that delivers food pellets and one that delivers fluid, after the rats have made the required number of responses. Under closed-economy conditions all consumption of food and fluid is obtained as a consequence of within-session labor supply. Experimental sessions last for an extended period of time (typically 20 to 24 hours), and there are no supplemental sources of food or fluid. As a consequence, body weight varies with labor supply and changes in wage rates and levels of earned consumption, and within-session earnings and labor supply are essential to the organism's well-being and survival. "Leisure-time" activities consist essentially of lying about, sleeping, and self-care activities; the rats were confined to their experimental quarter and had no programmed leisure-time activities.

Under these closed-economy procedures, unearned consumption was delivered at the beginning of an experimental session, during which time a single response was required for the delivery of food or liquid and the rat was free to decide how to allocate these responses. The total number of these responses was limited and fixed in advance. Although technically speaking consumption obtained here is not free since the animal must still respond to receive it, the response requirements were so low relative to the requirements at all other times (these were never less than 20 responses for the same amount of food and liquid) that earnings here effectively constitute free consumption. Once the free consumption was used up, the animal was free to respond, as much as it chose to, under the prevailing piecework wage rate.

Under open-economy conditions pigeons were placed in an experimental chamber for a 40-minute work period, during which time they were required to peck a response key for access to food rewards.[7] Value was induced on the job task through an extended deprivation period (typically 22 to 23 hours long), during which the pigeons were housed in their home chambers with no access to food but were provided with ad lib access to water. In addition, the subjects were maintained at a constant body weight (typically 80% ± a few grams). This was achieved through a regime of postexperimental feeding so that if, for example, an animal's earnings during an experimental session dropped to zero, it would receive larger than normal postsession rations, and if earnings exceeded the 80% maintenance level, the supplemental ration was reduced or eliminated. Although these sup-

---

[7] Consumption time did not count against total session time in these experiments, because the session control clock stopped during consumption.

plemental feedings were sufficiently delayed and irregular to maintain
a high induced valuation on the work activity within the experimental
session, they did permit the animal to compensate for reduced within-
session consumption by increased postsession consumption and vice
versa, an intertemporal substitutability of consumption and leisure not
possible under closed-economy conditions. As in the closed-economy
experiments there were no programmed leisure-time activities within
the work chamber. Under these open-economy conditions, we delivered a limited amount of unearned consumption periodically throughout an experimental session by simply providing the animal with access
to the food hopper for a brief fixed period of time.

Under both open- and closed-economy conditions a given set of
experimental conditions (wages and level of unearned income) were
maintained for a number of days and changed only when a predeter-
mined stability criterion in terms of responses and/or weight changes
had been satisfied. In all cases data analysis consisted of averages
computed over days satisfying these stability requirements. As such
our analysis of dynamic responses to unearned consumption are
applicable to dynamic adjustment models involving convergent adjustment processes (see, e.g., Conlisk, 1968). In other words, we are
talking not about short-run adjustment effects here, but about reasonably long lived effects.

Experimental results: The data reported in this section were obtained
as a byproduct of a series of compensated wage change experiments
and studies aimed at determining the effects of unearned consumption
on labor supply. The compensated wage change studies confirmed the
comparative–static predictions of the static utility model of labor
supply: Both pigeons and rats responded to Slutsky compensated wage
decreases by reducing labor supply and consumption under a variety of
wage rates and compensation procedures (Battalio et al., 1981; Battalio
and Kagel, 1985; Kagel, Battalio, and Green, 1987). Furthermore,
delivery of unearned consumption, holding real wage rates constant,
reliably resulted in reduced labor supply and increased total consumption, again under a variety of wage rates, supporting the assumption
that both consumption and leisure are normal goods under these
experimental conditions (Battalio et al., 1981; Battalio and Kagel, 1985;
Kagel Battalio, and Green, 1987).

The data in Table 6.1 are related to the issue of the long-run stability
of preferences after the delivery of unearned consumption. Each block
of data refers to a sequence of experimental conditions. Within each
sequence, wage rates for earned consumption were held constant while

Table 6.1. *Replicability of labor supply after the delivery of unearned consumption*

Maximum unearned consumption[a,b] (wage index)	Level of unearned consumption at replication point[a]	Labor supply[c]		
		Initial (1)	Replication (2)	Difference (1 − 2)
Pigeon 47				
166	0	4,963	4,941	22
(100)	50	2,205	2,100	105
	75	2,312	1,555	757
	100	1,360	1,065	295
100	0	3,274	3,046	228
(25)				
Pigeon 48				
261	0	6,356	5,650	706
(50)	39	4,069	4,590	−521
133	0	5,755	5,425	330
(200)				
Pigeon 49				
100	0	6,194	6,435	−151
(100)	40	2,895	2,740	155
50	0	5,376	5,520	−144
(25)				
Pigeon 50				
313	0	5,306	5,034	272
(50)	70	3,760	3,650	110
161	0	4,847	4,780	67
(200)				
Rat 921				
103	0	23,898	18,822	5,076
(100)				
37	0	45,347	47,289	−1,942
(44.4)				
Rat 922				
115	0	23,898	18,822	5,076
(100)				

[a] As a percentage of baseline earnings.
[b] Numbers in parentheses represent prevailing wage rate.
[c] Number of key pecks for pigeons, lever presses for rats.
Source: Kagel, Battalio, and Green (1987).

levels of unearned consumption were varied, starting from zero unearned consumption and increasing to some maximum value and returning to zero unearned consumption, with occasional replication points in between. Thus the only economic variable changing between replication points in a sequence was the level of unearned consumption.

The first column of the table reports the maximum amount of unearned consumption in the sequence (expressed as a percentage of earned consumption obtained under the initial zero unearned consumption condition at this wage). The prevailing wage rate for earned consumption in the sequence is reported in parentheses in the first column as well. (The wage rate is expressed as an index and is useful for comparing relative wages between sequences.) The second column of the table shows the level of unearned consumption in force at each replication point. This, too, is measured as a percentage of earned consumption obtained under the initial zero unearned consumption condition. The next two columns show the level of labor supplied (key pecks for pigeons, lever presses for rats) under the initial set of experimental conditions and upon replication after periods with delivery of substantially more unearned consumption (see first column). The last column of the table shows the difference between these two levels of labor supplied. A positive number here means that less labor was supplied upon replication (consistent with the welfare trap hypothesis); a negative number indicates that more labor was supplied (consistent with Conlisk's hypothesis).

The first sequence in the table reports four replication points for bird 47, under wage rate index 100, where the maximum level of unearned consumption in the sequence was 166% of earned consumption under the initial, zero unearned consumption condition. At all four replication points labor supply was greater initially, before the 166% unearned consumption condition, than following it. The second sequence for bird 47 contains a single replication point and was conducted under substantially lower real wages (wage index, 25). Here, too, labor supply was greater before delivery of unearned consumption than upon replication.

The pattern reported for bird 47 tends to be repeated across subjects. Thirteen of 17 replication points show reduced labor supply following the delivery of a high level of unearned income. As indicated by a binomial sign test, there would be less than a 2.5% chance of this happening if there were no systematic effect (under the null hypothesis that it is equally likely that replication values will show more or less labor supply than originally). The quantitative effect is small, however.

Replication points under conditions of zero free consumption indicate that reductions in labor supply average 4.8% of baseline labor supply and 3.2% for the pigeon experiments, where we have the most observations. The relatively small quantitative shifts in work levels associated with the receipt of unearned consumption in previous periods parallels findings from the U.S. economy; John Plant reports "a small welfare trap leading to more persistence (on welfare) than would otherwise be predicted [due to shifts in income earning opportunities]" (Plant 1984, pp. 679–80).

That our results tend to support a welfare trap hypothesis may well be due to the high income elasticity of demand for leisure, as opposed to consumption, found in response to the delivery of unearned income in these experiments (reviewed in Kagel, Battalio, and Green, 1987). The different income elasticities imply that increases in unearned consumption induce proportionately greater reductions in labor supply than increases in consumption. "Getting hooked" on leisure or consumption as a consequence of past choices may well be a function of the relative impact of unearned consumption on these two competing outcomes. As such it would be of considerable interest to test for comparable preference shifts under conditions in which unearned consumption or other economic forces produce proportionately greater increases in consumption than leisure. To the extent that we find comparable shifts in favor of "getting hooked" on consumption under these conditions, as Conlisk suggests, we will have identified relevant initial conditions for eliciting a welfare trap versus an earnings boost effect. Under any circumstances our results tend to validate the hypothesis that the primary force underlying the repeated presence of people on the welfare roles is an absence of income-earning opportunities relative to the welfare alternative rather than any nefarious shift in preferences, as underlies the welfare trap hypothesis.[8] In this case our results agree with the limited econometric evidence available.

[8] In an alternative version of the hypothesis, the welfare trap would result from the effects of welfare on recipients' human capital; presumably it deteriorates as a consequence of unemployment rather than shifts in preferences. These two effects are difficult to disentangle observationally, of course. Furthermore, to the extent that one can document that a welfare trap results from a deterioration of human capital stock, as compared with a shift in preferences, the public policy responses are quite different. We interpret our data as reflecting solely preference shift effects since the "pigeon capital" involved in learning how to key-peck is minimal or nonexistent.

6.3.2   *Temporal choice behavior: the cycle of poverty hypothesis*

The research hypothesis: It has been a well-established principle of animal behavior for some time that animals act as if they discount future benefits, sometimes at alarmingly high discount rates (for reviews, see Kagel and Green, 1986; Kagel et al., 1986).[9] In the economics literature there has been some concern with whether time discount rates vary inversely with the level of income or wealth, because this might have an important role in the perpetuation of poverty cycles. An early statement of the cycle of poverty issue is found in Irving Fisher (1907, quoted in Maital and Maital, 1977, p. 184):

The effect will be that . . . an inequality in the distribution of capital is gradually effected, and this inequality, once achieved, tends to perpetuate itself. The poorer a man grows, the keener his appreciation of present goods is likely to become.

Or more succinctly: "The smaller the income, the higher is the preference for present, over future income" (p. 185).

In dealing with the cycle of poverty hypothesis we cannot hope to recreate the full set of cultural and socioeconomic conditions that characterize poverty in different national economic systems. Rather what we aim to do is focus exclusively on the income and wealth effects of poverty by generating differences among subjects in this respect in the laboratory and determining the effects of this treatment variable on subjective rates of time discounting. If we can support Fisher's conjecture under these conditions we have direct evidence favoring income- and wealth-induced effects on preferences for present over future consumption, which to us, at least, is at the heart of Fisher's hypothesis. If we find no differences in wealth-induced effects on animals' discount rates, the data suggest that we look to other elements of the socioeconomic conditions commonly associated with poverty, such as discrimination and poor schooling, to explain the presence of poverty cycles within national economies. Distinguishing between these potential sources of poverty is essential to the design of public policy interventions, since a valid diagnosis of the source of the problem is essential for designing effective policy instruments to alleviate it.

[9] The economics literature on time discounting is quite contentious. Some even argue against the existence of a positive rate of time discounting (Stigler and Becker, 1977). Contrast the approach of Olson and Bailey (1981) with those of Thaler and Shefrin (1981) and Encarnación (1983).

Table 6.2. *Cycle of poverty experiments: experimental conditions*

Experimental condition	Small immediate alternative (SI)		Larger delayed alternative (LD)	
	Time delay[a] (sec)	Cups of saccharin[b] (0.05 cm³)	Time delay[a] (sec)	Cups of saccharin[b] (0.05 cm³)
A	6	1	10	3
B	2	1	6	3
C	1	2	20	3

[a] Time delays measured from point of response on lever. Note that time delays between choice trials are constant irrespective of alternative chosen.
[b] Reinforcement consists of a 1% sodium saccharin solution.

Experimental procedures[10]: In operationalizing the cycle of poverty issue, we employed a discrete trials choice procedure in which subjects chose between a smaller, more immediate reward (SI) and a larger, more delayed reward (LD). In all cases rats chose between a single pair of alternatives (shown in Table 6.2). For example, under treatment condition A the rats chose between a small immediate outcome (SI) involving a 6-second delay and one cup of saccharin and a larger delayed alternative involving a 10-second delay and three cups of saccharin. Choices were recorded and payoffs delivered in response to a single press on one of two choice levers. The time delays between choice opportunities were constant irrespective of the alternative chosen, so that choosing the SI outcome lever did not move up the start of the next choice trial.

We used different degrees of deprivation to operationalize the difference between high- and low-income wealth conditions. Two groups of four rats each were used. The low-income (high-deprivation) group received a total of 7 cm³ of liquid per day; the high-income (low-deprivation) group received a total of 28 cm³ of liquid per day. This was sufficient to ensure substantial weight differences between groups, the low-income group averaging 244 grams and the high-income group averaging 542 grams. Note that the low-income group, though substantially below full body weight, was healthy, routinely passing inspection by an animal care committee.

[10] These experiments are being conducted in our laboratory at Texas A&M University in collaboration with Ray Battalio and Len Green.

Choice conditions were such that, if the rats allocated all of their free-choice trials to the LD alternative, they would receive 5 cm³ of liquid within the experimental session. Additional liquid consumption was made up by measured amounts of *water* hung in the animals' home cage, available for consumption approximately one-half hour after the choice session had ended. In addition to the use of different liquids, the time discount rates induced a clear separation between within-experiment and postexperimental liquid intake; that is, the rats routinely responded to all choice trials as they become available. In using a 1% sodium saccharin solution as the reinforcer in experimental sessions, we employed a highly preferred reinforcer to offset potential negative feedback effects of satiation under high-consumption conditions.

Each experimental session began with 8 forced-choice trials followed by 28 free-choice trials. The forced-choice trials familiarized the subjects with the alternatives. During these trials only one of the choice levers was available. Sequences of forced choices across levers were fixed. However, the start point was determined randomly on a daily basis. During free-choice trials, the subjects could choose the lever on which to respond.

Choice alternatives remained the same for a minimum of 17 days and until choice frequencies satisfied a stability criterion. Under each experimental condition the LD and SI alternatives were switched between levers to control for potential lever bias. Choice frequencies were measured and reported in terms of average frequency of choice for the LD alternative measured over the least five days of a condition and averaged across side switches.

In terms of these choice measures Fisher's hypothesis implies that the high-income (low-deprivation) subjects will choose the LD alternative relatively more frequently than the low-income subjects. In measuring choices in this way we are assuming that lever bias, to the extent that it exists, is not systematically affected by deprivation levels. We also use choice frequencies to measure preferences. When the choice frequency for an alternative exceeds .5 by more than the day-to-day variability in the data, we interpret this as preference for the alternative in question. (This will generally hold at choice frequencies of .55 to .60 or better.) In measuring preferences in this way we are assuming that lever bias, to the extent that it exists, is an additively separable argument of the rat's utility function.

Experimental results: Table 6.3 shows choice frequencies for the LD alternative for both groups of rats in terms of the treatment conditions

Table 6.3. *Percentage of choice involving larger delayed alternatives*

	Low-income rats				High-income rats		
Subject	A	B	C	Subject	A	B	C
404	75	82	3 [2]	414	84	96	25 [15]
405	89	98	1 [24]	415	63	74	18 [16]
406	95	93	1 [44]	416	55	—	12 [10]
407	95	94	3 [45]	417	72	71	7 [49]
Average	87	92	2 [29]	Average	68	80	16 [23]

Note: Values in brackets are replication points.
Source: Kagel, Battalio, and Green (1987).

specified in Table 6.2. Bracketed values in Table 6.3 show replication points – a repeated application of the same set of experimental conditions several periods later. Choice frequencies of around .5 are characterized by virtually no response to the switching of the LD and SI alternatives across levers (as opposed to a 50% choice of LD on both levers) and are interpreted as indifference between the prospects on the animal's part. For example, rat 406 (in the low-income group) chose the LD alternative almost exclusively under treatment condition A (chose the 10-second delay/three-cup payoff 95% of the time, on average, over the 6-second delay/one-cup payoff). However, under treatment condition C the same rat chose the LD alternative (a 20-second delay/three-cup payoff) only 1% of the time compared with the SI alternative (a 1-second delay/two-cup payoff) and continued to choose the SI alternative relatively more frequently (albeit at a substantially reduced frequency) upon replication.

The results in Table 6.3 provide no support for Fisher's cycle of poverty hypothesis. If anything they support the *converse* of Fisher's hypothesis, because under experimental treatment conditions A and B the low-income group chose the LD alternative more often than did the high-income group. (Mean group differences under treatment condition A are statistically significant at the conventional 5% level.) Only under treatment condition C, in which rats preferred the SI alternative, did the high-income rats choose the LD alternative relatively more frequently. However, this result did not stand up under replication.

There are two additional points worth noting with respect to the results reported in Table 6.3. First, if the rats have a positive rate of time discounting and are in touch with the contingencies, in going from treatment condition A or B to C we should find a reduced choice of the LD alternative. This follows directly from the reduced spread between payoffs and the increased spread in the time delay between the LD and SI alternatives under treatment condition C as compared with A or B. The shift in choice frequencies were quite dramatic for both groups of rats.

Second, going from treatment condition A to B, we subtracted a constant time delay from both alternatives. Previous experiments with pigeons choosing among food reinforcements had suggested that this would result in the rats' preferences shifting in favor of the SI alternative. That is, we would observe temporally inconsistent choices (Strotz, 1956; Green, 1982; Kagel and Green; 1986). Note that for both groups of rats this did not happen; in fact, the rats' choice frequencies moved in the wrong direction relative to the temporal inconsistency hypothesis since they chose the LD alternative relatively more frequently under treatment condition B than under condition A. (These differences are not statistically significant, however.) Further manipulations designed to induce temporal inconsistencies, involving the addition of substantially larger constant time delays to both alternatives produced similar results: no preference reversals. This is quite surprising, given the robustness of the pigeon results, and is essential to follow up in terms of understanding temporal discounting processes in animals.

Further research on these issues will employ food reinforcers. The research issues of interest are the following:

1. Will we continue to obtain evidence favoring the *converse* of Fisher's cycle of poverty hypothesis using food payoffs instead of liquid, or will subjects' behavior now conform to the cycle of poverty hypothesis as scattered earlier research reports suggest (Snyderman, 1987; Eisenberger and Masterson, 1987)? Similar results with food-stuffs would suggest that income and wealth effects per se are not the primary factors underlying poverty cycles, but rather that other cultural and environmental forces associated with poverty, such as discrimination and educational opportunities, are at fault. If, however, choices over food payoffs generally conform to the cycle of poverty hypothesis, given that the converse of the hypothesis tends to hold with liquid payoffs, Fisher's wealth effect hypothesis might be correct outside the laboratory, but its validity is conditional on the commodities in the choice set. As such there is little chance, using animal experiments, to narrow down the circumstances within national economies in which the predictions of the hypothesis are likely to hold,

although we can reject Fisher's cycle of poverty hypothesis as a general economic phenomenon. However, this last result is still of inherent scientific interest.

2. Can we induce temporally inconsistent preferences in rats? Failure to induce temporally inconsistent choices with either food or liquid payoffs would require a fundamental reconsideration of the appropriate economic model to characterize intertemporal choice here, as well as the generality of the intertemporal inconsistencies identified in earlier pigeon experiments and the "self-control" literature developed on the basis of these pigeon experiments (for a review see Green, 1982; for some implications with a greater economic slant see Elster, 1979; Thaler and Shefrin, 1981).

6.3.3   Risky choice: Allais-type violations of the independence axiom

The research hypothesis: We have completed a series of experiments dealing with animals' choices among uncertain outcomes (Battalio et al., 1985). One question we posed was whether we could induce violations of the independence axiom of expected utility theory by mimicking conditions that resulted in systematic and replicable violations with human subjects choosing among hypothetical outcomes. Although systematic violations of the independence axiom have been reported for some time in the literature, starting with Allais (1953), virtually all reported violations have employed hypothetical choice alternatives. One of the last lines of defense of expected utility theory, as a descriptive theory of behavior, in the face of these violations is that they have involved choices among hypothetical as opposed to actual outcomes, and choices are likely to differ when subjects have to deal with the consequences of their behavior and have some experience with the outcomes (Machina, 1983a). With animals we were able to address these issues directly.

In conducting our experiments we took as our starting point the supposition that in choosing between prospects with discriminable outcomes, one of which dominates the other according to a first-degree stochastic dominance criteria, rats prefer the dominant alternative. This is a relatively robust result found in numerous experiments with different species of animals (Sutherland and Mackintosh, 1971).[11]

[11] The data here refer primarily to experiments in which animals chose between two alternatives that were identical with respect to quantity and quality of reinforcement but that differed with respect to probability of

Furthermore, before conducting our tests of the independence axiom, we found it necessary to examine what, in some circles at least, might be considered "well-established" principles of economic behavior, namely risk aversion and transitivity of choices among prospects with equal expected values, which differ by mean preserving spreads. There were several reasons for doing this. First, although there has been relatively little systematic work on choice under uncertainty aside from first-degree stochastic dominance issues and some recent work by Tom Caraco and his associates (reviewed in Caraco and Lima, in press), it is becoming increasingly clear that, given sufficient variance over outcomes for an uncertain prospect, animals do prefer a certain prospect with equal expected value to an uncertain alternative, at least when they have positive net energy balances. We wanted to calibrate our procedures and results relative to these outcomes.[12] Second, if transitivity were to break down in this setting (which it did not), it would be an important result to have obtained in interpreting the outcomes of the tests of the independence axiom. Third, since proto-cols generating violations of the independence axiom depend critically on the establishment of initial conditions in which subjects are risk averse in the sense of choosing a certain prospect in favor of an uncertain prospect with a higher expected value (see the $\lambda = 1.0$ condition in Table 6.4), we needed the information from the first series of experiments to establish the parameter values for the independence axiom tests.

Experimental procedures: A discrete trials choice procedure, similar to the one used in the cycle of poverty experiments reported in Section 6.3.2, was employed. In all cases rats chose between a single pair of prospects at a time. The prospects employed in the common ratio effect experiments are shown in Table 6.4. For example, under treatment condition 1 the rats chose between a certain 8 pellets (prospect A)

reinforcement. Failure to maximize in these experiments occurs only when a correction or guidance procedure is used so that, if subjects' first choice on a trial is not reinforced on that trial, it then receives reinforcement on the other alternative (Sutherland and Mackintosh, 1971). The data from these experiments clearly support a maximizing, as opposed to a probability-matching (Luce and Suppes, 1965), formulation, which is still adhered to in some quarters.

[12] This is not to say that we were not prepared to dispute these results, just that with respect to this question we had a basis for comparing our results with others and, if they differed, would have looked for a more suitable arena in which to determine the basis for these differences.

Table 6.4. *Tests of the common ratio effect: treatment conditions employed*

Condition	Prospects[a]			λ
1	A: 8 pellets, $p = 1.0$	or	B: 13 pellets, $p = \frac{3}{4}$ 1 pellet, $p = \frac{1}{4}$	1.0
	(8.0)		(10.0)	
2	C: 8 pellets, $p = \frac{1}{2}$ 1 pellet, $p = \frac{1}{2}$	or	D: 13 pellets, $p = \frac{3}{8}$ 1 pellet, $p = \frac{5}{8}$	$\frac{1}{2}$
	(4.5)		(5.5)	
3	E: 8 pellets, $p = \frac{1}{3}$ 1 pellet, $p = \frac{2}{3}$	or	F: 13 pellets, $p = \frac{1}{4}$ 1 pellet, $p = \frac{3}{4}$	$\frac{1}{3}$
	(3.33)		(4.0)	

[a] Expected values are in parentheses.
Source: Battalio, Kagel, and MacDonald (1985).

versus 13 pellets with payoff probability .75 and 1 pellet with payoff
probability .25. Note that the probabilities of the 8-pellet payoffs in
prospects C and E involve multiplying the probability in prospect A by
.50 and .33, respectively; those of the 13-pellet payoff in prospects D
and F involve multiplying the probability of that outcome in prospect
B by .50 and .33 as well. In both cases the 1-pellet payoff "soaks up"
the displaced probabilities. The term "common ratio" derives from the
equality of $p(8)/p(13)$ in A versus B, C versus D, and E versus F. An
expected utility maximizer must prefer either A, C, and E (if
$\lambda(1.0)[U(8) - U(1)] > \lambda(.75)[U(13) - U(1)]$) or else B, D, and F (if the
opposite were true). We refer to experimental conditions by the value
of λ associated with the different treatment conditions in Table 6.4.
Also shown under each prospect is the expected value, or actuarial
value, of the outcomes. Note that the expected value of each outcome
drops rather drastically as λ decreases.

Choices were recorded and payoffs delivered in response to a single
press on one of the two choice levers. Each experimental session began
with 16 forced-choice trials followed by 20 free-choice trials. Trials
were separated by a constant time interval of approximately one
minute irrespective of the choice made, the outcome obtained, or the
prospects under consideration.

The forced-choice trials familiarized the subjects with the alternatives. During these trials only one of the choice levers was available.
Furthermore, the empirical distribution function was forced to match
the programmed distribution function over each prospects trial set: The
random-number generator was constrained so that the average actual
outcome equaled the expected outcome across the forced-choice trial

set. Sequences of choices across levers and outcomes were fixed; however, the start point was determined randomly on a daily basis.

The free-choice trials measured preferences. During these trials, subjects could choose which level to respond on. For example, in condition 1, animals choosing between prospects A and B could devote all 20 of their free-choice trials to A, all 20 to B, or pick any combination (and sequence) of A and B outcomes they preferred, subject to the constraint of 20 choices. The empirical distribution function was *not* constrained to match the programmed distribution function here; the random-number-generating algorithm was allowed free reign, and the possibility of obtaining a given outcome on any trial was independent of outcomes on other trials.

Rats had no access to food between experimental sessions, had a water tube available in the experimental chamber, and were provided with ad lib access to water in their holding cages. Expected pellet payoffs were sufficient to insure the rat's health but well below satiation levels. In all cases, the rats would have readily accepted more choice trials (see Battalio et al., 1985, experiment 2).

Experimental sessions were conducted once per day, 7 days per week at approximately the same time on each day. Rats chose between the same pair of prospects, with prospects fixed behind the same lever, for a minimum of 15 and a maximum of 24 days. Within this constraint conditions were changed when visual inspection of the data indicated no trend in choices over a consecutive 5-day period. Conditions were commonly changed within 18 days.

Preference measures consist of the average proportion of choices of the less risky alternative over the last five days of an experimental condition. To control for lever bias, which can at times be severe for rats, we measured choice with prospects first on one lever (e.g., prospect A on the left lever, B on the right) and then switched prospects across the levers (B on the left, A on the right) and averaged the data for the last five days under each condition. This amounted to assuming that the utility function is additively separable with respect to position bias and risk preferences.

Experimental results: Table 6.5 shows the mean frequencies with which the lower expected value prospects (A, C, and E) were chosen at the various values of λ. Choice frequencies greater than .50 indicate preference for the prospects delivering 8 pellets (A, C, and E); frequencies below .50 indicate preference for the prospects delivering 13 pellets (B, D, and F). To distinguish preference from indifference, in each case we conducted two-tailed *t*-tests, based on daily data for the

Table 6.5. *Tests of the common ratio effect: frequency of choosing eight-pellet payoff alternative*

Subject	λ			
	1.0	$\frac{1}{2}$	$\frac{1}{3}$	1.0^a
304	57.0	55.0	46.0	56.0
	(1.57)	(1.11)	(−0.87)	(1.71)
324	47.8	41.0	36.0	—
	(−0.78)	(−2.94)*	(−4.00)**	
333	61.0	54.0	—	—
	(1.91)	(1.13)		
334	65.5	44.5	47.5	69.0
	(3.46)**	(−1.09)	(−0.56)	(16.9)**
Average across subjects	57.8	48.6	43.2	62.5
(standard error)	(7.53)	(6.94)	(6.25)	(9.19)

Note: The numbers in parentheses represent t statistics. Subject 333 died before it could complete the $\lambda = \frac{1}{3}$ treatment condition; 324 died before we could replicate baseline conditions.
[a] Replication point following $\lambda = \frac{1}{3}$ condition.
* Significant at 5% level.   ** Significant at 1% level.
Source: Battalio, Kagel, and MacDonald (1985).

last five days of each condition, of the null hypothesis that the choice frequency was .50, that is subjects were indifferent between the prospects under consideration. The results of these t-tests are shown in parentheses below the mean choice frequencies.

Two of the four rats show clear violations of the independence axiom in the Allais-type direction. Subject 324 starts out being indifferent between prospects in the $\lambda = 1.0$ condition but clearly prefers the prospect delivering 13 pellets at $\lambda = \frac{1}{3}$. Rat 334, in contrast, starts out with a clear preference for the certain outcome at $\lambda = 1.0$ but chooses the prospect delivering 13 pellets relatively more frequently at lower values of λ, indicating, at best, indifference between prospects. Furthermore, reinstatement of the $\lambda = 1.0$ condition shows preferences to be reversible and remarkably stable, even by the standards we have come to expect from rats. Similar swings in relative choice frequencies are reported for the other two rats as well. Thus although swings in choice frequencies are far from overwhelming, they are consistent across rats and in the Allais-type direction.

Having established violations of the independence axiom in the Allais-type direction, we are concerned with sorting out competing alternatives to von Neuman–Morgenstern expected utility theory that can account for these violations. One potential explanation for the results could be that the animals ignore the probability differences between prospects E and F and focus on the payoff differences and vice versa in choosing between prospects A and B. This is captured in prospect theory (Kahneman and Tversky, 1979) through the pre-editing and subjective probability aspects of the model. Machina's (1982, 1983b) generalized expected utility model explains the data through changing risk attitudes resulting from the different expected income levels associated with the different pairs of prospects – the "fanning out" hypothesis (hypothesis II in Machina, 1982; a similar "fanning out" hypothesis is embedded in Chew and MacCrimmon's, 1979, alpha utility model). Extensions of the procedures employed here can be used to distinguish between these and other nonexpected utility formulations. Whether these alternative formulations of choice under uncertainty have public policy implications that differ from expected utility theory or can be successfully integrated into game theory is an open question (see Machina, 1983b, for a discussion of this first point, and Weber, 1982, for efforts along the second line). Under any circumstances it is always gratifying to be right for the right reasons, and animal experimentation would seem to have a role to play in clarifying more accurate descriptive models of choice under uncertainty.

6.4   Concluding remarks

The history of animal experimentation within economics has focused, in terms of subject matter, on individual behavior. Much of economists' interest in individual choice behavior is based on its capacity to serve as a prelude to, or sensible starting point for, the study of market or group processes: supply and demand interactions, issues in industrial organization theory and policy, provision of public goods, and so on. In these subject areas, small-group experiments involving human subjects have dominated.

This limitation of animal experiments to individual subject behavior has been partly a matter of historical accident and partly a matter of efficient exploitation of existing experimental results and procedures established independently by psychologists. There is no inherent reason, however, to limit animal experimentation to individual choice behavior. In conjunction with Howard Rachlin we have designed, and are beginning to implement, experiments involving rat "duopolists." Ecologists are studying cooperative behavior in naturalistic settings

(Pulliam, Pyke, and Caraco, 1982), and Epstein and Skinner (1981) (also Epstein, Lanza, and Skinner, 1980) have established methodologies for studying exchange behavior. The methodological foundation for these investigations, their advantages and disadvantages, are similar to those characterized in the study of individual choice. We look forward to developments in these areas, as well as to continued research on individual choice behavior in certain and uncertain contexts.

References

Alchian, Armen A., "Uncertainty, Evolution and Economic Theory." *Journal of Political Economy 58* (June 1950), 211–21.

Allais, Maurice, "Le comportement de l'homme rationnel devant le risque, critique des postulates et axiomes de l'école Americaine." *Econometrica 21* (October 1953), 503–46.

Allison, J., "Demand Economics and Experimental Psychology." *Behavioral Science 24* (1979), 403–15.

Battalio, R. C., Dwyer, Gerald J., and Kagel, John H., "Tests of Some Alternative Theories of Individual Choice Behavior," in *Advances in Econometries*, Daniel Slottje (ed.), Vol. 5. Greenwich, Conn.: JAI Press (1986), pp. 3–30.

Battalio, R. C., Green, L., and Kagel, J. H., "Income–Leisure Tradeoffs of Animal Workers." *American Economic Review 71* (1981), 621–32.

Battalio, R. C., and Kagel, John H., "Consumption–Leisure Tradeoffs of Animal Workers: Effects of Increasing and Decreasing Marginal Wage Rates in a Closed Economy Experiment," in *Research in Experimental Economics*, Vernon L. Smith (ed.), Vol. 3. Greenwich, Conn.: JAI Press, (1985), pp. 1–30

Battalio, R. C., Kagel, J. H., and MacDonald, D., "Animals' Choices over Uncertain Outcomes: Some Initial Experimental Results." *American Economic Review 75* (1985).

Battalio, R. C., Kagel, J. H., Winkler, R. C., Fisher, E. G., Jr., Basmann, R. L., and Krasner, L., "A Test of Consumer Demand Theory Using Observations of Individual Consumer Purchases." *Western Economic Journal 11* (1973), 411–28.

Baum, W. M., "Choice in Free Ranging Wild Pigeons." *Science 185* (1974), 78–9.

Beer, Colin, "In Search of King Solomon's Ring." *Natural History 93* (June 1984), 30–32.

Bem, Daryl J., and Allen, Andrea, "On Predicting Some of the People Some of the Time." *Psychological Review 81* (November 1974), 506–20.

Ben-Portah, Yoram, "Economics and the Family – Match or Mismatch?" *Journal of Economic Literature 20* (March 1982), 52–64.

Caraco, T., and Lima, S. L., "Survivorship, Energy Budgets and Foraging Risk," in *Proceedings of Sixth Harvard Symposium on Quantitative Analysis of Behavior* (in press).

Chew, S., and MacCrimmon, K., "Alpha–Nu Choice Theory: A Generalization of Expected Utility Theory." University of British Columbia Faculty of Commerce and Business Administration Working Paper No. 669 (1979).

Conlisk, J., "Simple Dynamic Effects in Work–Leisure Choice: A Skeptical Comment on the Static Theory." *Journal of Human Resources 3* (1968), 324–6.

Cross, John G., "Some Comments on the Papers by Kagel and Battalio and Smith," in *Evaluation of Econometric Models*, J. Kmenta and J. B. Ramsey (eds.). Academic Press: New York (1980), pp. 403–6.

Dwyer, Gerald P., Jr., and Cotton, M. Lindsay, "Robert Giffen and the Irish Potato." *American Economic Review 74* (March 1984), 188–92.

Ebbesen, Ebbe B., and Konecni, Vladimir J., "Decision Making and Information Integration in the Courts: The Setting of Bail." *Journal of Personality and Social Psychology 32* (November 1975), 805–21.

Eisenberger, R., and Masterson, F. A., "'Effects of Prior Learning and Current Motivation on Self-Control," in *The Quantitative Analysis of Behavior*, M. L. Commons, J. E. Mazur, J. A. Nevin, and H. Rachlin (eds.), Vol. 5. Hillsdale, N.J.: Erlbaum, 1987, pp. 267–82.

Elster, J., *Ulysses and the Sirens: Studies in Rationality and Irrationality*. Cambridge University Press (1979).

Encarnacíon, J., Jr., "Positive Time Preference: A Comment." *Journal of Political Economy 91* (1983), 706–8.

Epstein, R., Lanza, R. P., and Skinner, B. F., "Symbolic Communication Between Two Pigeons (*Columbia sivia domestica*)." *Science 207* (February 1980), 543–5.

Epstein, R., and Skinner, B. F., "The Spontaneous Use of Memoranda by Pigeons." *Behavior Analysis Letters 1* (1981), 241–6.

Fischoff, Baruch, "Hindsight ≠ Foresight: The Effects of Outcome Knowledge on Judgement Under Uncertainty." *Journal of Experimental Psychology: Human Perception and Performance 1* (1975), 288–99.

Fisher, I., *The Rate of Interest*. New York: Macmillan (1907).

Friedman, Daniel, "Experimental Economics: Comment." *American Economic Review 25* (March 1985), 264.

Galef, Bennett G., Jr., "Mechanisms for the Social Transmission of Acquired Food Preferences from Adults to Weanling Rats," *Learning Mechanisms in Food Selection*, L. M. Barker, M. R. Best, and M. Domjan (eds.). Waco, Tex.: Baylor University Press (1977), pp. 123–50.

Green, L., "Self-Control Behavior in Animals," in *Research in Experimental Economics*, V. L. Smith (ed.), Vol. 2. Greenwich, Conn.: JAI Press (1982), pp. 129–50.

Green, L., Kagel, J. H., and Battalio, R. C., "Ratio Schedules of Reinforcement and Their Relationship to Economic Theories of Labor Supply," in *Quantitative Analyses of Behavior*, Vol. 2: *Matching and Maximizing Accounts*, M. Commons, R. J. Herrnstein, and H. Rachlin (eds.). Cambridge, Mass.: Ballinger (1982), pp. 395–429.

Grether, David M., and Plott, Charles R., "Economic Theory of Choice and the Preference Reversal Phenomenon." *American Economic Review 62* (September 1979), 623–38.

Griffin, D. R., *Animal Thinking*. Cambridge, Mass.: Harvard University Press (1984).

Heiner, Ronald A., "The Origin of Predictable Behavior." *American Economic Review 73* (September 1983), 560–95.

"Experimental Economics: Comment." *American Economic Review 75* (March 1985), 260–3.

Hursh, Steven R., "Behavioral Economics." *Journal of Experimental Analysis of Behavior 42* (November 1984, 435–52.

Kagel, J. H., and Battalio, Raymond C., "Token Economy and Animal Models for the Experimental Analysis of Behavior," in *Evaluation of Econometric Models*, J. Kmenta and J. B. Ramsey (eds.). New York: Academic Press (1980), pp. 379–402.

Kagel, J. H., Battalio, Raymond C., and Green, Leonard, "Matching Versus Maximizing: Comments on Prelec's Paper." *Psychological Review 90* (1983), 380–4.

"Consumer Demand Theory and Animal Behavior," mimeographed, University Houston (1987).

Kagel, J. H., Battalio, R. C., Rachlin, H., and Green, S., "Demand Curves for Animal Consumers." *Quarterly Journal of Economics 66* (February 1981), 1–15.

Kagel, J. H., Battalio, R. C., Rachlin, H., Green, L., Basmann, R. L., and Klemm, W. R., "Experimental Studies of Consumer Demand Behavior Using Laboratory Animals." *Economic Inquiry 13* (1975), 22–38.

Kagel, J. H., Dwyer, Gerald P., Jr., and Battalio, R. C., "Bliss Points vs. Minimum Needs: Tests of Competing Motivational Processes." *Behavioural Processes 11* (1985), 61–77.

Kagel, J. H., and Green, Leonard, "Intertemporal Choice Behavior: Evaluation of Economic and Psychological Models," in *Advances in Behavioral Economics*, L. Green and J. H. Kagel (eds.),Vol. 1. Norwood, N.J.: Ablex (1986), 166–84.

Kagel, J. H., Green, L., and Caraco, T., "When Foragers Discount the Future: Constraint or Adaptation?" *Animal Behaviour 34* (1986), 271–83.

Kagel, J. H., and Levin, D., "The Winner's Curse and Public Information in Common Value Auctions." *American Economic Review 76* (December 1986), 894–920.

Kahneman, Daniel, and Tversky, Amos, "Prospect Theory: An Analysis of Decision Under Risk." *Econometrica 47* (March 1979), 263–91.

Koo, A. Y. C., "An Empirical Test of Revealed Preference Theory." *Econometrica 31* (October 1963), 646–64.

Koo, A. Y. C., and Hasenkamp, G., "Structure of Revealed Preference: Some Preliminary Evidence." *Journal of Political Economy 80* (July–August 1972), 724–44.

Lea, S. E. G., "The Psychology and Economics of Demand." *Psychological Bulletin 85* (1978), 441–66.

"Animal Experiments in Economic Psychology." *Journal of Economic Psychology 1* (1981), 245–71.

Lowe, C. Fergus, "Determinants of Human Operant Behaviour," in *Advances in Analysis of Behaviour*, M. D. Zeiler and P. Harzem (eds.). Vol. 1. New York: Wiley (1979), pp. 159–92,

Luce, R. D., and Suppes, P., "Preference Utility and Subjective Probability," in *Handbook of Mathematical Psychology*, R. D. Luce, R. R. Bush, and E. Galanter (eds.). Vol. 3. New York: Wiley (1965), pp. 249–410.

Machina, Mark J., " 'Expected Utility' Analysis Without the Independence Axiom." *Econometrica 50* (March 1982), 277–324.

"The Economic Theory of Individual Behavior Toward Risk: Theory Evidence and New Directions," Tech. Report 433. Stanford University, Center for Research on Organizational Efficiency (1983a).

"Generalized Expected Utility Analysis and the Nature of Observed Violations of the Independence Axiom," in *Foundations of Utility and Risk Theory with Applications*, B. P. Stigum and F. Wenstop (eds). Dordrecht: Reidel (1983b), pp. 263–93.

Maital, S., and Maital, S., "Time Preference, Delay of Gratification and the Intergenerational Transmission of Economic Inequality: A Behavioral Theory of Income Distribution," in *Essays in Labor Market Analysis*, O. C. Ashenfelter and W. E. Oates (eds.). New York: Halsted (1977), pp. 179–99.

Matthews, B. A., Shimhoff, E., Catania, C., and Sagvolden, T., "Uninstructed Human

Responding: Sensitivity to Ratio and Interval Contingencies." *Journal of the Experimental Analysis of Behavior 27* (1977), 453–67.

May, K. O., "Intransitivity, Utility, and Aggregation of Preference Patterns." *Econometrica 22* (1954), 1–13.

Maynard-Smith, J., "Optimization Theory in Evolution." *Annual Review of Ecological Systems 9* (1978), 31–56.

McCrimmon, K. R., and Toda, M., "The Experimental Determination of Indifference Curves." *Review of Economic Studies 36* (1969), 433–51.

Nisbett, Richard E., and Wilson, Timothy DeCamp, "Telling More Than We Can Know: Verbal Reports on Mental Processes." *Psychological Review 84* (May 1977), 231–59.

Olson, M., and Bailey, M. J., "Positive Time Preference." *Journal of Political Economy 89* (January 1981), 1–25.

Phlips, L., *Applied Consumption Analysis.* New York: Elsevier (1974).

Plant, M. W., "An Empirical Analysis of Welfare Dependence." *American Economic Review 74* (September 1984), 673–84.

Plott, Charles R.,"Industrial Organization Theory and Experimental Economics." *Journal of Economic Literature 20* (December 1982), 1485–1527.

Prelec, D., "Matching, Maximizing, and the Hyperbolic Reinforcement Feedback Function." *Psychological Review 89* (1982), 189–230.

Pulliam, H. R., Pyke, G. H., and Caraco, T., "The Scanning Behavior of Junios: A Game-Theoretical Approach." *Journal of Theoretical Biology 95* (1982), 89–103.

Rachlin, H., "How to Decide Between Matching and Maximizing: A Reply to Prelec." *Psychological Review 90* (1983), 376–9.

Rachlin, H., Kagel, J. H., and Battalio, R. C., "Substitutability in Time-Allocation." *Psychological Review 87* (1980), 355–74.

Samuelson, P. A., *Foundations of Economic Analysis.* Cambridge, Mass: Harvard University Press (1947).

Schwartz, B., and Lacey, H., *Behaviorism, Science and Human Nature.* New York: Norton (1982).

Siegel, S., "Decision Making and Learning Under Varying Conditions of Reinforcement." *Annals of the New York Academy of Sciences 89* (1961), 766–83.

Silberberg, Alan, and Ziriax, John M. "Molecular Maximizing Characterizes Choice in Vaughan's (1981) Procedure." *Journal of the Experimental Analysis of Behavior 43* (January 1985), 83–96.

Simon, H., "Rational Decision Making in Business Organizations." *American Economic Review 69* (September 1979), 493–513.

Smith, V. L., "Experimental Economics: Induced Value Theory." *American Economic Review 66* (1976), 274–9.

    "Microeconomic Systems as an Experimental Science." *American Economic Review 72* (December 1982a), 923–55.

    "Introduction" in *Research in Experimental Economics*, V. L. Smith (ed.), Vol. 2. Greenwich, Conn.: JAI Press (1982b), pp. ix–xii.

Snyderman, M., "Prey Selection and Self-Control," in *The Quantitative Analysis of Behavior*, M. L. Commons, J. E. Mazur, J. A. Nevin, and H. Rachlin (eds.), Vol. 5. Hillsdale, N.J.: Erlbaum, (1987), pp. 283–308.

Staddon, J. E. R., and Hinson, John M., "Optimization: A Result or a Mechanism?" *Science 221* (September 1983), 976–7.

Stigler, G. J., and Becker, G. S., "De Gustibus Non Est Disputandum." *American Economic Review 67* (1977), 76–90.

Strotz, R. H., "Myopia and Inconsistency in Dynamic Utility Maximization." *Review of Economic Studies 23* (October 1956), 165–80.

Sutherland, Normal Stuart, and Mackintosh, Nicholas John, *Mechanisms of Animal Discrimination Learning*. New York: Academic Press (1971).

Thaler, R., and Shefrin, H. M., "An Economic Theory of Self-Control." *Journal of Political Economy 89* (April 1981), 392–406.

Vaughan, W., Jr., "Melioration, Matching and Maximizing." *Journal of the Experimental Analysis of Behavior 36* (1981), 141–9.

Weber, R., "The Allais Paradox, Dutch Auctions, and Alpha-Utility Theory." Unpublished manuscript, Northwestern University (1982).

Wright, Anthony A., Santiago, Hector C., Sands, Steven F., Kendrick, Donald F. and Cook, Robert C., "Memory Processing of Serial Lists by Pigeons, Monkeys and People." Unpublished manuscript, University of Texas Graduate School of Biomedical Sciences (1985).

CHAPTER 7

Dimensions of parallelism: some policy applications of experimental methods

CHARLES R. PLOTT

7.1 Introduction

The term "parallelism" refers to a vague notion about how observations of simple laboratory phenomena can help one understand and predict the behavior of a complicated and changing world. Of what use are experimental results to someone who is interested in something vastly larger and more complicated, perhaps fundamentally different than anything that can be studied in a laboratory setting? Questions such as this and the related notion of parallelism have probably existed from the earliest development of scientific experimental methodology, and although I found the term in a paper by Vernon Smith (1980) the notion itself pervades all branches of science and engineering.

The purpose of this chapter is to isolate some examples of how the issue of parallelism has been approached in economics. The chapter outlines several strategies that have been employed in attempts to use experimental research in actual policy decision making. The topic to be explored is how issues have been posed in these policy-related studies so that experimental methods could be applied. The discussion is limited to 10 instances in which I have been involved personally at some level.

Many different opinions exist about experimental methodology and the relationship between laboratory work, field studies, and policy decisions. The opinions are strongly held and are just as likely to be held by those with no experience at all in applying the methods as by those with much experience. For example, the textbook by Samuelson and Nordhaus (1983, p. 8) boldly claims that experiments in economics

The financial support of the National Science Foundation and the California Institute of Technology Program for Enterprise and Public Policy is gratefully acknowledged. I also wish to thank Alvin Roth and Howard Kunreuther, who provided comments on an early draft.

193

are impossible. Presumably these authors believe that some sort of
field study is the only way to approach an application of experimental
methods. Referee reports frequently reflect methodological philoso-
phies and related concepts of parallelism. Every experimentalist who
has submitted a paper to a professional journal has read a referee report
aggressively claiming that the experiments had nothing to do with the
"real world" or that the experiments were not "relevant" for some
reason or another. My impression is that such critics have very narrow
views about the connections between laboratory and naturally occurring situations, and they approach experimental methods with unrealistic expectations about what can be learned from applications.

This impression brings me to my point: Economists should keep an
open mind about experimental methodology and should judge work by
the statements of results rather than by methodological principles.
Methodological principles should evolve from our experiences with
what works and what does not work. That point is reflected in the title
and organization of this chapter. The topic is policy research as
opposed to basic research. The issues are: What was attempted, what
seemed to work and why, what was a flop and why?

The examples are organized according to what seems to have been
the principal strategy for using the experiments. Each strategy can be
viewed as a "dimension" or form of parallelism between policy
problems and laboratory experiments. Five different strategies are
identifiable. Each section treats a different strategy. The discussion
includes a general description of the strategy, the context of the policy
problem, and the role of the experiments in the final policy decision if
any decision resulted.

7.2   Ex post evaluation of a decision: the flying club

A policy decision was made. An action was taken. A result was
observed. What influence did the policy have on the observed result?
The question suggests a possible role for experiments in the ex post
evaluation of a policy decision.

The ex post evaluation of a policy decision motivated the agenda
experiments reported in Levine and Plott (1977). The policy decision in
this case was one that Mike Levine and I made to promote the use of
a particular agenda by a large flying club that was selecting a fleet of
aircraft. Unknown to all members of the club but ourselves, the agenda
was designed to influence the club to choose the fleet of aircraft most
preferred by Levine. The theory underlying the design of the agenda
was untested at the time the decision was made, and the preferences of

the members of the club were largely unknown. Nevertheless, the club used the agenda and chose the fleet the agenda was designed to secure. Was the agenda responsible for the group choice? Was the "policy" a success? The question can never be answered, but educated guesses can be made. The role of the experiments is to provide the foundation for making an educated guess.

The context of the decision will make the methodological issue clear. The flying club had a fixed amount of money to spend on aircraft. It had many options, including a variety of makes, sizes, and equipment. The club could buy several aircraft, each of which could be different, and the number of possible fleets was in the thousands. The preferences of the members of the club differed substantially. Since there were many possibilities and no unanimous opinion, how was the group to decide?

The agenda used by the club is shown in Figure 7.1. The first question addressed the primary or basic fleet to be purchased. After a primary fleet was chosen, the next issue was the number of aircraft. After that question was resolved, the group addressed the question of whether more than one type of aircraft should be purchased and how many. The final question was how the aircraft should be equipped.

Notice that each question partitions the options into two sets: a set to be rejected and a set to keep for further consideration. In order to understand this point consider Figure 7.2 The letter E represents a Bonanza E; F a Bonanza F; C a Cessna; and A a Bonanza A. For practical purposes after the basic fleet was decided, the remaining options were considered by a sequence of questions. First, the number of aircraft to be purchased was considered (six-plane fleet vs. seven-plane fleet). After that a series of questions addressed the composition of the fleet. Notice that the agenda can be represented in a tree form as shown and that a reordering or rewording of the agenda would lead to the formation of a different tree.

The agenda represented in Figure 7.2 was chosen to induce the group to choose the option EEEFFCC, which we preferred. This was a fleet of five small Bonanza Es and Bonanza Fs with two larger Cessnas. The basic idea was to use conflicts among members of the group and the majority rule to eliminate options at each stage of the agenda until the remaining choices would result in the option (EEEFFCC) that we wanted. Each different stage of the agenda uses a different majority to eliminate options that we wanted eliminated.

Our reasoning in designing this agenda involved aspects of theory that had not been tested directly, so the utility of our project could certainly be questioned. The agenda seemed to work according to plan, but how do we know? Perhaps the group's choice was fortuitous and had nothing at all to do with the agenda.

This is the agenda for the Group 111 equipment meeting. Your subcommittee has tried to define a series of problems facing the group and to give you an opportunity to express your preferences in resolving them. We suggest that you take a few moments to look over this agenda and familarize yourselves with the choices facing us, then come to the meeting, participate in the discussion, and vote by show of hands on the choices presented in alternatives 2–6. We would like to present the Board with the most comprehensive possible expression of Group III opinion. Please come.

1. INTRODUCTION:
   Availability, Type variety, Previous Depreciation problems, Needs of the Group vs. Cost, Safety, Radio Equipment.

2. PRIMARY AIRCRAFT TYPE:
   PROBLEM: Survey suggests that many Group III members perfer that the main part of the group fleet be four-seat Bonanzas. Should these be all the same age? If so, we could sell all existing Bonanzas and buy new F-33A's or we could sell only the V and F and buy used E-33A's. If they can be different ages, should we keep our E's and add new F's? Or do we want C-210's? Previous depreciation practices may affect these choices.

   INPUTS:
   Costs and rates for new F-33A's and refurbished E-33A's.
   Depreciation problems.
   Maintenance comparisons.
   Availability and price of used aircraft.

   VOTE: PRIMARY FLEET TYPE SHOULD BE:
   a. All new F-33A's at about *$29.00* hour;
   b. Refurbished E-33A's at about *$24.00* hour;
   c. Mixed new F-33A's at about *$28.00* hour and refurbished F-33A's at about *$24.00* hour;
   d. New C-210's at about *$25.00* hour.

3. SIZE OF GROUP III FLEET:
   PROBLEM: Survey suggests that membership considers present availability to be unsatisfactory. This summer we operated with a little over five aircraft available. We have based our rates on 500 hrs./yr./aircraft. With only five aircraft available, we are flying more than that. We can clearly operate six aircraft at 500 hrs./yr./aircraft. We might be able to operate seven at that rate. We almost certainly couldn't operate eight at 500. If we assume, conservatively, that a seventh aircraft would operate 400 hours and an eighth 300 hours, the question becomes, "how much availability do we want to pay for?"

   INPUTS:
   Alternative ways of paying for availability.

   VOTE:
   Cost increases associated with availability.
   a. 6   b. 7   c. 8

Figure 7.1. Flying club agenda. From Levine and Plott (1977).

SHOULD THE FLEET INCLUDE AIRCRAFT OTHER THAN THE PRIMARY TYPE?

PROBLEM: Most members indicated an occasional need for a five- or six-place airplane. Others indicated a desire to fly aircraft other than Bonanzas. There are advantages in scheduling, rate uniformity, majority choice, and type familiarity in keeping the fleet homogeneous. The advantages of operating more than one type include optimizing for different mission requirements and accommodating minority preferences.

INPUT:
Safety aspects of mixed fleets.
Survey input on desire for 5-place, 6-place, and mixed fleet.

VOTE: FLEET SHOULD BE:
a. All primary type;
b. Mixture of mostly primary type and some six-place.

IF SOME SIX-PLACE SHOULD BE INCLUDED, SHOULD THEY BE BONANZA A-36's or C-210's?

PROBLEM: Each of the two has advantages and disadvantages and different costs.

INPUT:
Weight and Balance and Performance comparisons.
Maintenance comparisons.
A-36 costs and advantages.
C-210 costs and advantages.

VOTE: SHOULD SECONDARY AIRPLANES BE:
a. A-36 at about *$31.50* hour?
b. C-210 at about *$27.00* hour?

ADDITIONAL EQUIPMENT.

PROBLEM: It has been club policy (and probably will be in the future) to equip aircraft alike. Most of the group has indicated a preference for glideslopes, and the cost discussions so far have included them. Others have discussed DME's, radio-coupled autopilots (no altitude hold), and encoding altimeters (to meet Group I TCA requirements starting 7/1/74).

INPUT:
Cost and uses of equipment. Increase in cost/hour.

VOTE:
Would you like to have the following equipment if it increased cost per hour by the following amounts?

YES   NO
——   —— DME at about $——hour.
——   —— Coupled autopilot at about $——hour.
——   —— Encoding altimeter at about $——hour.

SUMMARY AND RECOMMENDATIONS TO BE MADE TO THE BOARD

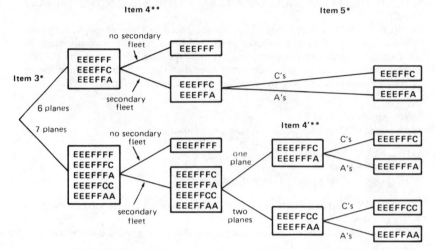

Figure 7.2. Schematic representation of flying club agenda. The item numbers marked with a single asterisk correspond to the numbers on the original agenda. The double asterisks indicate that the formal agenda listed only item 4, but the group correctly understood that it had two components–item 4 and item 4'. At the meeting the group did not vote formally on item 4, because no one advocated an unmixed fleet. The group simply moved to consider item 4' directly. From Levine and Plott (1977).

In order to test the effectiveness of our efforts, we designed a series of experiments. If the agenda failed to have an influence in a variety of experiments that involved conflicts similar to that of the flying club, we would be willing to say that our efforts had had no effect. If we found that we could use an agenda to influence group choice as we predicted, our confidence in the effectiveness of our efforts would be bolstered.

A questionnaire circulated by the club after the decision had been made provided data about the membership's preferences. The actual decision made by the group was checked against the prediction of the agenda model when applied to the reported preferences. The data were consistent with the model, but chance could still be an explanation. Next, we designed a series of experiments guided by the reported preferences. The objective was to see if the influence of the agenda could be demonstrated using those preferences in addition to preferences that would be even harder to manipulate.

Monetary incentives were included to induce preferences over an abstract set of options (letters of the alphabet). For example, an individual might receive $8 if the letter A was chosen, $5 if B was chosen, and so on. The amount a particular individual would receive given the group choice of an option was known only to that individual, reflecting the fact that the happiness or degree of satisfaction of any member of the flying club was unknown to others. The induced preferences were similar to those reported by club members. The agenda was the same as the club agenda, except that all reference to airplanes and related terms was removed.

During the experiments, we demonstrated the influence of the agenda decisively by changing the agenda while holding preferences fixed. First an option was picked by the experimenter. The model was applied to find an agenda that would influence the group to choose that option. The experiment was conducted with that agenda. Then a second option was selected and an agenda was constructed to induce the group to choose it. An experiment was then conducted with that agenda. The agenda certainly and predictably influenced the decisions in these experiments.

Did the agenda influence the outcome of the flying club meeting? Two assumptions must be made in order to draw an inference: (1) The preferences of the flying club were similar to those induced in the laboratory. (2) The relationship between the act of voting and preferences was the same for the individuals in the flying club meeting as it was for those individuals in the laboratory. If both assumptions are accepted, the agenda must have had an influence on the outcome of the flying club.

The issue now focuses on assumptions (1) and (2). If (1) is doubted, new experiments can be conducted in which the induced preferences more closely approximate those hypothesized for the club members. In principle all preference patterns could be examined, so assumption (1) provides no problem for the application of experiments. Any criticism along the lines of (1) is not an objection to the use of experiments; quite the contrary, it is a call for more experiments.

Assumption (2) involves a theory of behavior. In essence it requires the hypothesis that the voting decisions of all people, including those of the flying club and those in our experiments, can be reasonably captured by the model used to design the agenda. The acceptance of this general theory is a key to the application. To the extent that it can be demonstrated to be unreliable, the conclusions drawn from the theory about the cause of the flying club decisions can be challenged. Again, however, we discover that the challenge does not involve an objection to the use of experimental method. Instead, the challenge is a call for additional theory and perhaps more experiments. Additional theory would be simply an improved replacement of the old, and the additional experiments would be tests of it.

The basic theory of the agenda appears to work well in the laboratory setting. The voting decisions of individuals depend on the packaging of options in the agenda. In the design of an agenda, this dependence can be relied upon to induce a majority to accept or eliminate a set of options. The extent to which one is prepared to assert something about the voting decisions of the flying club seems to be an unavoidable matter of subjective judgment concerning one's confidence in the two assumptions. A variety of preferences have been checked and, so far, no exceptions to the behavioral theory have been exhibited.

7.3   Demonstration: landing slot allocations

On occasion the implications of theory are so clear and the results of previous experiments so unambiguous that professionals have little to learn from experiments. Nevertheless, a theory that seems obviously relevant to professionals is frequently abstract and complicated to those who have the power and responsibility to make decisions. Sometimes in a policy-making environment even the *word* "theory" is pejorative. In such cases experiments provide a way of demonstrating the ideas without resort to theoretical constructions. The role of experiments as a demonstration of theory was the basis of a Polinomics report (Grether, Isaac, and Plott, 1979) on the allocation of airline landing slots.

After the Airline Deregulation Act of 1978, staff members of the Civil Aeronautics Board (CAB) became concerned about the method of allocating the right to land at four major airports (Washington National Airport, Kennedy, La Guardia, O'Hare). The allocation decisions were made by committees. Each airport had a separate committee consisting of those airlines that had been certificated by the CAB to operate at the airport.

In 1968 the Federal Aviation Administration (FAA) had limited the number of slots (takeoffs and landings per hour) that could be conducted at each of these airports. The committees were charged with the task of determining by "agreement" the allocation of slots among the certificated carriers. What might happen if the committees failed to reach unanimity was unclear. The FAA might have administratively allocated the slots, but the criterion it would have used was uncertain and the role of politics in the process made the consequences of default uncertain. Since the committees had successfully achieved agreement every six months from 1968 until the time of the study (1979), what might have happened if the committees had failed was only a matter of speculation.

The situation changed with the Airline Deregulation Act. The CAB staff became concerned that the committees could be used as a barrier to new competition. I was contacted to study the committees because of my previous work on committee behavior. The question posed was related to the degree to which the committee process of allocating slots was compatible with the Airline Deregulation Act.

After we had undertaken some study and attended committee meetings, the nature of the committee behavior became clear and the structure of a reasonable process that could replace the committees became apparent. The appropriate model of the committee would have been immediately obvious to anyone with some game-theoretic and economic training. The committee operating under unanimity would attain some point in the "core" in the appropriate game without side payments. The location of the core would be very sensitive to the beliefs about what would happen if the committee defaulted. Simply put, an individual would rather veto an option than accept a committee decision less preferred than the option that would evolve as a result of the veto. The core would be an option preferred by everyone to the consequences of default. If such options existed, one of them would be chosen and, if not, the committee would default.

Since there were no side payments, an allocation in the core would not necessarily be efficient in an economic sense. That is, the airlines that would acquire the slots under the committee process would not necessarily be the carriers that valued the slots the most. In a cost–benefit sense the wrong carriers would get the slots. Furthermore, the allocation would be sensitive to airline beliefs about the consequences of default, and these beliefs would be sensitive to politics as opposed to economics.

Reasonable alternative processes involved markets with initial allocations determined by auction, or by lottery, or perhaps grandfathered with an aftermarket. Such alternative processes were very controversial and poorly understood by the airlines and public.

The role of the experiments was twofold. First, the experiments demonstrated the implications of the game-theoretic model used to evaluate the committee process. The emphasis is on the word "demonstrated" because the implications of the model were fully understood theoretically at the time, and previous experiments left little doubt that the substantive implications of the model would be predictive of committees operating under laboratory conditions. For those who had previously studied a wide range of committee experiments, very little was to be learned from additional experimentation.[1]

---

[1] Consult Fiorina and Plott (1978). These experiments and subsequent publications provide substantial support for the core as a behavioral model under

The audience, which consisted of CAB staff, Department of Transportation (DOT) staff, FAA staff, and the airlines, had no previous experience with committee experiments. Nor did the audience understand or have a tendency to accept game theory. Thus given the political and controversial nature of the issue, some demonstration that the theory had content was necessary. The purpose of the experiments was to demonstrate the major consequences of the theory when applied to the slot allocation committee process while avoiding any detailed discussion of the content of the theory, the axioms, or mathematical structure and also avoiding any long and academic discussions about why the theory might be true. The strategy was one of demonstration.

The parameters for the committee experiments were chosen to reflect beliefs about the actual committee parameters. Part of the study involved a demand-curve estimation for a certain period at Washington National Airport. These parameters, scaled down appropriately, were the ones chosen for the experiment. The subjects in most experiments were adults, preferably with some connection to the aerospace industry (e.g., aeronautical engineers). These decisions were made in anticipation of a claim that the committees under the field parameters would behave differently and/or that people from the industry are different from other people. In addition, participants in some commit-tees made several decisions together, reflecting the fact that sequences of decisions are characteristic of the slot committees.

Each individual was given a monetary incentive to acquire units of an abstract commodity, which from the experimenter's point of view represented the slots. In some experiments individuals participated in isolated committees. In other experiments individuals participated in more than one committee, and the value of slots received from one committee was dependent on the decisions made by the other committee. Such preference interdependencies or complementarities among the choice variables of different committees represented interdependencies among airports. A carrier might not want a slot to take off from O'Hare if it did not have a slot to land at Washington National Airport. The values of slots varied substantially among participants. These differences represented the different levels of economic potential that characterized different carriers.

Each committee had a fixed number of units to allocate. The rule was unanimity. In some experiments each individual was given a (different)

majority rule. Less experimental work existed on the behavior of the rule of unanimity, so technically speaking the experiments did have something to add.

quantity that represented the number of units he or she would get if the committee was unable to decide in the allotted amount of time (usually one hour). In other experiments the allocation was decided randomly in the event of a committee default.

The experiment made three points: (1) The outcome of the committee process is sensitive to the consequences of default; this point was made by experiments with identical preference parameters but different default rules. (2) The committee processes with different committee meetings for different airports could not deal efficiently with interdependencies among the airports. (3) The committee process would be insensitive to profitability of carriers and thus not promote an efficient allocation of resources. This point was made along with (1) by the inducement of high values for slots for some participants and very low values for others. The experiment demonstrated that, except for the bounds placed on decisions by the consequences of default, the value placed on slots by participants was unrelated to the allocation chosen. The allocation chosen was governed by the consequences of default and not participants' values.

The results of the committee experiments were not controversial. All three points were clearly evident in the data. Under unanimity a great pressure exists for equality of distribution, and unless a large allocation could be protected by a guarantee of a large quantity in the event of a default, participants had difficulty keeping it. For example, large carriers that should grow according to the economics of the situation never did so and usually contracted under the committee process. Inefficient carriers that should leave the airport never did so under the committee because they had no incentive to leave. The experiments provided a means by which the consequences of the theory of the core for the allocation of airport resources could be communicated without reference to the theory itself.

The report proposed the creation of a market for slots to replace the committees. Slots were to be auctioned by means of a first rejected bid, sealed-bid auction with an aftermarket. Markets and auctions had received some attention in the trade literature. Almost uniformly authors predicted that disastrous consequences would follow if markets were used to allocate the slots. This literature provided an excellent background for the experiments. The following questions were posed: (1) How do the committees perform relative to the proposed market process, and (2) do any of the disastrous predictions made in the trade literature actually occur if auctions are used?

Specifically the market experiments were conducted to demonstrate (1) that "rampant speculation" does not occur, (2) that the values placed on slots by the large carriers do not dictate slot prices because price is determined by the marginal buyer, and (3) that the problems poorly solved by the committee process would be solved more efficiently by a particular type of market process. All three points were clearly demonstrated by the experiments.

The report was adopted and promoted by the CAB. It was the subject of many public hearings and a notice of proposed rule making. The recommendations to replace the committee with a market process were very controversial, but the experiments were never criticized. In fact, the economic analysis was accepted in the sense that the critics chose to question the CAB's authority to implement such a scheme, and the tools used by critics to back up such claims were congressional and international political pressure.

The exact role of the experiments in this process is difficult to ascertain. The report was supplemented by detailed transcripts of three of the committee meetings. Quotations from these meetings were used to buttress the results of the theory and experiments. No doubt these were read carefully, and from these texts alone the logic of the theory could be detected. The experiments probably prevented certain types of claims from surfacing in policy debates and also gave confidence to governmental staff members who needed to support their views with data. Something other than pure theory was necessary.

Staff at the FAA were opposed to market policies from the beginning. They were certainly not convinced by the experiments and funded experiments from another group that they hoped would disconfirm our findings. The follow-up experiments conducted by another group were so complicated that no conclusions could be drawn from them. They attempted to use members of the industry who applied their own valuations brought from the field. In the sense of modern experimental economics, the study had no controls.

The recommendations of the Polinomics report were not implemented in 1979. However, attempts to implement variations of the recommendations have been made almost every year since then. The analysis of the committees has been almost completely accepted by all, including the airlines and even the FAA. The committees themselves began to deadlock by 1982. By 1984, the airlines had recommended that the committees be replaced with a modification of the Polinomics recommendation that I proposed as an alternative (*Aviation Daily*, 1983). This alternative grandfathered airlines at current slot holdings, created a market for slots, and provided that new capacity be auctioned. The FAA, which had assumed a leadership role in opposing all forms of market allocation, aggressively opposed this proposal in favor of its own plan to allocate slots administratively. In the fall of 1985 the

DOT issued a notice of proposed rule making to implement the proposal. That rule became law on April 1, 1986. Since then legislation has been drafted in both the House and the Senate that would reverse the rule.

7.4 Shifts in the burden of proof

Experimental data can influence the burden of proof in an ongoing policy debate. In this context experiments seem to be as much tactical as a means of gathering facts about the nature of the actual situation. The objective of the experiment is to establish the need for proponents of the other side of the argument to prove or disprove something before a policy discussion can proceed in their favor. Specifically, in the cases discussed in this section, proponents of the other side had made claims about a complex situation based on a very general economic model. The experiments were designed to check the accuracy of that model. If the model advocated because of its generality failed to be reliable in the simple case of the experimental markets, the burden of proof would presumably rest on the advocate to explain why it did not work. If a model is so general that it can be applied to some very complex situations, one would naturally expect it to be reliable in the simple situations. If the model performs sufficiently badly in the experiment, the burden is on the model's advocate to explain why the experiments were "special" or "different" from the complex case in which the model is supposed to work. Failing that, the generality of the model is in question and the application to the complex case is in doubt. Thus the experiments do not address the field situation directly. Rather, they address the theory that one side or the other has used to analyze the field situation.

The strategy is not foolproof. The side that should accept the new burden of proof might choose to ignore the results. Intellectual honesty notwithstanding, something must force the burden if the strategy is to work. The shift in the burden-of-proof tactic has been explicitly used in two studies. Some of the demonstration arguments used by Grether, Isaac, and Plott in the Polinomics airport slot study could be counted as a third instance of shift of burden-of-proof strategies.

7.4.1 Inland waterways barge traffic

Railroad companies were lobbying a high-level administrator to require barges to post rates with the Interstate Commerce Commission (ICC). The railroads argued that the public information feature of posted rates would make the industry more competitive, permit the railroads to compete more effectively against the barges, and aid the small barge owners who were allegedly secretly being undersold by the large barge companies. The administrator was skeptical of the arguments but had no basis for expressing his skepticism. He commissioned an experimental study (Hong and Plott, 1982) that became the first attempt to apply recently developed experimental methods to an actual policy problem.

The inland waterways barge industry is complex. Traffic exists on both coasts and in the Great Lakes region. Much of the industry exists on the Mississippi River and its tributaries. A great variety of products are hauled with boats, and firms are specialized accordingly. The first task of the study was to isolate a portion of the industry that had minimal complications. That portion would serve as a model for the creation of a laboratory industry.

A small portion of the Mississippi River was chosen. Only dry bulk cargo was incorporated into the basic model. Dry bulk was the major product for this stretch of the river. Parameters from governmental studies, judgments by industry people, and judgments by the researchers were used to characterize that portion of the industry during the year for which the best data were available. A laboratory experiment was conducted that represented a dramatically scaled down version of the industry.

The industry had about 15 grain shippers, the buyers of barge services. All were of approximately equal size. Between 25 and 35 barge companies existed. The size of a company could be measured by the number of boats it operated. Rough estimates of the volume of cargo shipped were available and served as the basis for demand and supply estimates.

The difficult part was determining an appropriate scale. Since a tow down the river took about a month, the number of boats translated into the number of tows a company could undertake. A unit in the experiment became one-half tow, and a period represented two weeks. A participant with a capacity to deliver five units in the experiment represented a company with more than five boats. The costs associated with units for sale in the experiment corresponded to engineering cost estimates for barges. An upward-sloping supply curve reflected a high marginal cost of upgrading marginal equipment and entry into the grain-hauling business by firms ordinarily hauling something else. The overall elasticity of supply was structured to reflect the best guesses about the industry. Elasticity of demand was similarly chosen. When the scale parameters were applied to the experimental parameters, the known industry aggregates were recovered.

A price-posting institution was used for two experimental sessions. The price-posting institution previously studied in laboratory work has many features similar to the rate-posting procedures used by the ICC. A second two experiments were conducted with a telephone market. All buyers and sellers were located in different rooms with telephones, and orders were negotiated and placed by phone. The telephone market was arguably analogous to the existing form of organization. Parameters were identical across all four markets.

In the price-posting markets, prices were higher, efficiencies were lower, and the small sellers made less profits than in the telephone markets. The results were exactly opposite to the predictions made by the railroads. Furthermore, the experiment provided estimates of the amount of business that would be shifted to the railroads if posted prices were required. The study was sufficient to make the administrator wary of the claims of the railroads. In private conversations they were challenged to explain the results. The administrator claimed that with evolving scientific evidence against their case he was not in a position to help them. The lobbying effort was diminished, and the policy advocated by the railroads was never pursued. The fact that a presumption existed against their case was sufficient to deter further lobbying efforts.

The administrator's use of this study was not widely supported within DOT. After the administrator left, the study was to have been published but was blocked by a staff economist who feared it would earn Proxmire's Golden Fleece Award and who in any case thought the idea of doing laboratory experiments in economics was foolish. At the time (1977) one could not use the authority of a large number of published papers to contest his belief. The study itself was then rejected by the *Journal of Political Economy*, which suggested that a paper with the details of the barge application removed and replaced by survey-oriented material might be acceptable. This suggestion came after the referees had mistakenly claimed that the results were due to an artifact of the experimental procedures.

7.4.2 The Ethyl case

The Federal Trade Commission (FTC) brought action against the major manufacturers of tetraethyl and tetramethyl lead, the lead-based gasoline additives that increase octane levels. The basis of the lawsuit was four practices widely used in the industry: (1) delivered pricing, (2) most favored nations clauses, (3) automatic matching of competitors' prices, and (4) advance notification of price increases. The experiments reported in Grether and Plott (1984) were conducted for the FTC to be used as rebuttal testimony in this case.

The government's claim was that these four practices when taken as a group increased prices in an "anticompetitive" fashion. The logic is as follows. Delivered pricing removes the potential for under-the-table price discounts in terms of free services. Delivery is the only major service provided to customers by producers. Most favored nations assure customers that no other customer is buying at a lower price. This policy eliminates a source of small price concessions in response to individual customer pressure. It is similar to the posted price of a rate bureau. What you see is what you get – there are no negotiations. Meet or release clauses tie prices to that of a competitor. It is the precommitment to a trigger-price policy. A company will not win customers away from a competitor by price concessions because as soon as the lower price becomes known the competitor lowers its price automatically. Advance notification requires a 30-day notice in advance of price increases. By giving a 40-day advance notice, competitors were aware of a 10-day window to bring prices up to the new level. If they failed to act in 10 days, the company that made the notice would necessarily retract it because of the practice of matching prices. Thus by giving a 40-day notice a company gives competitors a choice between all competitors having the higher price and there being no price increases by anyone.

The four defendants' reply to the charge that the practices had an anticompetitive effect was that they were an oligopoly. According to the defense, the practices had no effect on industry performance because there was no room for an effect. The industry enjoyed high (but not illegal) prices fostered by industrial concentration. According to the defendants' claim, any high prices and/or profits were accounted for entirely by industrial structure and therefore were unrelated to the four practices. The profits were not eroded by entry because the government's decision to phase out leaded gasoline served as an effective barrier to entry.

The experiments were designed by Grether and Plott to serve as a basis for rebuttal testimony for the government. Was the industry's claim true? Is it a fact that the practices necessarily have no influence when the industrial organization is that of the industry? If the answer is no, the defendants could not claim that the high profits and prices are necessarily unrelated to the government's case. A major tenet of their argument would be damaged.

Laboratory experiments were designed to match the numbers of suppliers and demanders, concentration ratios, demand elasticities, excess capacity, and so on, that are known properties of the industry. Special care was taken to anticipate questions that one could imagine during cross examination. Would the attorney attempt to make the experimental argument look foolish? The subjects were not undergraduates. For the most part they were employed adults preferably with an engineering background and/or some connection to the oil industry. The subjects participated in more than one experiment. Several different variations of the practices were studied. Consistency in design with that of previous experiments was sought so the weight of the authority of different types of experiments conducted by others could be used. Wherever possible, the consistency of the results with "the tradition of experimental research" was established. Testimony of respondents' experts was studied carefully so different forms of the rebutted theory would be recognizable within the experimental design. Many replications were done. Some experiments were blind in the sense that the experimenter conducting the experiment did not know the parameters. A double blind experiment was considered, but the experiment was so complicated that it could not be conducted by novices.

The results of the experiments were decisive in showing that the practices could have a substantial impact. The results were circulated to the respondents, but the government decided (correctly) that the case could be won without the rebuttal testimony provided by the experiments. Since these experiments were novel and since experiments had never before been introduced in any court, a decision was made not to enter the experimental results into testimony. Presumably there would have been no problem getting the experiments admitted as evidence (Kirkwood, 1981). The government won the case on the first round, but the defendants won on appeal.

After the trial a seminar on the experimental results was conducted at the FTC. Discussions with the defense lawyers following the seminar revealed some of their thinking. They had studied the several variations of the practices reported in the paper. One of the variations in which the practices were not strictly enforced resulted in prices slightly above the competitive equilibrium. Counsel for the defense asked if that treatment was the best approximation of the actual practices. The questions made sense because the practices as found in the industry were not perfect. Evidently, the first line of defense would have been to attempt to use the experimental data as evidence in support of the counsel's own position. In retrospect our experimental case could have been a better tool for the prosecution if we had built the detailed exceptions to perfect enforcement into the design. Given the nature of the imperfect practices found in the field, the experimental results would probably not have changed at all had this change been made.

An interesting feature of all three attempts to use the shift of burden of proof strategy is that the experiments were designed to mirror the industry as closely as possible. Relative sizes of buyers and sellers, demand elasticities, numbers of participants, and so on were all similar to those of the target industries. This was done to prevent the application of theories that attempt to show that the behavior of the laboratory industry will differ from that of the industry. Each imaginable difference between the experimental setting and the field is the starting point for a potential theory. An infinite number of such theories necessarily exists.

The logic is as follows. Individual A (railroads in barge study, the defense in the Ethyl case) has used a general theory T to infer something about the industry and its performance. Individual B (the experimenter) has noted that, under experimental circumstances E, theory T is not reliable. Thus T is not reliable in general because it is not reliable in E. Individual B then asks A to explain why T can be applied to the industry. That is, B places a burden of proof on A to show why T is applicable to the industry but not under condition E. Now B does not want A to have readily available some specified property of E that might be used to argue that E is an (uninteresting) exception to the general reliability of T. Each difference with the industry serves as a basis of a potential theory. For example, the laboratory results might be attributed to the special concentration ratios used in the experiment that differ from the industry's. The laboratory results might be attributed to the use of people experienced in the industry. The laboratory demand elasticity might differ from the industry, and so on. Such theories can be checked through additional experiments, but time and money are involved. The best strategy is to eliminate as many potential theories as possible so the burden of proof is not easily shifted back to its original position.

7.5   Direct extrapolation: air freight posting

Policy choices require making decisions, and the weight of the evidence is a subjective issue that rests with the decision maker. Studies designed to answer one set of questions might provide a decision maker with sufficient insight to act on a completely different set of issues. Such was the case with the CAB air freight rate decision.

Before 1980 air freight forwarders were required to post their rates with the CAB. Having studied the influence of posted prices in the early Plott and Smith (1978) study and the barge study (Hong and Plott, 1982), the CAB made the reasonable presumption that posted prices reduce market efficiency. On the basis of existing laboratory results and in the spirit of deregulation, the CAB issued a notice of proposed rule making to eliminate air freight rate posting. Seeing no claims that the presumption was incorrect, the CAB acted and eliminated the policy of rate posting.

7.6   Potential design: prepolicy research

Two experimental studies (Plott and Wilde, 1982; Lynch et al., 1984) were developed *as tools* with which to study policy options. Both were initially financed by the FTC, which has an interest in consumer protection. The staff of the commission is exposed to many competing policy prescriptions aimed at correcting alleged market failures.

The problem faced by the staff was that neither the "market failure" nor the influence of a "proposed remedy" can be clearly observed with field data. The experimental strategy was to create markets that would reliably "fail." Such markets could then be used to study the properties of proposed policy remedies as implemented in those markets. The experiments conducted were not focused on any particular industry or potential decision, nor were they designed to "test" any particular theory directly. Rather, they had characteristics of a variety of markets and alleged market problems that were the concern of the commission. The degree to which some theory or model might help explain their behavior was a secondary concern.

The experiments were complicated. The use of random devices and the associated training were nearly a separate experiment. Because of the nature of information acquisition and use, new types of market organization were imposed. Several different types of institution were studied that sometimes varied according to subtle aspects of when people were informed about their own preferences, the properties of commodities, and what they might do as a consequence. A full description of these experiments is far beyond the scope of this chapter.

The Plott and Wilde study focused on markets in which the consumer has only a limited capacity to evaluate the commodity (e.g., the services of a physician or perhaps the services of an automobile mechanic) and in which the seller might have a financial incentive to mislead the buyer. Experiments were conducted in which sellers offered two types of commodities (e.g., medical procedures). The relative value of these commodities to buyers depended on the state taken by some unobserved random variable (e.g., the infirmity). Only clues or statistics dependent on the state (e.g., symptoms) were observable. In some experiments the buyer could observe and interpret the clues. Sellers in these markets had a complicated supply response because of the multimarket nature of the setting, but they had no special function of information supply. When the sellers could interpret the clues and the buyers could not, the sellers had an additional important function. In addition to a supply response, the sellers gave advice to buyers and interpreted the buyer symptoms as part of the sale. The economic questions focused on models of the efficiency with which such markets operate. Would the buyer receive good information? Would the buyers act on it?

The Lynch et al. study also focuses on asymmetric information in markets. Markets were created in which low-quality products were delivered even though high-quality deliveries were Pareto superior. In this sense the study was very successful, because we were able to create such markets. The study then turned to the role of reputation and warranties in improving the efficiency of the markets.

An interesting feature of the Lynch et al. study is an experimental design involving sequential decisions. Recall that "theory tests" were not the primary purpose of the experiments. Instead, the strategy was first to try an extreme case in which almost all models predict that "lemons" would be produced. If the lemons phenomenon was demonstrated by the first phase of experimentation, the strategy was then to see if the most likely corrective policy as suggested by most theories would be effective. This policy involved the introduction of required, costlessly enforceable warranties. A failure at either end of this spectrum would have provided the background for a large series of negative results (about the applicability of theory) and subsequent experiments of a completely different sort. The positive results at the extremes that were actually observed were used as a foundation for exploring the more delicate phenomena between the extremes in which warranties were not required, enforceable, and so on.

Neither proposed legislation nor proposed rule making resulted from either study. The researchers learned much about the limitations of broad statements concerning behavior that have accompanied past policy decisions. The experiments also provided many insights into the nature of models that are being applied to consumer protection problems. The hope is that these background experiments will be the basis for additional experimentation and policy analysis.

7.7   Design

Sometimes economic problems require completely new types of organization and decision processes. In such cases history supplies no data, and a unique opportunity exists for experimental work. Experiments can provide some, perhaps limited experiences on which to base judgments about the nature of appropriate organizations and policy. Such situations are properly called problems of organizational design. Three instances are outlined here.

7.7.1   Slot exchanges

Following the slot allocation process study by Grether et al. (1979), the air controllers' strike occurred and the committees at the various airports began to deadlock. The number of constrained airports expanded from 4 to 22. A decision was made to create a "slot exchange." Air carriers were given temporary grandfather rights to their historic level of slots. The plan was to allow carriers to meet and exchange slots within and across airports on a one-for-one basis.

How should the process be organized? The problem was nontrivial because the size of the exchange was staggering. The number of commodities measured in the thousands, and the number of agents measured in the hundreds. The politics of the situation dictated that no buying or selling be allowed, so no numeraire existed. The logistics problem was enormous.

My role in this process was as a consultant for a carrier that wished to trade away from one airport to get to another. As a participant in all organizational meetings, I was involved in the design of the process.

The ultimate process was constructed on the basis of experiences with experiments with one-sided oral auctions. The only difference was that bids were to be tendered in writing rather than orally. Each carrier listed slots that it wished to acquire together with slots that it would take in exchange. The form of these proposed trades was that any slot in column A would be exchanged for any slot in column B. These lists of bids were collected and circulated to all carriers. With the list of proposed trades, carriers searched for chains of trades that involved their own proposals. At this stage of searching for trades, carriers were free to add new proposed exchanges that had the effect of a proposal being accepted or a chain of trades being completed.

The process was not well understood. However, pilot experiments had been conducted at the California Institute of Technology. The carrier that had employed me had practiced and had a strategy for dealing effectively with the process. Since our "team" had well-defined ideas about how the logistics of the process might work, we had little difficulty in convincing the group of all carriers to adopt the process. The process and improved variations were used many times, including a brief period when monetary transactions could take place and a period in which "many-for-one" trades were permitted. The entire affair was similar to a large experiment, and given the constraints it worked rather smoothly.

7.7.2   Westchester County Airport

The county of Westchester in New York decided to auction access to its airport terminal. The terminal is small and safety codes limited passenger usage to a maximum of 40 enplane and 40 deplane passengers in any 15-minute period. In addition, a maximum of four aircraft could use the parking pads at any time, and at most, two of these could be large aircraft.

When the county had taken action to limit the use of the terminal to the stated capacity limitations, it became involved in a lawsuit. The judge ordered the county to devise a mechanism for allocating the available capacity that was consistent with the Airline Deregulation Act. The county chose to develop an auction system that was to be used in the event that a settlement could not be attained.

The auction was designed by Glen George, a graduate student at the California Institute of Technology, and myself. It was important to avoid many potential criticisms of auction processes that litigants might raise, and it was necessary to conform to the realities of politics. The carriers might more readily accept a process that tended to allocate rents to carriers, so a one-price auction was used. In a discriminative auction, sellers pay what they bid. In a one-price auction, the high bidders pay the value of the excluded bid. If the demand curve is "steep," the former generates greater revenue to the seller than does the latter (Miller and Plott, 1985). Because the continuum of time was unwieldy, the day was divided into 15-minute segments. Capacity was divided into five passenger enplane blocks and five passenger deplane blocks. Thus two separate markets existed every 15-minute period of the day in which eight passenger blocks were sold in each. Carriers wished to tie purchases together, so provisions for special constraints that tied enplane purchases to deplane purchases were designed. Carriers were also allowed to submit multiple bids tied together with a constraint that canceled all other tied bids if one of the set was accepted.[2]

The number of markets together with the possibility of constraints resulted in a very large and potentially complex auction. Experiments

---

[2] Many of the ideas were motivated by Rassanti, Smith, and Bulfin (1982). The combinatorial auction was not feasible because of practical and technical problems.

were conducted using demand conditions similar to those believed to exist at Westchester County Airport. The purpose of the experiments was to answer some very practical questions: (1) Were the instructions clear about how to tender bids and use the constraints? What types of confusion were we likely to encounter? (2) Did unusual strategies exist that might undermine any efficiency properties of the auction process? (3) Were we likely to encounter a computational problem in determining the winning bids? We could imagine problems that would exceed our computer capacity. The solution to the auction involves a large integer programming problem, the dimensions of which are very sensitive to the number of constraints. The use of bids and constraints is not governed by the logic of the problem, so we had no a priori way of determining the size of the computational problem without actually trying the auction.

The experiments were invaluable. Many problems were uncovered at every stage. The instructions were not clear. We did not have a firm grasp of the game theory, and the experiments provided insights about the strategic possibilities. Computational problems did exist. The whole process was redesigned several times after bugs surfaced during the experiments. Experiments are still being conducted to improve the process.

The process was not used at Westchester County Airport. The respondents settled by adopting the process I proposed for Washington National Airport (*Aviation Daily*, 1983) discussed in Section 7.3. The original laboratory experiments and the field experiments with the slot exchanges have provided convincing evidence that markets in slots will "work." All of this evidence made carriers happy with a market for slots, although the FAA remained adamantly opposed. Now the New York Port is considering an auction process for the three major airports in New York City. The research and refinements on the Westchester County problem are relevant to the Port's problem.

7.7.3 Space station

The National Aeronautics and Space Administration (NASA) is planning to place a manned space station in orbit. The station will be used as a research laboratory, as a manufacturing facility, and for a variety of other purposes. The users will be the U.S. government, foreign governments, and private corporations. The Reagan administration wants the capacity to be allocated by some sort of pricing system. A team of economists at the Jet Propulsion Laboratory has been given the task of designing a pricing mechanism.

The task is complicated by the existence of nonconvexities, externalities, large common costs, much uncertainty, and other factors. In addition, NASA cannot operate for a profit or even take money for that matter, so profit centers and related decentralized schemes do not seem to be feasible. Matters are further complicated by the fact that the space station design is in a continuous state of evolution, and the design of the system itself should be affected by the pricing scheme.

The proposed role of experiments in this project is much different from that in previous research. Some testing of institutional influences is underway (Banks, Plott, and Porter, 1986), but the central role is to be slightly different. The experiments are to be used as a heuristic – a tool for organizing thoughts and questions as opposed to a tool for answering questions. Most experimenters have noticed that the process of designing experiments makes the researchers aware of complications and interdependencies that would have otherwise escaped notice. The space station project is intended to capitalize on this feature of the method.

The space station is just finding its way to the drawing boards. The variables are not even known, much less the costs. The experimental plan is to conduct simulations of pricing policies under experimental conditions that reflect much of the physical, institutional, and motivational aspects of the space station. The ultimate subjects will be the NASA personnel who are building the station. The purpose will be to instruct the personnel on the nature of competing policy options by providing them with some experiences with their operation. It is hoped that such exercises will generate insights about the features of the station, its cost, engineering structure, service capacities, and so on and thus make the simulation of policy options useful.

7.8   Closing remarks

The theme of this chapter is that "parallelism" involves many different dimensions that reflect the nature of policy analysis. Parallelism takes different forms, but there seems to be no formula for choosing an appropriate one. Instead, the use of laboratory methods in policy contexts seems to be an art involving a skillful and very subjective choice of experimental conditions. The laboratory results are sources of experience under conditions that it is hoped will be useful to those responsible for making decisions. The role of experiments in policy contexts is an activity more akin to practice than to some sort of scientific pursuit of truth. Experimentation is a source of experience similar to the experience one acquires as one practices the piano before a concert or that a team acquires as it practices before a game. The connections between such experiences and final performance can have many dimensions. The kinds of useful practice undertaken in preparation for a football game can range from ballet to scrimmage. The scrimmage itself can involve plays that the coach thinks the opponent will use as well as plays the coach is sure will not be used but are nevertheless educational. Similarly, experiments that provide the best insights about the nature of upcoming options might include faithful reproductions of the anticipated situation, but certainly there is no reason to believe that good experiments necessarily take that form.[3] In fact, there is no a priori reason to believe that faithful reproductions would be of any use at all.

Having compared this type of research with practice, it may come as no surprise that I am particularly uncomfortable with the concept of external validity. First, the word "external" involves a needless commitment to the proposition that there are no general principles of behavior that govern simultaneously both laboratory and "other" situations. If both laboratory behavior and field behavior are governed by the same principles as is believed to be the case in economics, it makes little sense to think in terms of "external" and "internal" behavior; all of the behavior is "internal." Second, the word "validity" sets a standard that is impossible to meet in policy contexts. An economic policy decision will constitute a unique event in history. The exact circumstances will not be repeated. Many unobserved parameters will be in operation. There is in principle no way to "validate" theories about what might happen. Simple judgment cannot be avoided. The experiments simply shape the thought processes, the data, and the arguments that form that judgment.

I do *not* intend to suggest that policy applications of experiments involve only rhetoric. Although opinions of policymakers are clearly important, the research objective is not simply to alter opinions. The objective is to make a correct guess about what will happen if a policy is put into operation. The purpose of the experiment is to make the guess as informed in the light of experience as possible.

---

[3] My own thoughts about how one might learn something from experiments were influenced by environmental engineers at the California Institute of Technology. The engineers were attempting to determine the flow of effluents that might result from a change in release in the ocean near Los Angeles. They were studying currents in a large pool constructed in the basement of a building on the campus. Of course, their pool looked nothing at all like the Pacific; yet it taught them something about their models, and it was the models that helped them learn something about the Pacific.

My approach to applied work has been to forget the concept of external validity and not to take the concept of parallelism too literally. Instead, the approach has been pragmatic in the sense that the use of experiments in each project has been justified by whatever arguments seemed appropriate given the context. What kind of experiment would make the guess work inherent in policy decision making more informed? The purpose of this chapter was to survey some of what was done to see to what extent some order or method actually existed after all. Laboratory studies and policy problems are connected by a many-dimensional correspondence. This chapter has outlined a few of those dimensions.

References

Aviation Daily (Washington, D.C.). July 25, 1983, back of pp. 124 and 127.

Banks, Jeffrey S., Plott, Charles R., and Porter, David P., "An Experimental Analysis of Public Goods Provision Mechanisms with and without Unanimity," Social Science Working Paper No. 595. California Institute of Technology, January 1986.

Fiorina, M., and Plott, Charles R., "Committee Decisions Under Majority Rule: An Experimental Study." *American Political Science Review 72* (June 1978), 575–98.

Grether, David M., Isaac, R. Mark, and Plott, Charles R., "Alternative Methods of Allocating Airport Slots: Performance and Evaluation," prepared for the Civil Aeronautics Board. Pasadena, Calif.: Polinomics Research Laboratories, Inc., 1979.
"The Allocation of Landing Rights by Unanimity among Competitors." *American Economic Review 71* (May 1981), 166–71.

Grether, David M., and Plott, Charles R., "The Effects of Market Practices in Oligopolistic Markets: An Experimental Examination of the Ethyl Case." *Economic Inquiry 22* (October 1984), 479–507.

Hong, James, and Plott, Charles R., "Rate Filing Policies for Inland Water Transportation: An Experimental Approach." *Bell Journal of Economics 13* (Spring 1982), 1–19.

Kirkwood, John B., "Antitrust Implications of the Recent Experimental Literature on Collusion." In *Strategy, Predation, and Antitrust Analysis*, edited by Steven C. Salop, pp. 608–21. Washington, D.C.: Federal Trade Commission, September 1981.

Levine, Michael E., and Plott, Charles R., "Agenda Influence and Its Implications." *Virginia Law Review 63* (May 1977), 561–604.

Lynch, Michael, Miller, Ross M., Plott, Charles R., and Porter, Russell, "Product Quality, Informational Efficiency and Regulations in Experimental Markets," Social Science Working Paper No. 518. California Institute of Technology, March 1984.

Miller, Gary J., and Plott, Charles R. "Revenue Generating Properties of Sealed-Bid Auctions: An Experimental Analysis of One-Price and Discriminative Processes." In *Research in Experimental Economics*, edited by Vernon L. Smith, vol. 3, pp. 31–72. Greenwich, Conn.: JAI Press, 1985.

Plott, Charles R., and Smith, Vernon L. "An Experimental Examination of Two Exchange Institutions." *Review of Economic Studies 45* (February 1978), 133–53.

Plott, Charles R., and Wilde, Louis L., "Professional Diagnosis Versus Self Diagnosis: An Experimental Examination of Some Special Features of Markets with Uncertainty." In *Research in Experimental Economics*, edited by Vernon L. Smith, Vol. 2. Greenwich, Conn.: JAI, 1982.

Rassanti, S. J., Smith, V. L., and Bulfin, R. L., "A Combinatorial Auction Mechanism for Airport Time Slot Allocation." *Bell Journal of Economics 13* (Autumn 1982), 402–17.

Samuelson, Paul A., and Nordhaus, William D., *Economics*, 12th ed. New York: McGraw-Hill, 1983.

Smith, Vernon L., "Relevance of Laboratory Experiments to Testing Resource Allocation Theory." In *Evaluation of Econometric Models*, edited by J. Kmenta and J. Ramsey. New York: Academic Press, 1980.

DATE DUE

DEMCO 38-297